Direct Selling

FOR

DUMMIES®

A Wiley Brand

by Belinda Ellsworth

FOR

DUMMIES®

A Wiley Brand

Direct Selling **For Dummies®**

Published by: **John Wiley & Sons, Inc.,** 111 River Street, Hoboken, NJ 07030-5774, www.wiley.com

Copyright © 2015 by John Wiley & Sons, Inc., Hoboken, New Jersey

Published simultaneously in Canada

No part of this publication may be reproduced, stored in a retrieval system or transmitted in any form or by any means, electronic, mechanical, photocopying, recording, scanning or otherwise, except as permitted under Sections 107 or 108 of the 1976 United States Copyright Act, without the prior written permission of the Publisher. Requests to the Publisher for permission should be addressed to the Permissions Department, John Wiley & Sons, Inc., 111 River Street, Hoboken, NJ 07030, (201) 748-6011, fax (201) 748-6008, or online at http://www.wiley.com/go/permissions.

Trademarks: Wiley, For Dummies, the Dummies Man logo, Dummies.com, Making Everything Easier, and related trade dress are trademarks or registered trademarks of John Wiley & Sons, Inc., and may not be used without written permission. All other trademarks are the property of their respective owners. John Wiley & Sons, Inc., is not associated with any product or vendor mentioned in this book. The Power Hour™ is a trademark of Step Into Success and is used with permission.

LIMIT OF LIABILITY/DISCLAIMER OF WARRANTY: WHILE THE PUBLISHER AND AUTHOR HAVE USED THEIR BEST EFFORTS IN PREPARING THIS BOOK, THEY MAKE NO REPRESENTATIONS OR WARRANTIES WITH RESPECT TO THE ACCURACY OR COMPLETENESS OF THE CONTENTS OF THIS BOOK AND SPECIFICALLY DISCLAIM ANY IMPLIED WARRANTIES OF MERCHANTABILITY OR FITNESS FOR A PARTICULAR PURPOSE. NO WARRANTY MAY BE CREATED OR EXTENDED BY SALES REPRESENTATIVES OR WRITTEN SALES MATERIALS. THE ADVICE AND STRATEGIES CONTAINED HEREIN MAY NOT BE SUITABLE FOR YOUR SITUATION. YOU SHOULD CONSULT WITH A PROFESSIONAL WHERE APPROPRIATE. NEITHER THE PUBLISHER NOR THE AUTHOR SHALL BE LIABLE FOR DAMAGES ARISING HEREFROM.

For general information on our other products and services, please contact our Customer Care Department within the U.S. at 877-762-2974, outside the U.S. at 317-572-3993, or fax 317-572-4002. For technical support, please visit www.wiley.com/techsupport.

Wiley publishes in a variety of print and electronic formats and by print-on-demand. Some material included with standard print versions of this book may not be included in e-books or in print-on-demand. If this book refers to media such as a CD or DVD that is not included in the version you purchased, you may download this material at http://booksupport.wiley.com. For more information about Wiley products, visit www.wiley.com.

Library of Congress Control Number: 2015948800

ISBN 978-1-119-07648-3 (pbk); ISBN 978-1-119-07618-6 (ePub); ISBN 978-1-119-07620-9 (ePDF)

Manufactured in the United States of America

10 9 8 7 6 5 4 3 2

Contents at a Glance

Introduction **1**

Part I: Exploring the Direct Sales Industry **5**

Chapter 1: Direct Sales 101 7

Chapter 2: Choosing the Right Direct Sales Company 31

Chapter 3: Working with Different Direct Selling Models 41

Part II: Building the Skills to Create a Successful Business **53**

Chapter 4: Keeping a Positive Attitude 55

Chapter 5: Creating a Vision, Setting Goals, and Boosting Your Productivity 71

Chapter 6: Always Be Ready for Business 91

Part III: Putting Sales Strategies into Practice **107**

Chapter 7: Building Your Business on Bookings 109

Chapter 8: Planning a Launch Party or Show 139

Chapter 9: Hosting Successful Parties 149

Chapter 10: Coaching Your Host 165

Chapter 11: Social Selling: Direct Selling on Social Media 177

Chapter 12: The Power of One-on-One Selling 209

Chapter 13: Sustaining Growth: The Fortune Is in the Follow-Up 221

Part IV: Building an Organization **237**

Chapter 14: Attracting New Team Members: Recruiting and Sponsoring 239

Chapter 15: Conducting Interviews 261

Chapter 16: Sponsoring New Recruits and Leading Teams 269

Chapter 17: Group Recruiting: Holding Opportunity Events 289

Part V: Operating and Maintaining a Successful Business **299**

Chapter 18: Managing Your Money Wisely...............................301

Chapter 19: Meeting and Communicating 309

Chapter 20: Networking to Grow Your Reach 319

Part VI: The Part of Tens 331

Chapter 21: Ten Mistakes to Avoid..333
Chapter 22: Top Ten Resources for Direct Sellers 339
Chapter 23: Ten Benefits of Direct Sales...345

Index 351

Table of Contents

Introduction *1*

About This Book 1

Foolish Assumptions 2

Icons Used in This Book 2

Beyond the Book 3

Where to Go from Here 3

Part I: Exploring the Direct Sales Industry *5*

Chapter 1: Direct Sales 101 7

How Direct Sales Works 8

Understanding the Three Different Direct Sales Models 10

Network Marketing 10

Party Plan 11

Hybrid 12

Who does best with each model? 13

Your First Steps in Direct Sales 14

Why the Direct Sales Model Succeeds 17

Personal Attributes and Skills

Needed for Direct Sales 19

Belief in the product 19

Vision and goals 19

Superior communication skills 19

Patience 20

Interpersonal skills 20

Presentation skills 20

Ability to recognize buying cues 21

Customer care 21

Technological aptitude 22

Commitment to personal development 22

Different Ways to Work Your Business 23

Live presentations and home parties 23

Trade shows and vendor events 23

Event parties 24

Online marketing and online parties 25

Fundraising 25

Re-servicing 26

Personal shopping experience 26

A Brief History of the Direct Sales Model 27

Traveling salesmen 27

The Internet age 27

The emergence of social selling 28

Chapter 2: Choosing the Right Direct Sales Company.............**31**

What to Consider When Choosing a Company.................................33
The Three P's of Every Company 35
    Products...35
    Profitability...36
    Programs...37
Special Considerations for Start-up Companies 38
    Advantages 39
    Disadvantages 39
Debunking the Myth of Saturation 40

Chapter 3: Working with Different Direct Selling Models.........**41**

The Network Marketing Model 41
    Recruiting in Network Marketing...42
    Sharing the product and the opportunity 44
    Who is best suited for Network Marketing? 45
    What does it take to be successful? 46
The Party Plan Model..47
    Recruiting in Party Plan 48
    Sharing the product and opportunity 49
    Who is best suited for Party Plan?...50
The Hybrid Model..51

Part II: Building the Skills to Create a Successful Business **53**

Chapter 4: Keeping a Positive Attitude........................**55**

Staying Successful: Attitude Is Everything..................................55
    Sharing your enthusiasm with everyone 56
    Being excited while out and about 58
    Learning to deal with no 59
    Finding the silver lining in everything......................................60
    Staying positive on social media...62
    Being a strong role model for your team 62
Overcoming Self-Doubt 63
    The four cornerstones of belief 64
    Starting with self-talk..65
    Building confidence and self-esteem 65
Getting Out of Your Own Way...66
    Settling for less...66
    Avoiding resignation 67
    Managing perfectionism and procrastination.........................67
    Staying away from denial and blame...68
    Taking risks: Getting past the fear 69
    Comparing yourself to others 70

Chapter 5: Creating a Vision, Setting Goals, and Boosting Your Productivity..................................71

Vision: Your Big Picture of Why 72
   My vision in direct sales 73
   Your vision will change.................................73
   Being a leader and helping
      others with their vision 74
Goals: Milestones to Success 75
   Goals don't have to be scary 75
   Setting intentional goals: The five Ds 76
Be Rewarded: Strive for Company Incentive Programs.................78
Productivity and the Power Hour.................................79
   Your 15 minutes on host coaching 81
   Your 15 minutes on booking 81
   Your 15 minutes on recruiting 82
   Your 15 minutes on customer service 83
Developing Important Skills 83
   The power of focus.................................84
   The power of commitment 86
   The power of consistency.................................86
   The power of organization, or lack thereof.................................88

Chapter 6: Always Be Ready for Business 91

Always Be Ready to Give Out a Business Card.................................92
Keep Catalogs with You.................................94
Have Host and Opportunity Packets Handy 95
Plan Your Show-on-the-Go.................................96
Create Your 30-Second Commercial 99
Dress for Success.................................102
Know Your Next Available Dates.................................103

Part III: Putting Sales Strategies into Practice 107

Chapter 7: Building Your Business on Bookings 109

Understanding the Importance of Bookings 110
Keeping Control of Your Calendar 111
   Setting a schedule.................................111
   Booking for sooner, not later 112
   Setting goals for your calendar 112
   Knowing your next available dates.................................113
   Weave dating your calendar.................................113
Scheduling Appointments and Bookings.................................113
   Jump-starting your bookings.................................114
   Practice, practice, practice.................................114
   Building momentum for your future business 115
   Building your Booking Lead Notebook 116

Securing Bookings or Appointments 118
   The casual approach 118
   See the people 119
   Enlist your friends 121
   Host your own party.. 122
Why People Book — Or Don't... 123
Three Power Questions to Get the Reluctant to Say Yes 125
Planting Booking Seeds... 126
The Booking Talk.. 127
Tips for Securing More Bookings 128
Overcoming Common Objections 130
   "Let me check with my friends first"... 130
   "My friends are partied out".. 130
   "My house isn't big enough"... 131
   "I don't have any time — I'm too busy" 131
   "I think I just want to do a catalog party" 131
Tips on Finding New Business 132
   Using your social network for referrals 133
   Getting leads from leads 133
   Go where your customers are.. 134

Chapter 8: Planning a Launch Party or Show 139

Understanding Why Your Launch Party Is So Important..................... 141
Preparing for Your Launch.. 142
The 1-2-3s of Inviting 144
Having a Back-Up Launch 145
After the Launch: Introducing My Two-Booking Method.................... 145
   Your first two parties 146
   Your second two parties... 146
   Your third two parties... 146

Chapter 9: Hosting Successful Parties.........................149

A Brief History of Home Parties... 149
Understanding the Appeal of Home Parties.. 150
Creating Desire 152
Giving Your Opening Talk 153
   What not to do 154
   Creating a powerful opening talk.. 155
   Example opening talk 156
Giving Your Presentation 156
   Presentation tips.. 157
   Building more desire for the product 157
Giving Your Booking Talk.. 158
   Choosing what to say 158
   Building desire for hosting 160
The Recruiting Talk.. 161
Upselling, Checkout, and Closing 161

Chapter 10: Coaching Your Host **165**

Understanding the Host's Motivation...166

Coaching on Attendance and Outside Orders 167

Keeping Your Host Excited, Engaged, and Informed 168

    Building excitement..169

    Keeping your host engaged 170

    Keeping your host informed...170

    The day you book your host 171

    The day after the first contact 171

    The first phone call..172

    When the invitations are sent 172

    The booster call 173

    The day of the party..174

    Closing the party..174

    Thank-you note immediately after...175

    Two weeks after the party 175

Host Coaching Online 176

**Chapter 11: Social Selling: Direct Selling
on Social Media** **177**

Choosing the Right Social Media for Your Business...............................179

The Five Cs of Social Media...180

Facebook for Direct Sellers 182

    Reviewing Facebook's strengths...182

    Setting up a Facebook Business Page 185

    Using your personal Facebook account
        for personal branding...187

    Hosting Facebook parties 189

Instagram and Pinterest: The Power of Photos 194

Twitter: Community Presence 195

    Building your audience on Twitter..197

    Hashtags everywhere...198

Capturing the Social Sale..200

The Virtues of Blogging 201

    Increasing visitors to your website 202

    Increasing search engine visibility 202

    Positioning yourself as an industry expert..202

    Creating customer relationships 203

    Selling through your blog 203

    Getting your blog noticed 204

There's an App for That..205

    Designing your own graphics and invites...205

    Organizing your material 206

    Keeping an eye on time management...206

    Incorporating business services..207

Chapter 12: The Power of One-on-One Selling................209

Selling with One-on-One Appointments.................................210
Getting One-on-One Appointments 211
Perfecting the Details: What to Do and Say............................213
Selling While Out and About 214
Executing a show-on-the-go....................................215
Starting conversations...215
Distributing promo cards 216
Using wear-to-share and other promotables.............216
Having product handy...217
Enhancing the Personal Shopping Experience 218
Identifying the target audience 219
Finding the right service to introduce your product 219

**Chapter 13: Sustaining Growth: The Fortune
Is in the Follow-Up...221**

Warm and Cold Markets..222
Being likable and trusted...222
Getting referrals..223
Being systematic about customer service.................223
Following Up with Booking Leads 224
Following Up with Hosts 226
Following Up with Customers 227
Following Up with Recruit Leads...228
Hot and warm recruit leads.....................................228
Brrr! Cold recruit leads 230
Removing the Guesswork: Using the 2+2+2 Method
of Follow-Up 231
2-day follow-up 231
2-weeks later 233
2-months later 234
Re-Servicing: Customer Care Is Key.....................................235

Part IV: Building an Organization........................... 237

**Chapter 14: Attracting New Team Members:
Recruiting and Sponsoring......................................239**

The Rewards of Recruiting..240
The Rules of Recruiting...243
Always invite 243
Never prejudge...244
Always do the recruiting talk no matter what............245
Look for leads instead of recruits.............................246

The "Why" of Recruiting: What's in It for Them 247
    Financial freedom or income..248
    Flexibility of time 248
    Friendships 251
    Recognition..251
    Personal growth and self-esteem..................................252
Getting People Interested...253
How to Lose a Recruit Lead 256
Using Follow-up and Good Customer Care 259
Recruiting on Social Media...259
    Facebook...260
    LinkedIn..260
    YouTube..260

Chapter 15: Conducting Interviews. 261
Setting the Stage: Creating Interest......................................261
Asking for an Interview 262
    How to ask 263
    Who to ask 263
Interviewing a Potential Recruit: Phase 1..............................264
    What to say..264
    What to do about indecision 265
    What no really means..265
Interviewing a Potential Recruit: Phase 2..............................266
    What to say..266
    The beginning of training...267

Chapter 16: Sponsoring New Recruits
and Leading Teams 269
Getting a New Team Member Off to a Great Start 271
What It Means to Be a Leader 274
    Setting goals and building vision in others 274
    Becoming a trainer 275
    Knowing when to coach..276
Mentoring Team Members 278
Working with Different Personalities 279
    Electronic/Digital communication.................................280
    Phone calls and video-conference calls.........................280
    Snail mail..281
    Face-to-face meetings 281
Using Team Facebook Groups 282
Challenging Your New Recruits 283
    Challenge: Announce your business to the world...........284
    Challenge: Explore your virtual office............................284
    Challenge: Get organized 285
    Challenge: Make a graphic..286

Challenge: Your "why" story 286
Challenge: Invite some friends 287
Challenge: Fortune is in the follow-up 288
It's Always a Learning Process 288

Chapter 17: Group Recruiting: Holding
Opportunity Events **289**

Looking at the Best Types of Opportunity Events 290
Recruiting at Events 291
Explaining the business model 292
Emphasizing the five needs direct sales fulfills 293
Sharing the three Ps: Products, programs, and profits 294
Encouraging them to make a decision 296
Planning and Staging Events 296

Part V: Operating and Maintaining
a Successful Business 299

Chapter 18: Managing Your Money Wisely **301**

Getting Spousal Buy-In 302
Paying Yourself and Keeping Track 303
Watch Out for Overnight Success 304
Opening Your Eyes to Taxes 306
Withholding, refunds, and loaning the IRS money 306
Tax benefits of a home-based business 306

Chapter 19: Meeting and Communicating **309**

Attending Your Company's Conference 310
Planning and Attending Successful Meetings 311
Motivation 312
Recognition 312
Sharing information and important updates 313
Training 314
Friendship 314
New products 315
Culture of opportunity 315
Communicating with Your Leader and Your Team.............316
Communicating with your leader 316
Communication with your team 318

Chapter 20: Networking to Grow Your Reach **319**

Introducing Yourself 320
Business Best Friends 321
Finding the Right People to Network With........................323

Attending community events 324
Using social media 324
Creating friendships 326
Tips for Power Networking 327
Maintaining Connections After Meeting 328
Set Up an Advisory Board 329

Part VI: The Part of Tens 331

Chapter 21: Ten Mistakes to Avoid .... .333
Not Starting with a Strong Line-up of Events 333
Being Afraid to Ask for a Party or Appointment 334
Failing to Set Goals 334
Lacking Commitment and Persistence 335
Prejudging Customers and Prospects 335
Not Treating Your Business like a Business 336
Lacking Focus 336
Skipping Training and Development 337
Neglecting Business Relationships 337
Depending on Friends and Family for Too Long 338

Chapter 22: Top Ten Resources for Direct Sellers .... .339
Step Into Success 339
Time Management 340
Organization and File Sharing 341
Team Communication and Online Meetings 341
Social Media Communication and Management 342
Video Creation 342
Images and graphics 342
Newsletters and Email 343
Business Expenses and Money Management 343
Website and Blog Creation 344

Chapter 23: Ten Benefits of Direct Sales .... .345
Increase in Income 345
Flexible Schedule 346
Be Your Own Boss and Work from Home 346
Friendships and Relationships 347
Incentives and Recognition 347
Business Skills 347
Personal Growth 348
Mentorship 348
Discount on Products 349
Tax Benefits 349

Index 351

Introduction

Welcome to *Direct Selling For Dummies!* I have been a direct sales trainer for the last 20 years (after 15 years as an independent representative), and for the last 20 years, people have been asking me to write a book. Well, something always held me back, and I never did it, until . . . the Dummies folks approached me to write a book on direct selling. I jumped on it. I had already written many guides for individual companies, but I knew the direct sales industry needed a step-by-step, plainly written guide to navigating direct sales and building a successful business.

Despite what you may read on Facebook, creating and maintaining a successful direct sales business involved a lot more than posting product shots and pleading with people to "join your team." Direct sales is like any other business — it takes work. But the benefits of increased income, flexibility, recognition, and personal growth all make it worth it.

If you picked up this book, I assume you have been bitten by the direct sales bug and are ready to take a chance on *you.* Just know that even though you are looking to go into business for yourself, because you bought this book, you are not alone. I am here for you every step of the way.

About This Book

Direct sales companies do their best to provide their representatives with relevant information about the industry and training guides to help them succeed. But until now, there's been no book or guide out there like this one, simple and comprehensive. No other book on the shelves will take you from the beginning of your direct sales journey all the way through to success. This book is full of my training on every aspect of the business, from your very first party or appointment to building a multimillion-dollar organization.

Keep this book on a shelf in your office or somewhere close by. It is perfect to reference whether you are struggling with filling your calendar, recruiting new team members, increasing sales, or working with a team member.

Anyone can succeed in direct sales, but the fact of the matter is, the industry is currently very female, and I acknowledge this in my use of feminine pronouns in the book. Rest assured that even though I may be using *she* and *her* all over the place, the industry does have its share of men, especially in the Network Marketing and Hybrid end of the spectrum (see Chapter 3 for more on these models). That said, the bulk of this book is aimed at the Party Plan model of direct sales, and I made the decision to allow the language to reflect that.

Foolish Assumptions

I can't presume to know your hopes and dreams. What I do know is that you picked up this book, which means you are at least interested in earning income from home while running your own business and staying as busy as you want. If you decide to go ahead and take the plunge, get ready to change your life. Whether you're looking to pay for dance lessons for your daughter, buy your first car, or pay off debt, this industry can help you, and so can this book.

Now I don't know what company you are interested in, whether you prefer the Party Plan or Network Marketing models (see Chapter 3 for more on those), or if you have any experience with this industry. If not, great — and if so, great. There is something here for you either way.

I do assume that you have a vision of a better life for yourself. That you want to chase your dreams, better your family situation, and experience personal growth. I assume that you're looking for a little something (or a big something) to finally call your own. And I assume that you are motivated and a self-starter.

Icons Used in This Book

Tips contain nuggets of useful, practical advice earned from years of experience in the field and training representatives.

Material next to this icon is stuff you should keep in mind for future reference.

This serves to alert you to things that could cause trouble or cost you time. It is meant to help you avoid common but costly mistakes.

Beyond the Book

Once you read this book, you will be hungry for even more content.

In addition to the material in the print or e-book you're reading right now, this product also comes with some access-anywhere goodies on the web. No matter how long you have been in the direct sales industry or how great your leader or company is, you'll likely come across a few questions where you require extra help. Check out our free eCheat Sheet at `www.dummies.com/cheatsheet/directselling` for some additional references you can bookmark to keep handy.

In addition, there's also some extra content that wouldn't quite fit within the confines of the book. Think of these as a kind of book version of "extras" that come on a DVD. At `www.dummies.com/extras/directselling` you'll find articles on promoting leaders and training your team, building out your skill set, running your business, and putting sales strategies into practice. You'll even find an extra "Part of Tens" chapter on using Facebook to promote and expand your business.

Where to Go from Here

You may be thinking, *if I can start anywhere, where should I start?*

This book wasn't designed to be linear. It's a friendly reference, not a tutorial, which means you can start or stop wherever you please. Take a look through the table of contents or index to discover the areas that interest you most. Or check for the sections that cover the topics you need the most help in.

If you're new to direct sales, the beginning is a great place to start. You will learn a little bit about the direct sales industry, get some info on what type of company may be best for you and your situation, and check out my new representative checklist. No matter where you start, I hope you have fun exploring the book and soaking up my 35 years worth of direct sales knowledge and expertise.

Part I
Exploring the Direct Sales Industry

getting started with

Direct Selling

In this part . . .

✔ Getting yourself oriented in the world of direct sales

✔ Figuring out which company, and kind of company, may be right for you

✔ Introducing the three main direct selling models

Chapter 1

Direct Sales 101

In This Chapter

▶ Understanding how direct sales works

▶ Checking out the three types of direct sales models

▶ Getting off to a great start with a checklist

▶ Working on the right skills to succeed

▶ Getting an overview on ways to work your business

▶ Knowing a bit about the history of direct sales

You may have been drawn to start your direct sales business for any number of reasons, or perhaps you're still conducting research before you move forward. Either way, I welcome you to direct sales, a distribution model that has changed many lives.

Direct sales or *direct selling* refers to the sale of products or services away from a fixed retail location. These products are marketed and sold directly through independent sales representatives, also known as consultants, presenters, distributers, and a variety of other names.

Direct sales reps are not employees of the direct sales company. Rather, they are independent business owners who enjoy all of the benefits of being self-employed with the added perk of being a part of a company that handles operations like shipping, product development, marketing, and more.

You are in business for yourself, not by yourself.

Direct selling gives both men and women the opportunity to be in business for themselves, add to their families' incomes, and create the life they have always imagined. The direct sales industry is filled with success stories from stay-at-home moms paying for dance lessons, women retiring their husbands, and families buying their dream home. Whatever your goal is, direct sales is probably an industry that can get you there.

Was your mother a Tupperware lady when you were a kid? Did your neighbor sell Mary Kay? Did your family know an Amway millionaire? Even if not, you're probably quite aware of some of the legendary companies that have used this network style of marketing their products. Direct sales companies include some major household names and global brands nearly as familiar as Coca-Cola, McDonald's, General Mills, or Kraft. Here are a few examples:

- ✔ Cutco
- ✔ Kirby Vacuums
- ✔ Avon
- ✔ Tupperware

You may have noticed friends on Facebook posting about making extra money, earning free trips, or perhaps even quitting their day jobs! Plenty of people have been successful with businesses like these. Regular people just like you continue to build thriving businesses in direct sales today.

You may be interested in starting your business to generate extra income while working part-time —or maybe you aim to ultimately rely on direct sales as your primary income. Or you could be like a lot of people who have fallen in love with a product, and watched a friend or acquaintance work their business, and decided that you, too, would like to earn free product and some income by sharing something you're passionate about. If you're like the vast majority of people who join direct sales companies, your reasons may involve a combination of these possibilities.

The world of direct sales has been very significant in my life for more than 35 years. I am sincerely grateful for all it has provided me and my family. The income and rewards of direct sales companies have afforded me a lifestyle I couldn't have imagined and have led me to treasured lifelong friendships.

The direct selling industry can help you achieve what you want out of life. The details of what *a better life* looks like are completely up to you.

But how does direct sales work, and what does becoming an independent direct sales rep involve? Read on.

How Direct Sales Works

In direct sales, as mentioned, the products are sold by *independent representatives,* not employees. These salespeople purchase a business starter kit to join a direct sales company. A *business starter kit* typically requires a low-cost fee for materials, the details of which differ among companies. This starter kit often includes products that you can use to display at your parties and demonstrate for your clients. The kit also includes necessary paperwork and training materials that will help you get your business off to a fantastic start. Your kit has everything you need to run a successful business. This purchase, along with signing the company's standard agreement, sets you up as a member, or independent representative.

As a representative (or consultant, or brand ambassador, or perhaps other title, depending on the company), you are an independent contractor who works on a commission-only basis, running your own small business. Because you are truly independent, you don't report to a supervisor. You set your own hours. You decide when, whether, or how often you will work. If you feel like it, you can increase your efforts and earn more money—in effect, giving yourself a raise—or you can pursue a more advanced job title. With direct selling, all job titles, promotions, and pay raises are based solely on production.

You are independent, yes, but you also have a built-in support system from the company and from your team. You are part of a team of other independent representatives who have a vested interest in your success—your *upline.* Your upline includes your *sponsor,* the person who helped you join the business (whom you get placed directly under in terms of organizational structure), along with other experienced people whose businesses are connected to your business through a sponsorship line. These upline mentors can really help you. They know how to create success in the business and have sponsored many other independent representatives. They can show you how to do the same. Your access to this mentorship is built in to the direct sales business model.

In addition to being taught how to sell products, you will be trained on how to meet people outside your own personal circle to sell products to and how to introduce people to the benefits of becoming a representative as well.

You can feel comfortable turning to your upline for support because the business model pays them commissions based on the success of the people in their sponsorship line. They are eager to see you succeed and they understand the details of your business better than anyone. Your success contributes to their success, so they have an incentive to provide you access to the tools and information you need to run your business well.

With a very low starter kit purchase, direct sales offers the average person a way to earn income with an established business model and a marketable product line. It works almost like a mini-franchise without the initial investment. It can cost a new business owner tens of thousands or even millions of dollars to open a brick-and-mortar franchise like a donut shop or fast-food restaurant. With direct sales, you benefit from your affiliation with a company that has created the concept, conducted research and development, incurred the manufacturing costs, and invested the money in starting the larger business and brand. This provides you with a low-risk opportunity to earn more money than you could realistically by starting from scratch alone.

The company also absorbs the ongoing expenses of warehousing the product, developing new products, creating marketing materials, complying with government regulations, and taking care of a number of other high-ticket costs that you'll never even have to think about, let alone be responsible for. This arrangement removes some headaches for you and eliminates the need to hire a staff of your own or become an expert in these other areas. When things work well, representatives can focus solely on marketing the products, taking great care of their customers and teams, and recruiting new people into their teams.

So, what's in it for the company? Independent representatives are the sales and marketing arm of the company, and the company only pays commissions for actual sales. Instead of paying for advertising and other expensive marketing, the company only pays the independent sales force after a sale has been made. That is appealing to companies, especially when they have products they believe will do better with word-of-mouth advertising and in-person demonstration.

Understanding the Three Different Direct Sales Models

Within the direct sales business model, there are three main kinds of company structures. They are called Network Marketing, Party Plan, and Hybrid. Chapter 3 goes into a lot more detail on these, but this section provides a quick overview.

Network Marketing

Network Marketing refers to a company structure designed to move consumable products through a network of independent representatives, through both personal use and sales to end consumers. When a Network Marketing company is building its sales force, it is focused on building a network of consumers. The company doesn't distinguish between those who join as independent representatives to earn money and those who join merely for a discount on their personal products.

(Network Marketing has also been referred to as *multi-level marketing* or MLM, but that is a misnomer—actually, all of direct sales is structured with multi-level compensation plans to pay their representatives, and all direct sales companies are therefore multi-level marketing companies.)

One strength of the Network Marketing model is that companies can grow very large and sell huge amounts of products through a vast network of people who have, in many senses of the word, joined as members. Many members set themselves up for a subscription to receive their products each month — an arrangement often called *auto-ship.* These continuous re-orders through a network of people affiliated with the company by choice can lead to consistent sales growth, as long as people in the network continue to see the benefit of the product.

Examples of companies that use the Network Marketing model are Isagenix, USANA, and Amway.

Party Plan

Party Plan refers to a model focused on efficiently selling to groups of people who have been gathered together by a host they know personally, either in person or virtually (online). These types of gatherings are typically referred to as *parties.* However, some companies personalize the term they use for their parties in order to make the experience more unique. For example, jewelry bars, tastings, cooking shows, makeovers, and so on.

These parties are hosted at a customer's home, and this customer is known as the *host.* The host traditionally is rewarded with a series of discounted and free products as well as host-exclusive specials. The host invites her friends over as guests to attend the party. The party usually consists of light refreshments, socializing, and a presentation done by the representative. The purpose of a home party is to create a fun, relaxing, home shopping experience with friends.

Toward the end of the party, the rep collects payment (usually through credit cards or cash) for the products the host and her guests want to order. These orders are placed through the rep's *virtual office* (which is provided to her through her company). Chapter 9 discusses in detail how to conduct a successful party.

This model lends the power of the host's personal recommendation to the products and facilitates *social proof,* which means the weight of influence carried by a group of people. Once one person decides to buy, it increases the likelihood that the rest of the guests in attendance will also buy — that's social proof in action.

The model is called Party Plan, but many companies who use this structure prefer different terminology. Some companies refer to the gatherings as *parties,* whereas others will call them *shows, demonstrations, classes, mixers, tastings, trunk shows,* or *showcases.* Some direct sales companies even actively discourage the use of the word *party.* Regardless of what they are called, Party Plan parties are quite effective in generating sales, attracting recruits, and teaching others how to sell.

One clear strength of the Party Plan model is the easy-to-understand emphasis on selling products to customers. This structure can include one-on-one sales and a variety of other ways to sell, but the majority of training conducted by these companies focuses on the most efficient and enjoyable method of sales — which is, of course, the party. New independent representatives can easily grasp the concept of this fun method of commerce, and that makes it a very accessible business model for the average person.

Examples of companies that use the Party Plan model are Jamberry, The Pampered Chef, Scentsy, and Stella & Dot.

Hybrid

This is the new kid on the block. As you might guess, it blends the practices of Network Marketing and Party Plan. In Hybrid companies, as with those in the Party Plan model, independent representatives have hosts gather their friends and family to experience a product demonstration, in-person or online. But with Hybrid, the emphasis is as much on the business opportunity as it is on sales of the product. The structures of the compensation plan tend to borrow traditional elements from both Party Plan and Network Marketing.

One significant difference is that with Hybrid companies, it is common for the representative to encourage the host to have an *impromptu* gathering, rather than scheduling it weeks in advance. They might say, "Sure, I'd love to demonstrate how this product works. I absolutely love it and I think you will, too. You can get it for free, too, and I can show you how. Why don't you and a few friends come over and watch while I show it to you tonight or tomorrow?"

Hybrid companies typically represent tangible products that are consumable, such as health and wellness or beauty products. As in Network Marketing, these products lend themselves well to auto-ship, the subscription order model where independent representatives and customers get monthly replenishment orders shipped to their homes automatically.

In Hybrid companies, auto-ship usually offers a price break for the customer, (sometimes referred to as a *preferred customer rate*). You will see programs that offer *vanishing auto-ship* or *free auto-ship* for customers who refer other customers through referral programs. These referral programs can also include free auto-ship for independent representatives who have a certain number of customers on auto-ship, meaning that the representative's own monthly consumption of product is covered. These referral programs, which attractively combine the customer-focused Party Plan outlook with the Network Marketing-style auto-ship approach, have been very successful and have led to significant growth for the companies and leaders involved.

Examples of companies that lend themselves to a hybrid model are Nerium, ItWorks, and Thrive Life.

Who does best with each model?

Direct sales appeals to people interested in earning extra money outside of a traditional job. Some choose to work part-time with a direct sales company as a way to pay for the extras that challenge their budget, often in addition to a full-time job. Others are looking for a way to make additional money while still attending to priorities in their lives like parenting, caregiving, school, or charitable work and appreciate that they can control their calendar and plan events, parties, and *one-on-one appointments* (where you meet with clients individually instead of in a group setting, like a home party) around their schedules.

According to the Direct Selling Association of the United States, 83 percent of representatives in direct selling are women. In the past, generally speaking, men tended to be drawn more to the Network Marketing model, with women feeling more comfortable focused on the Party Plan style of business.

Perhaps sharing products they are passionate about comes more easily to most women. In any case, there's no question that Party Plan selling is very popular among females. In general, women enjoy gathering with other women and tend look for reasons to do so. Having a Party Plan business or hosting a party provides an excellent excuse to get together.

In recent years, with the growth of the Internet, the increase in dual-income families, and product lines that are more appealing to modern women (weight loss, skincare, and energy products), there has been a noticeable increase in Hybrid and Network Marketing companies targeting a female salesforce.

In addition, busy people of both genders see the benefit of Network Marketing's reputation for ongoing *automatic* income (also known as *residual income*) from a business that can fit into the nooks and crannies of their schedule and be handled by phone and keyboard, instead of with a schedule of home parties. This could explain why many married couples choose to build a business together in the Network Marketing model.

Party Plan is still going strong and continues to be the top choice of people interested in earning profits and creating cash flow from even the early stages of their business. Quite often, representatives in Party Plan get paid for some or all of their sales the night of each party. For people looking to alleviate day-to-day budget shortfalls, the Party Plan model is especially attractive.

With the changes in the industry through the Internet and social media, as well the globalization of the industry, direct sales is growing. And with multiple ways to touch your business, all three models are becoming more appealing.

Your First Steps in Direct Sales

Much of this book is devoted to helping you work through the many details of direct selling, and I devote whole chapters to explaining the many facets and supporting you in making decisions.

Let's say for a second that you've picked your product and company and have decided to join up. What happens then? What are you in for? Here is a simple checklist you can follow as you take your first steps in your new business.

While waiting for your kit:

- ✔ Get a date book or calendar big enough to write in. This is where you will schedule your meetings, appointments, and parties.

- ✔ Mark all the dates that you want to work for the next two months and add any personal conflicts to your calendar. If your goal is to work Tuesdays and Thursdays, then put a star on each of those dates. This will help you offer dates to clients who want to set parties or appointments with you.

- ✔ Schedule your launch party. Your *launch party* is a party you host yourself that will launch your business to your family and friends. For best results, you'll schedule two launch parties within three days of each other. Chapter 8 talks all about launch parties.

✔ Make a working list of people you know (50–100 names) and their contact info. (See Chapter 7 for help on creating your list of 100.)

✔ Post your plans on Facebook and tell your friends and family how excited you are about your new business. (For more information on how to utilize social media in your business, head over to Chapter 11.)

✔ Invite as many people as you can to your launch party(ies) (check out Chapter 8 for more information).

✔ Schedule four to five additional home parties (see Chapter 9) or appointments (Chapter 12) in a 30-day time frame. In this case, you will ask people who could not attend your launch parties to host parties of their own. See Chapters 7 and 8 for more information.

✔ Invite a friend to start a business with you. Statistics show that when you start the business with a friend, your chances of success are much higher. (See Chapter 14 for more on recruiting.)

✔ Set up your personal website that your company provides. Your company will provide you with step-by-step instructions on how to do this. This is a website you will be able to share with your customers and use for marketing purposes. Customers will be able to order directly from your website and find out more information on hosting a party or joining the business.

✔ Get to know your virtual office. Your virtual office is the portal your company will provide where you can place orders, access training, and get other company information. Don't get overwhelmed by your virtual office. Ask your leader to walk you through placing your first order and navigating your way.

✔ Set up a space that you will use as your personal office (see Chapter 5 for tips on organization).

✔ Attend one or more of your sponsor's or leader's parties or interviews in your area. Learning from others who are already experienced in this business is a great way to become more comfortable with the presentation, selling, and recruiting aspects.

✔ Create an outline for your presentation (see Chapter 9).

Once your kit arrives:

✔ Set up your kit display and take a photo. Post it on Facebook to show your friends and family.

✔ Familiarize yourself with the catalog and products.

✔ Place your first order.

✔ Order additional business supplies.

✔ Set up your kit and practice your presentation and invite someone to come over to help you get some practice. Your presentation will include your product demonstration as well as the other elements of a successful party, like the opening talk, booking talk, and closing. For more information on all this, see Chapter 9.

✔ Open a separate checking/savings account for your business.

✔ Invite more friends to try the business with you. Recruiting or sponsoring new team members is usually a component of your company's "Fast Start" program. You should be able to attract new recruits from your launch party and other parties (see Chapter 14 for more on recruiting).

✔ Familiarize yourself with your company's Fast Start program. This program is designed by your company to help you succeed in your first 90 days of business.

✔ Familiarize yourself with your company's compensation plan. Your leader will be able to walk you through this.

✔ Learn how to coach your first host. Check out Chapter 10 for more on host coaching.

It may seem confusing, or even overwhelming. Don't worry. That's why I wrote this book. Most people join a company and then ask themselves, *What do I do first? What does this jargon being thrown around even mean? And what do I really need to know, right now, to get moving so I can earn some money?*

My Introduction to direct sales

I was bitten by the direct sales bug at a young age. When I was 14, my mother was invited to a Mary Kay cosmetics party, and I really wanted to go. Most likely, she was looking forward to a nice evening spent with other adults, because she said I couldn't come. But as a teenage girl, I simply could not resist the appeal of makeup and a party, so I hopped on my bicycle and rode over to her friend's house. My arrival was perfectly timed — it was too dark for her to send me home alone on my bicycle.

The Mary Kay director (a top position in a direct sales company) quickly assessed the situation and graciously asked me to be her special helper for the evening. Apparently, she was pleased with my assistance, because at the

end of the party she asked whether I would be interested in helping her a few days a week after school. Of course I said yes. At the time, I had no idea that accepting that part-time fun "job" as well as meeting company founder Mary Kay Ash a year later would lead to a 35-year-long career working in direct sales, as an independent representative just like you, in corporate roles, and as a sought-after-speaker, trainer, and expert.

I love this industry and it is my pleasure to share its power with people like you and help you experience as much success as possible by providing practical training, specifics on how to grow a successful business, and tips on what to avoid on your business journey.

That is where the list of steps comes in. Keep coming back to it if you begin to feel lost. You will have a shorter learning curve and feel more confident if you pay attention to the list, read the related chapters in this book, and seek additional guidance and training from your company — and especially from your sponsor and your upline.

Why the Direct Sales Model Succeeds

Direct sales models are successful because they offer the company an opportunity to market products directly to consumers. In direct sales, as mentioned, the products are sold by *independent representatives* who are not employees. These reps are independent contractors who work on a commission-only basis.

Because the independent representatives are the sales arm of the company, the company only pays commissions for actual sales. Independent representatives are also the main way the company advertises and markets its products. Many traditional companies with ordinary sales channels utilize social media, for example, to help increase brand and product awareness. But direct sales companies don't use typical advertising strategies like radio or TV to market their offerings. Direct sales companies mainly utilize their representatives to help market their products because they believe the products will do better with word-of-mouth advertising and in-person demonstrations.

As you explore the different products available through direct sales, you will find that the products are often positioned as cutting-edge, unique, made from superior raw materials, and basically better than products that are available in stores. Although that may not always be the case, generally speaking the products do stand up to scrutiny and tend to inspire a type of "super fan" convinced of the supremely high quality of each product.

It is a fact that direct sales product lines often are the first to bring new ideas to market. The companies are often led by mavericks or risk takers who are looking to get out ahead of the pack and incorporate the latest research and the newest "miracle" ingredients. People in this distribution model who have been laughed at in the past are the same people who first brought things like super foods, vitamins, healthy energy drinks, and supercharged, nutrient-enriched shake powders to market. All of these things are now, of course, carried widely in health food and grocery stores around the country and are no longer considered *fringe*.

There is also a lot of truth to the cost-savings and cost-reallocation made possible by skipping the middle man and delivering your products direct to the consumer through *volunteer* sales people (independent representatives). Rather than pay a big portion of company revenue for advertising, which, studies show, continues to have less and less real impact on consumer decisions, these companies can and do spend a higher percentage of their budgets on creating high-quality products through product research and product development.

Combine products that are typically superior to what's available elsewhere with a sales model that leverages social connections, and you have a social selling model that has been proven to be very effective and profitable over time, for both the companies themselves and the independent representatives who build businesses with them.

Today, you can find a vast array of products and services sold through direct sales. Here are some popular products:

- Cosmetics, beauty products, and skincare products
- Clothing and fashion
- Food and wine
- Home decor, including candles and fragrances
- Jewelry
- Kitchen items and cookware
- Nutritional supplements and diet aids
- Organizing and scrapbooking supplies
- Personal protection
- Romance and relationship enhancers
- Tools for home repair
- Weight management and workout supplies

And it's not just about products. Services sold through direct sales can include the following:

- Utilities and energy
- Financial planning
- Insurance products
- Legal products
- Personal business services
- Telecommunication

Those lists are just a sampling. There are hundreds of categories of items you can market or purchase through direct sales companies.

Personal Attributes and Skills Needed for Direct Sales

Succeeding in direct sales calls for a certain combination of personality traits and skills. Despite their apparent differences, the same personality traits and skills come in handy with all three of the business models:

- Resilience and persistence
- Strong work ethic and discipline
- Ability to accept rejection and work outside your comfort zone
- Enthusiasm

Beyond those generally applicable traits, you'll find that possessing or cultivating many other skills and talents will be of immense help to you in direct sales. This section discusses those and why they are important.

Belief in the product

It is imperative that you authentically and completely believe in the product you represent. Without that, your skills will fail to convince others, and the experience will be so lacking in satisfaction that it will all feel like hard work.

Vision and goals

You need a clear and specific vision of what you want to achieve with your business. And you need to define, in writing, your income goals, production goals, progress up the company ranks, and what having this business will do for your life and how it will feel (read more about this in Chapter 5). You'll hear people refer to this as your *why*. Having this strong *why* will help you overcome the challenges you will inevitably encounter.

Superior communication skills

If you're naturally a great communicator, you're in luck. But even if you're not, if you're determined, it is possible to significantly improve your communication skills and reap the benefits in your life and in your business. This includes becoming a better listener who asks questions to gain clearer understanding; a better connector, because people do business with those they know, like, and trust; and presenter, because being able to demonstrate your products or explain your opportunity with confidence is essential.

Patience

Rome wasn't built in a day and regardless of the model you choose (see Chapter 3 for a rundown on the three different direct sales models), gaining mastery and building your business so that it provides a steady, reliable income take time. In Network Marketing, people often give up too soon, because their small initial checks make them feel unsuccessful. In Party Plan and Hybrid, a lack of patience often leads to frustration because achieving a rhythm of parties booked and getting better at consistently running them will take time, as well. People do get better at the activities of their businesses, but there is no substitute for practice — and practice takes time.

Patience is also helpful in your interactions with customers and prospects. Statistically speaking, it takes seven exposures before someone makes a buying decision. Learning to feel calm during this process can be a great help.

The *yes* you're looking for can feel like it takes a long, long time. The more you practice some detachment to the outcome and just stay the course and maintain patience, the more enjoyable your business will be.

Interpersonal skills

You should have a desire to build relationships with others, including your new contacts, party guests, hosts, team members, and recruit leads. The better you are at working with others and building relationships, the farther you'll go in any business, and the better results you'll experience.

When you put relationships first, business follows naturally — sometimes directly, and sometimes through referrals.

Presentation skills

In Party Plan and Hybrid, you'll do not only product presentations, but also presentations designed to encourage others to become party hosts and team members.

The key to great presentations is *to be brief*. The primary reason people attend an in-person home party is to socialize with their friends — shopping while they do it is an added bonus.

You can review a standard party plan presentation in Chapter 9. Practice is key when it comes to presentation skills.

And though it is true that the Network Marketing model relies on tools to make these presentations, as you build a team you'll be called on more to present to groups. You'll also present over the phone to your team member's prospects. Developing solid presentation skills is valuable in that model, too.

Ability to recognize buying cues

To succeed, it helps greatly if you're able to recognize small, tell-tale signs that someone is interested in exploring opportunities to purchase, join your team, or host a party. Often, people won't directly ask for more information on hosting or joining the business. Instead, they may simply *lean in* to listen intently as you mention a benefit. Or they may ask you about how much time you spend on your business or how much money can be earned. Sometimes, the clue is as subtle as offering to help you collect your demonstration products and put them in your car, connect with you on social media, or even just sit next to you at a luncheon.

In general, when someone gives you a conversation opener, they are exhibiting interest. And, as tempting as it is to let all your enthusiasm show, you'll find that your best results occur when you give small pieces of information in an upbeat manner and avoid overwhelming them.

Customer care

More of a scheduled habit than a skill, this is crucial, nonetheless. Each month, or at least every other month, you should contact your customers and ask how you can serve them. What you're also doing is reading their temperature. Start these conversations by asking how they're enjoying the products they purchased. In following months, offer them products they may be interested in for themselves or for upcoming holidays. At least twice a year, offer them the opportunity to earn free or discounted products by hosting a fun party for their friends.

These periodic conversations keep you connected to your customers and provide them the opportunity to share their product testimonials with you, express interest in your income opportunity, or provide you referrals.

Chapter 13 talks in detail about providing excellent customer care.

Technological aptitude

You don't need to be a computer geek, but companies are turning to technological solutions more and more. Currently that means e-commerce, mobile phone apps, and leveraging social media at the corporate level — and encouraging their independent representatives to do the same. They're using apps, running webinars, and conducting online conferences. Some companies (most often in Hybrid and Network Marketing) even boast that you can "work your business from your phone." To keep up, you're going to need to plug in and connect online. See Chapter 11 for more on how to run a successful online business.

Commitment to personal development

Efforts to build your vision, become a better communicator, and develop a more patient personality all fall under *personal development.* An essential part of your job in direct sales is to improve your attitude, resilience, interpersonal skills, and leadership skills.

You've got to realize that, although the time spent developing these skills may not appear to have an immediate or direct impact on your business, it makes a significant difference in your experience and your results. Reading books, listening to motivational audio, and seeking out additional training will all help with your personal development.

I always laugh at the idea of a child walking into a stable filled with manure and gleefully shouting, "I know there's a pony in here somewhere!" I laugh because life usually trains that optimism out of us. Personal development is a simple way to put it back in. Whether it's a magazine article on how someone overcame the odds to achieve a dream or a podcast that helps bring to mind principles you already know, personal development material really does remind you that good things happen when you don't give up.

Surrounding yourself with people you want to be like and observing them will improve your skills. Each day is new, regardless of what you did or didn't do yesterday, and you get to start fresh.

Be persistent, be patient, help others, keep an open mind, develop a positive attitude, and you will go far!

Different Ways to Work Your Business

One of the most exciting aspects of direct selling is the flexibility and variety of options that are available. In fact, you should use several different methods of touching your business and generating new contacts. (By *touching*, I mean interacting with.) The more different things you try, the more you'll create a broad base of profit that will sustain you — and the more you'll appeal to a broader number of prospective team members. Conduct business in multiple ways, and you'll be presenting options that appeal to the desires of prospects who may not be exactly like you.

I urge you to choose a few favorite methods from the options given in this section and try them. Keep the others in the back of your mind. Then if a day comes when new leads are decreasing, or you need more bookings, you can revisit the options for ideas of other ways you can expand your business.

Live presentations and home parties

When people get to attend a party and interact with other guests, they experience that great energy that comes from people having a good time together. The right balance of fun, the excitement of seeing friends make similar purchases, the information provided in the brief presentation, and the added bonus of your expert advice all combine to create the social proof mentioned earlier in the chapter. Social proof can create stronger sales, result in more bookings, and even make recruiting new team members easier. In my experience, holding parties regularly results in higher sales and recruiting numbers.

Trade shows and vendor events

Trade shows can help you reach out into your community and meet people you may not have met otherwise. Here's something surprising: I've found that smaller, less expensive events tend to provide a bigger return on your investment.

I've also discovered that there's a key ingredient to creating success: Decide on your purpose for that particular event. If it's to get bookings, then don't focus on selling product. Concentrate on engaging people so that you get bookings. That means you'd most likely have just display product and only a small amount of product to sell. Your focus will be on creating an urgency to book a party with you, perhaps with a *Book Today* special.

If your goal is to earn enough to pay for your booth as you expand your contacts, you'll want to focus on selling product you have on hand. You'll experience the best results if, instead of bringing along your catalog or a variety of items, you instead offer a specific *Show Special.* A Show Special is a particular item or bundle of items that you're highlighting for that particular event. You'll have a supply of this to sell cash-and-carry to people who visit your booth.

If your goal is recruiting, make a gift basket that goes to a new team member and make sure all your conversations include the message "I'm looking for people to join me."

Event parties

Event parties are an exciting new twist on the home parties that have been the bastion of the Party Plan industry for decades. Event parties are held outside the home, and are growing more and more popular. There are two basic types of event parties: those held at an office, restaurant, or coffee shop and those held in partnership with a retail establishment. The first type has been around for years. It is really just a home party held in a different venue.

The second type seems to be growing in popularity, as more shops are starting to pair up with representatives on a monthly basis. A boutique, gym, or bookstore might want representatives that offer tea or food samples, or even an unrelated but still non-competing product. A cafe might like to invite representatives of jewelry, clothing, or home decor companies to display their products.

For example, a cafe near my home features a different party each month, displaying a flyer every day until the event. They let the selected representative set up a display of products, and the cafe owners and the representatives both tell me they love it.

Because both the store front and the representative promote the event, it becomes a blending of their customers. The representative's customers return to the store, and the store's customers become the representative's customers, too.

Want more examples? Appliance stores let cookware representatives do cooking demonstrations. Women's gyms love partnering with nutrition supplements and weight-loss product representatives. Some boutiques who don't carry jewelry allow jewelry reps to set up their displays and meet their clientele during key weekends. Libraries have been known to allow food and beverage reps to distribute samples during book readings. The key is for the establishment to provide added value for their customers, while also using your business to drive more people to their location. Of course, the added benefit for you is the exposure to a new clientele.

Online marketing and online parties

These days, one of the most touted aspects of direct selling is the benefit of doing business online. There's no question that online parties can be a great boost to your business. They allow you to reach people outside your general vicinity and offer the convenience of being able to cover your responsibilities at home while popping over to the computer to host an online party on Facebook.

When it comes to doing a great online party, you use exactly the same skills as an in-home party. The difference is in how you utilize those skills. To succeed with virtual parties, you need to engage guests, make it fun, and show them how your product really answers a need they have. Successful online parties also demonstrate why hosting a party is exciting and rewarding and how becoming a representative meets a need that each guest has.

You'll find that doing a combination of virtual parties and live parties is often the best fit for both you and your hosts. You may need to be home on a certain evening, and she may believe her house isn't large enough to do a live party — that's a great time to utilize an online party. You don't have to leave your house, you can put the kids in bed and sit down and do your virtual party. She doesn't have to rush around cleaning — she simply grabs her laptop and helps you engage her friends.

Fundraising

Fundraising is a $19 billion market. The great part of fundraising programs is that people want to support their community. Fundraising can introduce you and your products to an entirely different crowd. Many companies offer a fundraising program that divides your normal profit so that the bulk of it goes to the school or organization. But if not, you can develop your own program. Focus on offering about a dozen top items on a flyer rather than using the entire catalog. Make sure the receipt offers an opt-out option for future contact and that the products are delivered with your contact information included. People who come from a long-term corporate background find this model of doing business very successful and appealing.

Re-servicing

This is a piece of the business that many people leave out, and that's a huge amount of cash to leave on the table. *Re-servicing* is more than simply posting on Facebook "I'm putting in an order, does anyone want anything?" Re-servicing is true customer care, meaning it involves contacting customers by phone with a simple, short conversation to ensure that they're doing well and like the products, and to determine whether they need more or would like to try the monthly special.

If your company doesn't offer a monthly special, create one for just your customers. Or look at each customer's previous purchases and suggest something tailored just to them. Re-servicing can turn into an independent stream of income. I made thousands of dollars in sales by focusing just one day a week on re-servicing. You can also schedule about 15–20 minutes a day for this task.

For more details on re-servicing, see Chapter 13.

Personal shopping experience

Consider providing a service as well as selling products. For example, for those who sell food-storage products, you might tell your prospective customers something like "For a fee, I will come in and organize your pantry." The customer then pays the fee, and you come in, show them how to organize and what products should be used — and tell them they can apply their fee as a credit toward their order. Representatives that offer cooking tools can offer to streamline kitchens. Those offering clothing can also offer seasonal wardrobe-organization services. For many companies, it's appropriate to offer this service twice a year.

Personal shopping may not be something you can base your entire business on, but it is one more layer you can add to it. Though you may have time to do just one party a week, perhaps during the middle of the day you can do a couple of personal shopping experiences.

Some representatives overlook this opportunity. They fail to recognize that there are people who will *not* have a party, but they *will* buy your products. Recently, I overheard a conversation between a well-to-do professional and an eager representative. When the prospect mentioned that she'd love to have the representative come help her one-on-one, the representative replied, "You can have a party!" From the prospect's objections, it was clear that she had no interest in hosting, but *was* ready and willing to buy products. The representative was so focused on persuading the woman to host a party that she missed an opportunity to make what could have been a very lucrative sale.

A Brief History of the Direct Sales Model

Nearly every culture shares a heritage of direct selling. What they sold direct to consumers varies from era to era, continent to continent, and community to community, but around the globe, as far back as history is recorded, individuals have sold goods to their neighbors and countrymen. These networks of commerce were direct-selling distribution channels, much like the direct sales companies of today.

Traveling salesmen

Salesmen, hawking their wares, would gather in the center of the village or town, and the community would come to listen to the presentations and then purchase the items they needed. Some would work only in their own town, whereas others traveled from town to town, seeking new markets and new customers.

The archetype of a traveling salesman is universal. When people need something and it is brought *to* them, they purchase. In essence, that is the long tradition that modern direct sales is built on.

Later, as the practice evolved to match the changes in the ways communities and families lived, door-to-door selling developed. With home parties showing up on the scene in the 1950s, the image of the traveling salesman was expanded to include another image: the career woman venturing out to build a different kind of career for herself (with Mary Kay or Avon) and the stay-at-home mother (with Tupperware) earning income either for her own fun, for extras, or to supplement the family budget.

These days with the Internet and smartphones, the demographics of who is earning money with direct sales has shifted again. The common denominators are a desire on the part of individuals for more income on their own terms, for more flexibility, and to promote products and/or a business opportunity they feel passionate about.

The Internet age

Just as direct-to-consumer salesmen adapted over the years to the changes in communities, direct sellers are a resilient bunch. Over the years, the methods of sales have evolved to reflect the trends of the time, as well as demographic shifts.

From the door-to-door sales practices of companies like Fuller Brush and Avon, which enabled people to *shop from home,* to the emergence of home parties, which allowed guests to socialize while shopping and catered to a burgeoning population of women eager to get out of the house and earn their own money, one thing is clear: As the times change, the methods of commerce do, too.

Nowadays, the home party is going strong due to its effectiveness, but people can also work their businesses completely online (more in Chapter 11). Many representatives can operate successful businesses and build networks and connections through the Internet and their social media channels.

Besides making it so much easier to place orders, ship direct to the customers, run sales reports, and track your income with company-hosted software, the digital age has opened up new horizons for staying connected, creating buzz, and sharing valuable information (I discuss this more in Chapter 11). There has never been a more exciting or more efficient time to be involved in direct selling.

New technologies, mobile apps, and social media channels are constantly emerging and are changing the way we grow our brands. Social networks, especially Facebook, Instagram, and Pinterest, are changing the way we socialize, buy, sell, make money, do business, bank, and do all kinds of other stuff. I really could go on forever, because in reality, social media is changing the way we do *everything*.

So, if the business landscape is changing, we have to change. It's as simple as that. Social media is becoming an integral part of the direct sales industry, even down to the way we communicate with our company's corporate office, our teams, and our customers.

The emergence of social selling

Much like Groupon, LivingSocial, Uber, Fabletics, Airbnb, and a number of other e-commerce ventures, direct sales is a form of *referral marketing*. The difference is a lot of these high-tech companies are new to the game in comparison to direct selling, which has been relying on referral marketing for decades. Over the past several years, a new term has been circulating: *social selling.*

Social selling can refer to someone who just wants to sell socially to friends and family. But it's most often used to describe people who sell mainly through social networking. *Social selling* is the use of social media networks to interact directly with customers, leads, and clients. Platforms like Facebook and Instagram give independent representatives the opportunity to build friendships, be visible, and answer questions.

Social proof is simply the weight of influence carried by a group of people. Social proof can show up in online communities and is visible and at play in social selling. But the prime example of the power of social proof in direct sales is the Party Plan model. *Party Plan* refers to a direct sales model that is focused on efficiently selling to groups of people who have been gathered together by a host they know personally, either in person or virtually online. (Chapter 2 talks a bit more about the different models of direct selling.) This lends the power of the hosts' personal recommendation to the products along with harnessing and facilitating social proof. In the party environment, whether during an online party on Facebook or at a traditional in-home party, once one person decides to buy, it increases the likelihood that the rest of the guests in attendance will also make a purchase.

Social selling continues to gain prominence and is beginning to look like the modern way to do business. With your direct sales business, you have that power built right into the distribution model.

Chapter 2

Choosing the Right Direct Sales Company

In This Chapter

▶ Contemplating the benefits of direct selling

▶ Exploring products, profits, and programs

▶ Choosing a start-up company

▶ Debunking the myth of saturation

*B*eing a business owner is something many people dream about — four out of five people say they want to own their own business — yet only about 8 percent ever do. What keeps the other 72 percent from stepping out and becoming entrepreneurs? Most of the time, it's not even the courage to start or the self-discipline required to succeed that holds people back. In reality, it's usually the cash outlay for overhead and the length of time before revenue meets and exceeds it that prevents most people from owning their own business.

Depending on which field you're talking about, starting a traditional small business can cost a lot of money. If you want the ease of a franchise, you may be looking at even more money. Of course, one benefit of a franchise is the system the company has in place to support the entrepreneur. This can include everything from purchasing to marketing and selling. These proven methods of operation help create lasting success for entrepreneurs, and make the return on investment (ROI) more likely and more profitable.

What many people don't realize is that direct sales is a low-risk way to start their own business. And it offers many of the same benefits as a franchise. Like franchises, direct sales businesses have proven systems for marketing and selling that they share with their independent representatives. They also help take care of inventory, shipping, product development, and so on.

But they also offer something more — or rather, less. Direct sales allows you to get started for minimal costs. In fact, many starter kits for Party Plan businesses will run you less than $200.

The training for representatives is also often low-cost or free. Most direct sales companies provide a simple program that, when followed closely, help you earn commission (which will help you recoup the cost of your kit) and earn additional products to add to your kit within your first three months of business. Most such companies also typically offer free ongoing training in the form of conference calls, webinars, and meetings. And many offer marketing materials such as catalogs, business cards, social media graphics, posters, email campaigns, and so on.

Direct sales companies have a vested interest in you and your success, which is why they provide you with the training, marketing, and other techniques needed to be successful.

The direct sales model is definitely a powerhouse business model, though it differs in some ways from a traditional retail business model. Both models source products or services to sell to consumers. But a traditional retail business hires salespeople, gives them marketing materials, and tells each salesperson when and where to work. Even if the salesperson is on 100 percent commission, the company requires the salesperson to report to work at a specific time, sell a preset amount, and report to a supervisor. These salespeople receive pay increases and promotions based on their supervisors' decisions.

Direct selling around the world

Direct selling is a global business model. That doesn't mean that every direct sales company operates in every country. It means that the business model operates here in North America, as well as in Central and South America, Europe, Asia, Australia, and Africa. In fact, global estimated retail sales topped US $178 billion in 2013, according to the World Federation of Direct Selling Associations. That was up over 8 percent from 2012. The WFDSA also reported that there are over 96 million independent direct sales representatives worldwide.

The United States is currently the leading market for direct selling, with an estimated $32 billion in retail sales during 2013. Here's something that may shock you: Direct sales generates about one in every six dollars of retail sales, globally.

Direct sales, on the other hand, is very different in terms of flexibility of time and work. When you start a direct sales business, you are in business for yourself. You determine how much you want to work and how much you want to get paid. You are recognized by your efforts when you achieve certain benchmarks in the company, such as achieving a certain level of sales and bringing on a certain number of new team members.

Even though you are in business *for* yourself, you are not in business *by* yourself. Your company is with you every step of the way, motivating and training you to achieve success.

What to Consider When Choosing a Company

Nowadays, an extra stream of income, the lack of job security at a regular job, and the desire for additional tax breaks make a home-based business very appealing. And there are many great companies out there. You may like several of the product lines and could be well suited for any of them. So how do you choose?

Most people select a direct sales company that they've already heard about or had some contact with, whether as a customer or host. Another way that people become interested in a certain company is that a friend or family member joins and invites them to learn more about the opportunity.

Belief in your product, programs, and profits is important when deciding whether a company is right for you. You also need to be passionate about what you offer your clients. Many people discover this passion after they've sampled a product, become a loyal customer of a company, or hosted a party themselves.

If you are interested in learning more about what companies are available to join, aside from the ones you already know, the Direct Selling Association is a great resource. It offers a list of many different companies, organized by category. Visit www.dsa.org for more information.

Many people ask me what the best company would be for them to join. I always answer by mentioning the three Ps: *The best company is the one that pays special attention to products, programs, and profits.*

It should deliver a quality *product* in a timely fashion. It should also support you as a representative with *programs* that train you, help you reach short-term goals, and build long-term habits for success. And of course, *profit* refers to compensation, and in direct selling, that's more than just commission. Some of the profitable rewards are, for example, car incentives and trip incentives.

For profits, you should take incentives into account and choose based on what is important to you. Some companies pay a higher commission on personal sales, and if that's what you are looking for, then that will be appealing. Some focus on the rewards and have excellent trip incentives, which are easy to earn. Some may have a simple and easy car program, so if a car is desirable then this could be for you.

All companies use the exact same dollar; it's how they choose to divide it that makes them different. Sometimes it comes down to the passion that you have for the company, their products and programs, and their profit focus. People always ask me, who has the best compensation program that works? I always respond: *They all work if you work their program.*

One of the key ingredients to success is enthusiasm. People are drawn to it — they want to be a part of it. When someone sees that you are enthusiastic or passionate, it piques their interest. So, it's important that you are enthusiastic.

It can be very difficult to fake that excitement. I have heard people say over and over that you need to *fake it till you make it.* People can say that all day long, but it's not an easy thing to do. Others see through it, and you may not feel as comfortable doing it. I like the statement *honesty is the best policy,* and I do believe that when people see that you are sincere and excited about your product, company, or opportunity, then they will naturally want to do business with you.

How I got started in direct sales

My start in direct sales was due to a combination of the season in my life and my enthusiasm about the product. I was 18 years old when I first started in the business. I was really just looking for a way to supplement my income as a musician. So when I was asked to have a crystal party to help someone out, I readily agreed.

Now I was single and in a rock and roll band and didn't really have a big need for crystal at that time. However, I really was drawn to the product. I loved it and even though I would later leave and choose another line of products, I still am drawn to beautiful glass. I love decorating with it and I love beautiful serving pieces for entertaining. (And nowadays I entertain more with crystal than I did when I was a drummer in a rock band.) I am still mesmerized by the beauty of crystal.

While I was hosting the party to help a friend, the consultant who did the party said to me, "You ought to do this! You would be really good at it." It would have never been on my radar to seek out an opportunity to sell crystal, but because she believed in me and I liked the product, I did it.

After years of success, I fell in love with the industry, and I believed in the opportunities that it offered others. Eventually I decided to leave my crystal business and switch to jewelry. Though I didn't *love* it, I did like it. I also realized that other people did love jewelry, and at that time I was very interested in building a team and achieving large profitability.

The best company really just depends on you, your likes, and your lifestyle; and finding what is going to fit with that.

The Three P's of Every Company

There are several factors to consider when choosing which direct selling company you want to launch your business from. It's absolutely important to look at the "three Ps" mentioned in the last section. In fact, they're so important that I'm going to look at them much more closely in their own section here.

Products

It is extremely important for you to really like the product that you are going to represent, especially if it is your first time in direct selling.

Most people actually join a company because they really believe in the product. For others, they may have experienced great results from a product and have a great testimonial and really want others to have that same experience. And then there are those for whom it is a product they really need, will use, and want to be able to get at an ongoing discount. For others, it's the season in their life, what their interests are, and what their circle of friends are into at that time. And for still others, it's simply that someone believed in them and thought they would be good at doing something different combined with the idea of being able to make some extra income.

But it's still important for you to like the product.

There is an incredible amount of variety in products and services in the direct selling industry. In fact, almost every product you can purchase through a retail outlet can be purchased through a direct seller. You can choose nutritional supplements, discount memberships, financial services, clothing, accessories, kitchenware, décor, cosmetics, entertainment, essential oils, food and wine, and much, much more.

I suggest you choose a product you're passionate about, or that you know many others are passionate about. I wouldn't worry about "the next big thing" so much as finding a product you believe others will want to purchase. I've heard people recommend only selling consumable products, but I know from both experience and anecdotally that products like jewelry draw people who are passionate buyers, even though they haven't used up their existing supply.

When considering a business, think for a minute: Do you like the product? Do you think the product is marketable to a large group of people? From that perspective, it doesn't really matter how much the commission is — if you can't sell it to anyone, then you won't have much success.

Ask yourself these questions:

- ✔ How marketable is the product?
- ✔ Does it appeal to men and women, and to a variety of ages?
- ✔ Is it a consumable?
- ✔ Will you be able to re-service your clients?
- ✔ Is there room for growth?
- ✔ Will customers be able to continue to add to the collection?
- ✔ Is it at a good price point for the majority of people you will be dealing with?

As mentioned before, I personally have never sold a consumable product. But I was still always very successful at getting repeat business because of the emphasis I put on re-servicing customers and the relationships that I developed with them. Chapter 13 talks a lot more about these topics.

Another thing to consider is that products that benefit from an explanation or demonstration usually do better being sold through direct sales channels than simply sitting on the shelf in a big box discount store. So if you love a product and know that when you can explain its appeal, it will sell, you may have found a good company for yourself.

Profitability

Profitability is a product or service's ability to consistently sell and deliver a good wage. I knew customers who would regularly purchase from the collection I was selling. These were also the people who tended to put me in touch with other women who loved jewelry or crystal, too. That helped increase profitability.

When selecting the right direct selling company for you, keep an eye on profitability. Commissions or profits are very important because 80 percent of people join a company with the hopes that they will be able to make a nice additional income.

When considering a direct sales company, ask these questions about profitability:

- How much are you going to be paid for working?
- What is the percentage you will receive for personal sales?
- How much will you have to sell personally to get any bonuses?
- What does it take to move up the ladder?
- What does the career plan look like?
- Are you compensated quickly for bringing others into the business?
- Because commission is based on a percentage of sales, is that based on wholesale or retail?
- If commissions are based on a volume model, how many points of volume are you getting for each dollar in sales?
- What is an average sale per customer?
- What is the average party?

These are things that you need to know, but again you can still be successful as long as you understand the structure of compensation and work with the program to reach those benchmarks.

Programs

Finally, consider what programs the company has in place for you to be successful. Determine what rewards are offered to you and your hosts and customers.

It's important to find out what programs a company offers. Ask the following questions:

- Does the company offer benefits or incentives to the people that will host a party in their home?
- Does the company offer a referral program where hosts are given free product when one of their guests books a party?
- Does the company provide a merchant account so you don't have to get your own to accept credit and debit card payment?
- Does the company handle sending out all the products?
- Do you have a personal website provided and what are your ongoing costs, if any (for example, monthly website fee, newsletter subscription fee, processing fee for commission checks or direct deposit, annual renewal fee, monthly minimums, and so on)?

Depending on what's important to you, many programs may be as important as the cash you earn. Find out the following:

✔ Does the company offer a car program?

✔ Do they offer trip incentives?

✔ Is traveling important to you?

One of the most important factors in deciding which direct selling company to join is how appealing the kit program is and whether it's easy and affordable to join. This will matter as you attract others to the business. You'll also need to know what type of training the company provides and how easy it is to access.

Another added perk is whether the company provides a professionally written newsletter that you can send to your customers or a continuous email campaign. These are just a few that you may want to look at.

Regardless of which direct selling structure you choose — Party Plan, Network Marketing, or Hybrid — the company will offer several types of programs. First and foremost should be a good training program. Training should include a plan for your first months in business as well as ongoing support.

Most companies have a program that offers additional products to add to your kit while you're earning your money back. Most of these programs are 90-day programs that have benchmarks at the 30-, 60-, and 90-day marks.

Other programs will recognize you for your efforts, awarding you titles or gifts for achieving sales or recruiting goals. *Recruiting* means adding representatives to your team. Chapter 14 covers recruiting in detail.

Special Considerations for Start-up Companies

One of the most exciting things you'll hear in direct selling is: *This is a ground floor opportunity!* Joining a company that's just starting up can be very rewarding — but it can be risky too.

The United States has seen some phenomenal growth among direct selling start-ups in the past decade. According to the industry trade journal *Direct Selling News,* a Hybrid company founded in 2011 reached sales of $100 million in 2012, then doubled that in 2013, and then more than doubled again in 2014. In fact, the journal's Global 100 list, which ranks the retail sales of direct selling companies across the world, cited 11 companies that grew by $100 million or more in 2014 — several of which were less than ten years old.

But there are also some very real down sides, too. Examine everything closely before making your decision.

Advantages

The primary advantage of selecting a start-up company is that you really can be in on the ground floor. I would consider that joining any time during the company's first five years puts you in on the ground floor. I promise you that representatives who joined Mary Kay when it was a fledgling company of four to five years old and then kept working and building her business are very professionally satisfied people.

As one of the people on the ground floor, you will be in the exciting position of having plenty of *downline* (the people under you in your organization, including your personally enrolled team members and people *they* have brought into the business) helping build your paycheck as you continue to recruit and help them build theirs.

Another benefit is being able to introduce a new product and its advantages to people who haven't heard of it yet, or who perhaps haven't seen or heard the business presentation. This gives you a great chance to create excitement and give them a chance to experience something new.

Disadvantages

There are also disadvantages to being part of a start-up company. With a new company selling new products, it takes time to get effective marketing materials in the representatives' hands, get a robust website off the ground, deliver strong training programs, and work out the bugs in the new operation.

It also takes money. Start-up companies are rarely staffed with a full creative team. They may lack industry expertise as well as corporate expertise, an accounting department, event team, marketing staff, warehouse staff, and so on. This means that you'll likely face some frustrating delays in areas that seem very important to the business.

Debunking the Myth of Saturation

I'm frequently asked about saturation of a market. There are always people worried about this, and people often ask, "How many representatives are in my area?" For some reason, they seem to believe that their area reaches market saturation when there are five people selling in their town.

To those worried about saturation, I ask what the population of their area is. After they tell me, say, 50,000, I quickly do the math for them. Even if you had 17 representatives, then you'd have to do 200 parties per month per consultant — a number that is very unrealistic and, actually, unattainable.

But even with the number game aside, look at your own circles: friends, family, acquaintances, coworkers, kids' friends' parents, doctors, lawyers, real estate agents, instructors, coaches, and so on. Chances are, the majority of these people will not be selling for the same company that you are. You have a larger reach than you think you do, especially when you factor in their network and circles.

It takes a lot to reach saturation. I frequently tell people that one thing you will almost never have to worry about in direct sales is saturation. That's because direct sales companies don't limit you to specific territories. So, when you aren't finding customers on your street, your block, or even your city, you can simply contact friends in another area by logging on to social media.

And let's face it, not everyone that joins in this business stays. In fact, a third of the people on your team are usually leaving. This isn't a negative reflection on you or on the industry — it's simply that they don't feel it's a good fit for them, or they just don't enjoy it, or maybe life circumstances are causing them to refocus their attention.

In fact, because there are always changing lives and circumstances among your team members and prospects, there are always going to be people you can sell to or recruit. Every year, a whole new group of people are graduating, buying a home, getting married, having a baby, and so on. People continue to go through new cycles of life, and these are opportunities for you. Five years ago, your best friend might not have been interested in purchasing from your home decor business, but with her new home and new circumstances, your products will become some of her favorites.

The most important thing to remember is, establishing relationships with your customers and clients is key. Build strong rapport with your networks and they will continue to purchase from you and recommend you to their circles of friends.

Chapter 3

Working with Different Direct Selling Models

In This Chapter

▶ Understanding Network Marketing

▶ Checking out Party Plan

▶ Zeroing in on the Hybrid model

*F*or many years, there was a big distinction between the Network Marketing business model and the Party Plan business model. In recent years, the two models have started to come together, and in large part, that is where we get the term *Hybrid.* Companies take the best attributes of both models and bring them together in one company. I have also heard people refer to their company as a *hybrid* because of the type of compensation plan they have created. And many of the Network Marketing companies are becoming more product focused, whereas they used to focus almost exclusively on the business opportunity.

At the end of the day, what they all have in common is that direct sales is where the representative sells direct to the consumer or customer without the aid of a retail establishment.

There are many strong opinions about which model is best. So I felt it was important to just cover a bit more about the differences and who may be best suited to you — and along the way dispel some myths about direct selling in general.

The Network Marketing Model

Network Marketing is characterized by a number of factors that are consistent across companies. Companies using the Network Marketing model market readily consumable products like vitamins, skincare products, and subscription services that lend themselves well to auto-ship. The idea is to generate orders every single month, build income consistency and growth, and create a "customer for life."

The emphasis in these companies is frequently on the income opportunity as much or even more than it is on the product. Because the cost of joining as a "member" is often quite low, and can be offered without a kit or product included, many people who would normally just be customers join as independent representatives, often with their first order. That means that when a product becomes popular, there is the opportunity for exponential growth in company size, team size, and income.

There can be a significant benefit to joining earlier, because the structure of the sales force can mean that you may be rewarded by "getting in first" when people who join after you are put into your team, sometimes without any effort on your part. Timing can matter in Network Marketing, and you'll sometimes hear this "getting in first" process referred to as *getting your spot* or *position*.

Income can appear low at first because the strength of this model is in the residual income. *Residual income* results from repeat purchases from the same customers, often on auto-ship. These customers are sometimes retail customers of yours, as well as independent representatives who make up your team of both consumers and marketers. Due to the ongoing consumption in your network or team, your income can continue to grow even as your personal selling and recruiting plateaus or drops.

There is a strong online component with a high level of e-commerce in the Network Marketing model, so customers and independent representatives will often re-order online or stay on auto-ship indefinitely, bringing you the same income that you received from their original orders, with no additional effort from you.

Recruiting in Network Marketing

With such a strong focus on the business and income opportunity and how common it is for customers to just go ahead and join right at the beginning, in Network Marketing, you will commonly be offering the business opportunity to your contacts at the same time you offer the product. Often in these companies, the *opportunity* is strongly considered to actually *be* one of the most compelling "products" you offer. So, you'll sometimes present the income opportunity before they even try the product, or soon after they become your customer.

Is Network Marketing a pyramid scheme?

One of the most frequent questions I'm asked is how to address the misconception that direct selling is a pyramid scheme. A *pyramid scheme* is based on people making money when more people invest in the scheme after them. In direct sales, people earn money when people who join after them sell products. But a pyramid scheme only pays out for a limited amount of time, because people are paid on investment of dollars by new people brought into the scheme, and eventually that arrangement collapses. In direct selling, you get paid for supporting people who are selling actual product to end consumers and who are recruiting others to do the same, which generates revenue that is divvied up among the people who get paid commissions on those particular sales and the company itself.

The Direct Selling Association — the industry organization that advocates for the direct sales model with government, media, and consumers — heavily regulates compensation plans and commission payouts to ensure payments aren't being made based solely on bringing new people into the networks. This is also one reason the association discourages purchases of large amounts of inventory by people who are joining the business (they call this *inventory loading* or *front-end loading,* and it is typically prohibited by the companies themselves).

There have been fraudulent companies claiming to use the direct sales business model, when in practice they are not about selling anything at all. These companies emphasize a significant investment in large amounts of product or services, as well as persuading other people to join the company and invest in similar amounts of product or services. Training for finding customers to purchase the product is practically nonexistent in these companies. Within these operations, it is possible for a representative to purchase enough product that they, in effect, purchase a promotion, rather than earning it through personal and team sales (this is also called *bonus buying,* and most companies prohibit this practice, as well).

When recruiting into your Network Marketing business, you look for people who are seeking a business opportunity, who are interested in earning money, and/or people who absolutely love the product. Due to the consumer network nature of your Network Marketing business, people who are not interested in promoting the business at all can still provide excellent contributions to your network due to their sheer enthusiasm about the product. Product *superfans* who talk about the product and either sign their friends up "by accident" or refer their contacts to talk to you can be just as effective for the growth of your network as people intent on making an income.

Your main objective when seeking new, independent representatives for your team is to naturally and organically gain access to other people's networks and therefore expand your own network. This expansion into the people your contact knows and the people *they* know (and so on) is part of what drives the exponential growth in network marketing.

Each of the people who join will experience at least a small financial benefit from their own referrals, so it ends up being a winning situation, even for those who are just in the network to get a discount or because they are in love with the product for their own personal use.

Sharing the product and the opportunity

Products and the opportunity are shared in a few different ways in Network Marketing.

Testimonials

Network Marketers are urged to *become a product of the product* — which means that they use the product regularly so that they can have their own testimonial regarding its benefits. With so many of the products being in skin-care, weight loss, wellness, and business and utilities services, it's believed that when you are using your company's product to its maximum recommended "dosage," it will become apparent in your physical appearance or in your life.

Before-and-after images and stories are a hallmark of the Network Marketing sales approach because, as is commonly repeated in these companies, *facts tell, stories sell*. So, rather than talk about all the details and specifics of the product the company is offering, independent representatives are encouraged to share their individual positive experiences and let the emotion and authenticity of that sharing attract sales and recruits.

Presentations

Instead of relying on hosts who gather their friends for a presentation (as in the party plan and hybrid models, covered next), most Network Marketing presentations are conducted one-on-one, either over the phone, using Internet presentation tools, or in person as a business presentation. These are also often called *appointments*. Often in these presentations, the business opportunity is emphasized as much as the products or services.

In recent years, many Network Marketing companies and leaders are promoting the value of having new independent representatives kick off their businesses with a "Launch Party" or "Grand Opening" event. They have discovered that in-home events to launch someone's business are a simple, accessible, efficient, and fun way for the new team member to effectively introduce the products and opportunity to a large group of friends, family, and associates all at once.

Systems, tools, and sampling

Network Marketing is also known for the practice of relying on *sampling* to spark interest in the products and using *tools* to share information, including about the business opportunity. These tools are often websites, videos, magazines, audio recordings, and even smartphone and tablet apps. With a belief that the average person can be successful if they follow a system, Network Marketing encourages the independent representative to let the product and the tools do the talking. This lends itself well to long-distance recruiting and sales, as well as a strong reliance on the Internet and phone for even personal sales and recruiting.

You can mail samples almost anywhere and follow up online or by phone to take orders or point interested people in the direction of tools to answer their questions or a website for them to join. Network Marketers often have enough product on hand to supply their personal use and sampling, typically mailed to their homes through an auto-ship program.

Customer orders are typically shipped directly by the company to the customers after an order is placed online, so representatives stocking inventory is no longer necessary and is actively discouraged. In fact, reputable Network Marketing companies ban the practice of purchasing enough product to earn a promotion or advance to a higher job title (or *rank*) and do their best to sanction representatives who place these kinds of orders (also called *bonus buying*).

Years ago, companies began to recognize that though it may appear to increase sales, having a high percentage of sales coming from representatives purchasing an inventory of product that just sits around instead of selling products to end consumers burdens the sales force and weakens the company. Companies now measure their ratio of retail customers to independent representatives and use that measurement as a gauge of healthy growth.

Who is best suited for Network Marketing?

The Network Marketing model is best suited for people who fit the following profile:

- ✔ Enjoy networking one-on-one
- ✔ Like building relationships over time
- ✔ Find comfort in following a very specific system

The people who do best in this model are people who are comfortable allowing the product and the business opportunity to take center stage. They then see themselves more as a *messenger* of the tools that share the information, rather than being the star, expert, or source of information themselves.

This is not to say that they have no appetite for recognition, but rather that they can comply with a system that is already in place and has a proven track record. Often, the process of effectively building a network involves deferring to the expertise of others with the sole purpose of demonstrating the "system" to the prospects.

The key to lasting and satisfying success in Network Marketing is the art of duplication. To attract a lot of recruits and foster duplication in your network, your business practices must be duplicable. Being the *expert* is not easily duplicable because it leads to attracting only people who already believe they are capable of being or quickly becoming the expert, too. That slows your recruiting and network growth.

People who need to "know it all" (and a lot of us fall into that camp) do best in this business when they can preserve their knowledge for supporting their team in the building of their businesses. Your team, also known as your *downline,* is your line of sponsorship who looks to you for guidance. You are considered their *upline* or *sponsor.* You can share your wisdom, your tips, your extensive product knowledge and much more in support of them.

Other traits that are a good match for Network Marketing are:

- ✔ Desire for a residual income stream, delivered regularly (often weekly) via direct deposit
- ✔ Willingness to take a small risk now for potential substantial payoff later (which is true for every direct seller, no matter what type of model).
- ✔ Ability to delay financial gratification and work harder now for a small initial income that could grow in the future

What does it take to be successful?

Are you someone who takes action? Are you a risk-taker with a positive attitude, and you just believe deep down that you will succeed? If the word *no* doesn't faze you, if you are decisive, and if people are attracted to your energy, you may be a fantastic fit for success in the Network Marketing model.

With that said, many people are under the misconception that you have to *be* a certain kind of person to get involved in Network Marketing. The truth is you don't. Average people can do well in Network Marketing, as do people who are focused on improving themselves, those who need some encouragement to step outside of their comfort zones, and people who tend to be shy when in groups.

Part of what makes Network Marketing so successful is that it is so system-focused, that average people can experience better than average results. The load isn't all on *your* shoulders to be an incredible presenter or a great salesperson. The model itself is designed to rely on tools and on existing relationships and networks so that you can create a business following the steps of the people before you.

You can recruit to your weaknesses. If you are the most know-it-all of know-it-alls, you may recruit someone who is more humble, more coachable, and more willing to comply with the system — they can become a recruiting magnet on your team, and *you* benefit. Terrified of speaking in front of groups? Recruit a friend who is a natural host and connector, partner up, and the next thing you know, your team has doubled in size.

In Network Marketing, as in both Party Plan and the Hybrid Model, what is most important is a burning desire for success, a strong work ethic, persistence, and resilience. Use the tools and the system that is already in place, and maintain the discipline to stick with it.

The Party Plan Model

Party Plan places less emphasis on recruiting new team members than the other two models do. In general, women — who make up the vast majority of Party Plan independent representatives, hosts, and party guests — are often more comfortable sharing products to create income than they are recruiting to create income. Fortunately, finding interested recruits becomes almost a natural side bonus of a well-run home party. You get in front of enough women enough times and you will encounter many who are looking for something like a Party Plan business.

So, despite a common discomfort with recruiting, when trained properly, women often discover that helping other women succeed by recruiting and training them brings great satisfaction in addition to boosting their business income.

Party Plan is characterized by a number of factors that are consistent across companies. First, most of the product sales and recruiting takes place during events (parties), both in-person and online, where groups of people (called *guests*) have been gathered together by a host they know personally.

The emphasis in these companies is typically on the products and the gatherings themselves. Hosts act as partners with the independent representative to boost attendance and sales. The parties are the primary source of new contacts and leads.

Parties serve a dual purpose:

- ✔ They generate sales
- ✔ They introduce the independent representative to new, fresh contacts on a regular basis

Many representatives earn all the money they want through their parties and through re-orders from their customers. They find they can continue their businesses successfully as long as they like with little or no recruiting. Their commissions on their personal sales are often quite satisfying, even in the beginning.

The specials provided for customers and perks offered to the hosts of parties are typically provided at no cost to the representative and can be leveraged to get more parties booked and increase initial sales and re-orders.

Instead of being paid with a periodic direct deposit of commissions for their personal sales, Party Plan representatives often receive their sales commissions directly the night of the party or within a few days of submission of the sale, depending on the company's order-taking structure.

Recruiting in Party Plan

The natural life cycle for new recruits in Party Plan is to start out as a guest and customer, become a host next, and later join as a representative. It is common to find potential recruits at the party and invite them to be hosts so they can learn more before approaching them with the business opportunity.

Recruiting in Party Plan is a skill set that piggybacks on the party structure. Each well-run party, in addition to being a sales event, is an *opportunity event.* The party is the ideal place to showcase exactly what your business looks and feels like. It gives each guest who might be interested in earning money the chance to see how simple, easy, and fun it can be.

In recent years, recruiting in Party Plan has increased exponentially due to the introduction of social selling through online platforms and social media. See Chapter 11 for more information on running a successful online business.

Sharing the product and opportunity

Products and the opportunity to join are shared in a few different ways in Party Plan.

Party presentation and customer re-orders

The product presentation at the party is the primary source of sales for the independent representative. The party is where new customers are found, and through ongoing customer care and establishing a relationship, representatives gather future orders and re-orders and book future parties.

Guests as your best customers

An independent representative meets a few or many new people at each party, which provides both immediate sales and a steady supply of future customers and hosts. Presenting products once to a group of people is an efficient way to sell, and the energy of the group usually leads to larger orders by each customer than if the customer were approached independently. Because the guests at the party are a self-selected group who chose to attend after being invited, they are open to the product line before the representative even begins the presentation.

Guests as your new recruit leads

Parties also mean a constant stream of fresh eyes and new potential team members. By structuring the party to include an invitation to take a closer look at the business potential, an independent representative deliberately increases her pool of recruit leads. These leads are the strongest because they have already been exposed to your primary business function and have even begun unconsciously training by observing you in action. See Chapter 9 for more on party structure and Chapter 14 for all about recruiting.

Hosts as your most likely next recruit

A trademark aspect of Party Plan is that the representative helps the host have a successful party through coaching (called *host coaching,* the topic of Chapter 10). The host earns perks and rewards based on the results of the party and is therefore grateful for the support and has an incentive to promote the party. This process of prepping for a great party (Chapter 9) often reveals which hosts would make good representatives and serves as an opportunity for the host to learn more about the business, which often piques their interest in becoming representatives themselves.

Who is best suited for Party Plan?

Party Plan is a great fit for those who enjoy helping others discover new things, people who love to share the things they're passionate about, and for those interested in supporting the success of others.

There are two types of personalities who tend to succeed in the Party Plan model of direct selling. The first type is the one you probably already have in mind: confident, outgoing, never at a loss for words, with a strong personality and no fear of public speaking. The second personality type may be a bit of a surprise: the introvert who almost seems to shun the spotlight, possibly soft-spoken, but with a passion for the product and willingness to share that passion.

To succeed in the Party Plan model, you need to know your product, but you don't have to memorize every fact. It's perfectly okay to say, "I don't have that answer, but I do know I can call my upline or the company to get it. May I call you tomorrow to let you know what I learn?"

Another factor that will help you succeed in the Party Plan model is a willingness to engage people in purposeful conversations. By *purposeful* conversation, I mean finding out what is important to them so you can help them achieve what they define as success. Being someone they can look to for guidance and expertise in the areas related to your product line is also key.

As with the Network Marketing model, being passionate about the product is important to succeeding in the Party Plan structure.

Here are some other traits that are a good match for Party Plan:

- ✔ Desire for a part-time income stream without a formal part-time job
- ✔ Relatively immediate need for that income (new Party Plan reps can begin making income with their very first parties and often receive their commissions the night of their party or soon thereafter)
- ✔ Comfortable being the "expert" or personal shopper and advisor
- ✔ Desire to get out of the house and socialize
- ✔ Love of the product and enjoyment in talking about the product line
- ✔ Knack for entertaining and demonstrating

The Hybrid Model

As the name suggests, the Hybrid model is a combination, in both pay structure and business practices, of Network Marketing and Party Plan. In Hybrid companies, as in Party Plan companies, most product is sold through gatherings where hosts have invited their contacts, in-person or online, to learn more about a product and the income opportunity.

With its frequent focus on online demonstrations and how-to videos and a reliance on e-commerce and auto-ship, the Hybrid model is the most flexible of the models when it comes to schedule and structuring a business around other priorities, while still getting paid primarily for selling product through presentations to several people at once.

Hybrid recruiting methods rely on the party approach and on emphasizing the business opportunity as strongly as the products during these parties. The use of testimonials, tools, and systems is almost identical to the way things are done in Network Marketing.

Because the Hybrid model combines some of the best features of both Network Marketing and Party Plan, it seems to draw both men and women equally. It also appeals to couples who want to work a business together.

This model seems to attract all demographics. Baby Boomers usually aren't as familiar with this model as they are with the other two, so they tend to enthusiastically engage because it appears to be something different, about which they haven't already developed strong opinions. Generation X adults seem to appreciate the authenticity of the product emphasis that also allows for building a significant income fairly quickly. Millennials, also know as Gen Y, like the balance of product and opportunity, which seems realistic and exciting, as well as the reliance on new technologies.

If income is important to you, but you still want to be focused on and passionate about a product that meets a real need, you may prefer a Hybrid company. If you enjoy low-pressure gatherings, online and in-person, that can provide social proof that encourages purchases and presents the benefits of a new venture in a comfortable, casual environment, the Hybrid may be a better fit for you than straight Network Marketing, which relies more on one-on-one presentations. If you are readily able to connect with others through your passion for an interest or for a product you love or through the possibilities of a lucrative opportunity and the lifestyle that results, you may prefer the Hybrid model.

The Hybrid model is such a natural blending of the Network Marketing and Party Plan models, that if you suspect that you have some of the traits of success for either or both of those, a Hybrid company may also be a good fit for you.

Because things change so fast in direct sales companies, more and more companies are of a Hybrid nature. There are Party Plan companies who have developed auto-ship programs, and there are Network Marketing companies who have adopted the Party method, even though neither may refer to themselves as Hybrid.

Part II
Building the Skills to Create a Successful Business

Top Personal Attributes and Skills Needed for Direct Sales

- Resilience and persistence
- Strong work ethic and discipline
- Ability to accept rejection and work outside your comfort zone
- Enthusiasm

Find out how you can practice your skills at www.dummies.com/extras/directsales.

In this part . . .

- ✔ Understanding the importance of staying positive at all costs
- ✔ Setting goals and improving your productivity
- ✔ Being ready to do business at all times

Chapter 4

Keeping a Positive Attitude

- -

In This Chapter

▶ Understanding that success is all in your attitude

▶ Breaking through self-doubt

▶ Avoiding self-sabotage

- -

*W*hen you first start your business, you want to see as many people as you can. And when you see these people, you need to be enthusiastic about your new adventure because others will mirror the energy you put out. If you want others to be drawn to you and the products and services you offer, you must be positive.

Having a positive attitude makes you likeable and it makes others feel confident about doing business with you. Even in the midst of challenging times and obstacles, you need to challenge yourself to assume the best about your company, your products, and your ability to be successful.

Staying Successful: Attitude Is Everything

For almost everything, I estimate that 80 percent of your success is wrapped up in your attitude. And I know for a fact that the attitude you choose to have will either attract people to you or cause them to not want to do business with you.

Every morning when you wake up, you have the power to decide what type of day you're going to have. If you wake up thinking you will have a horrible day, then you will continue to have a horrible day. If you say things like, "I have nothing going for me. I have no bookings, no sales, and no recruiting leads," then that's how you're going to feel, and that is what will manifest in your life.

You must always act in a way that will attract people towards you. Choose to look at your day in a positive way. Say to yourself, "This is a great day! My business is coming along nicely, and my calendar is already half full." The choice is yours whether you want to be optimistic or pessimistic. How you see yourself and your life is what you will get — so always be positive and energetic.

Sharing your enthusiasm with everyone

Enthusiasm is contagious. People will mirror your attitude, your tone of voice, and your body language. If you're enthusiastic, people will be enthusiastic with you; if you're confident, people will be confident with you; if you're unsure, people will be unsure with you; if you're hesitant, people will be hesitant with you. You get the point.

That is why it is important to always remain excited about your business. Be passionate and confident about what you are doing, your success, and your business, because people will mirror that same reaction.

If you call a past host and say, "Hey Mary, it's Belinda. I know it's been a while since we did a party, but I wanted to let you know that I have a new catalog. I'd like to show it to you. What do you think?"

Mary will probably respond with something like, "Send it to me and I'll ask around. If I get any interest, I'll call you back."

On the other hand, if you call Mary having already decided to be excited about your new catalog instead of sounding indifferent, your conversation might go something like this: "Oh my gosh, Mary, I can't wait to show you our new catalog. Your friends are going to love it! We have so many amazing new products that you are absolutely going to love. My calendar is already filling up fast! You do not want to miss out on this. I only have Tuesday, May 5th and Saturday, May 23rd open. Does either of those work for you?"

Her reaction will most likely be, "Okay! Let's book the 23rd!" instead of being unsure or hesitant. If you show Mary that you're excited, then she will be excited.

Many new representatives are nervous about trying to secure bookings or get new business. This is because they lack confidence. They feel unsure and they don't want to seem pushy. Instead of keeping a positive attitude and sharing her excitement for her business, a new rep usually says something like this:

> "Hi Sally, this is Carol." (*Lots of small talk.*) "Well, I don't want to keep you. I know you're busy . . . and you may or may not be interested . . . but I went to a _____ party and really liked the products, so I decided to join the company. I just have to do six parties to really get my business off the ground. I don't know if I'll get any bookings after that. If not, it's okay. I don't like to pressure my friends, as you know, but if you would help me out, that would be awesome."

This rep comes off as shy, afraid, and unsure how to handle her business. If you remind yourself why you got into this business and remain excited and positive, your conversation with others would be very different.

Ask yourself why you started. Did you want to pay for camp this summer? Go on a well-deserved vacation? Maybe pay off some debt? Whatever your reason for joining the business, be sure to keep it in mind at all times. Write down your vision and goals and keep it somewhere easily accessible. Put it on your fridge, mirror, desk — and anywhere else you look. Keeping yourself focused on what you want and staying committed to achieving it will help you remain positive and excited while working with your customers and clients.

When you commit to having a positive attitude about your business, your conversations will begin to sound more like this:

> "Hi Sally, this is Carol. I'm so glad I caught you. I'm sure you're busy, so I won't keep you. I just had some exciting news to share. I went to a _____ party on Thursday and was so impressed with the products. It was something I could really see myself sharing with others, so I decided to join the company as a way to meet new people and earn extra income for our family. Sally, I'd absolutely love for you to get your friends together for a fun party. This is something I think they would really enjoy, and it will also give you an opportunity to receive some special thank-you gifts. This would really help me out. What do you think?"

Not only will you feel different about yourself and your business after having a conversation that begins like this one, so will your hosts. Even if your host agreed to a party when you sounded unsure, she likely won't turn out to be an enthusiastic host and will have that same attitude when inviting her friends to the party. Her call would most likely sound like this:

> "Hey Joanne, it's Sally. I'm having this party for my friend Carol just to help her out with her new direct sales business. You don't have to buy anything. Just come for the food."

That is certainly not the way you want anyone to talk about you or your business. Instead, by remaining positive and sharing your enthusiasm and excitement with leads, not only will you have a higher chance of booking parties, you will have a greater chance of having successful ones because your host will be excited too.

Being excited while out and about

It's important to be excited about getting new business, and that means being enthusiastic when you're out. Here are the three most important things to remember before you go out:

- **Look and feel your best:** When you look your best, you feel your best. Being excited about your business ensures that you are always prepared to get business, and that means looking professional. Remember, many of these people will be inviting you into their homes to do parties with them and introduce you to their friends, so it's important that you look presentable.

  If you run to the grocery store in your sweatpants and t-shirt and overhear someone talking about needing what you sell, what are the chances that you will approach them? Probably very slim. Not only will you not approach that person, you will probably spend the rest of your day complaining about how you lost a lead. If you stay excited about your business, then you will live in an excited space. You will get ready before you leave the house and leave the house saying, "Today is going to be a great day! I have blitz cards in my purse and catalogs in my car. I am going to get a lead today!" (Blitz cards are also known as promo cards — small cards that contain product information about a popular item or line, as well as some information about the business opportunity; see Chapter 12 for more.)

- **Be ready with your 30-second commercial:** You put on a clean blouse, styled your hair, and put on some make-up. You're feeling and looking good and you're remaining optimistic about your day. But be sure you're prepared for new business. Have your 30-second commercial ready to whip out at any opportunity (Chapter 6 talks more about this). In brief, your 30-second commercial is designed to share with your leads exactly what you offer while creating a desire for it. The more excited you sound about your business, the more excited they will be.

- **Learn to engage in conversations:** It's important to be energetic and to network. And that means starting conversations with people. An easy way to start conversations with someone is by complimenting them on something. A compliment gets people feeling good about themselves and more inclined to continue a conversation with you.

> Starting a conversation can be difficult, sure — but you have to force yourself to do it, because when you do, you have the opportunity to get some amazing results in return.

 If you can wear your product or have it with you, great. Otherwise, you may want to have logo wear on or you may want to carry a bag with your logo on it. (Chapter 6 talks more about the importance of logo wear and *wear it to share it.*)

Learning to deal with no

One thing you need to learn quickly in this business — in any business, for that matter — is that people are going to tell you no.

There are people who will not like or want your product. They won't want to book a party, and they won't think direct sales is for them. And that's okay. You can't let them bring you down, because getting a no actually means you are closer to getting a yes.

When someone tells you no, remind yourself that they aren't saying no to you because they don't like you as a person. They are saying no to the experience or to the product, maybe even because they don't understand it.

To get good things, expect good things

In life, you need to expect good things to happen. Many people believe in the law of attraction — that by focusing on positive or negative thoughts, you can get positive or negative results. People also want to connect and do business with like-minded people. Your personal and business brand should always help you connect to your target audience. It's important to be the kind of person you want to attract. And most people are attracted to positive people with a great outlook.

When you wake up in the morning or before you go out, you need to expect that something good is going to happen. Have the expectancy that you are going to get into a conversation with somebody at the bank, the hair salon, or the grocery store. Expect to make a sale, book a party, or find a recruit lead.

When you expect things and remain positive, you challenge yourself to be prepared. Maybe you decide to take five blitz cards out with you because you expect to meet five amazing people. When you leave the house with that attitude, you are more likely to start conversations with people and get the ball rolling. You will feel more confident about your business and what you offer, and so will the people you meet.

I think sometimes people are so fearful they're going to get a no that it prevents them from getting a yes. The truth is, to get a yes, you need to get a number of no's. If you ask ten people and one says yes, that means nine say no. So, when you get the no, be excited about it — because you know that a yes is just around the corner!

Many tend to take rejection personally and let it affect the way they think about their business. The first few times you hear no from your friends, family, or coworkers, or if no one shows up to your launch party, you may want to abandon your dreams. You will want to lose your positive attitude. You will start convincing yourself of things like these:

- ✔ Well, I really just wanted the products in the kit anyway.
- ✔ I guess it wasn't meant to be.
- ✔ I'm actually too busy with my other job.
- ✔ I've earned back the cost of the kit, so it's no big deal.

In fact, many people talk themselves out of the business before it even starts. This is why you need to remain positive and committed to your goal. To get the results you want your for business, you have to stay focused, give your business the time and attention it deserves, and don't let the no's bring you down.

As with any new job, there are going to be times when you feel uncomfortable and unsure, especially at the beginning. But as long as you remain positive about your business — even through the no's — you will find yourself attracting people you want.

Finding the silver lining in everything

Learning to find the silver lining means learning to find the best in everything that happens. If you do your best and look for the good in every situation, then good things will come to you.

I remember when I was in the field, I booked a party with a woman who was over 90 years old and lived two hours away. I went all the way there, and no one showed up. I could tell she was upset, so I stayed with her for two hours looking at photos of past vacations and things her grandchildren had made her. I could have gotten upset and written the evening off as a horrible night with money lost. Instead, I put my focus on her and making her feel good. I was hopeful that something good would come from the situation, and it did. She not only collected an abundance of outside orders, she helped me create the biggest booking chain of that summer.

Sometimes when we do something, we want an exchange of effort or a result right away. If you do good and help people, it comes back to you in other areas of your life. It might not come back to you at that exact moment, but eventually you will see the fruits of your labor.

Being solution oriented

You *will* have something go wrong in your business at some point. Instead of focusing on what's wrong, focus on what you can do to fix it. Every time you see a problem, immediately make it your goal to find a solution.

I remember once when I was traveling to Toronto, I was sitting beside a couple whose flight had just been cancelled. I heard them say things like, "What are we going to do now?" "I can't believe our flight got cancelled. Now we are going to miss picking up Jacob." Automatically, they looked at their situation with a negative attitude and started to list how this one thing was going to ruin everything else.

I have always been very solution oriented, so I was already coming up with solutions for them. I interrupted them and apologized for overhearing and gave them some options. I let them know that the Windsor airport was only 45 minutes away and that maybe they could get a flight from there. I reminded them that Detroit to Toronto was only a four-hour drive, so they could possibly rent a car. After I mentioned these options to them, they calmed down, and their attitude changed.

The fact is, most people don't think in a solution-oriented manner. Many people keep themselves from moving forward toward their goal. Instead they give up at the first sign of trouble and let one small thing ruin their day.

Letting go of the things you can't change

Sometimes things aren't meant to be, and there is nothing you can change, no matter how solution-oriented you are. You need to move forward and find the positive in that.

Don't be upset about the things you can't change. Something like an order being delayed in shipping is completely out of your control. But what *do* you have control over? You can connect with your customer and reassure them that their order is coming. Nine out of ten times your customer will completely understand. If they don't, you can work with them to make them happy.

People spend so much time and energy on the things they have no control over. That's why it's important to find the silver lining and stay positive about everything.

Staying positive on social media

People are watching what you do and say on social media. They are deciding what type of person you are, whether they like and trust you, and whether they want to do business with you.

Your social media platforms should not be places to air your dirty laundry, complain about your day, or in any other way be unprofessional. When you do any of these things, you come off as a negative person — and people don't want to do business with negative people.

Even if you choose to use your social media pages only for personal use and *not* for business, never forget that there are still potential customers, hosts, and recruits viewing you online. Someone who is interested in your product or your business will most often check out your social media pages to decide whether or not you are someone they want to do business with.

No matter how you are running your business — as hobby, part-time, or full-time — it's important to always be ready for business because it can turn up everywhere. That is why it's important to always be professional, respect-ful, and positive on your social media pages. Show your friends and follow-ers that you are friendly and approachable, and that you are someone they would love to do business with either as a customer, host, or team member.

You also don't want to run from negative comments either. Deleting a nega-tive comment about your business on your social media pages is one of the worst things you can do because it shows your customer (and others watch-ing) that you are not confident enough to handle the situation. Plus you make your customer feel like their opinion or situation doesn't matter.

Instead, use a negative comment as an opportunity to show off your amaz-ing customer service. We all make mistakes, so continue to be positive and help find a solution for the situation. (Chapter 11 talks a lot more about using social media in direct sales.)

Being a strong role model for your team

As a sponsor or leader, it's important to be an example for your team. You want to create a space for them that is positive, uplifting, and motivational. Often, your team members are already fighting with negative self-talk and self-doubt, so it's important for you to have a positive attitude.

The service recovery paradox: When mistakes turn out great

The *service recovery paradox* is the idea that customers will be more loyal to you after you have made a mistake and made up for it with great customer service. It turns out that your customers understand that you and your company make mistakes. What most people are looking for is to be validated and heard. They want to make sure that they matter to you and that you will do what it takes to fix the situation for them.

One time I went to dinner with a group of friends to a new restaurant. Even though we had made a reservation, it took over an hour to seat us for dinner. I remember how hungry we all were, not to mention how upset and frustrated I was. As we were waiting for our waitress to come over, my friend turned to me and said, "Well, we're definitely never coming back here!"

When our waitress came to the table, she was accompanied by the manager. The manager apologized for the wait and brought us a sample of almost every appetizer on the entire menu. He wanted to make sure that we felt taken care of and that we enjoyed the remainder of

our evening. The food was fantastic, and we were so blown away by the service that even to this day, the restaurant is still a place we recommend to everyone.

That is the service recovery paradox. I became a *more* loyal customer after having the staff make up for a mistake because I got to see how professionally they handled a negative situation and how fast they turned it around. The manager believed in the experience and food — he knew we would enjoy the appetizers that he brought out for us. You need to have this same attitude about your business, your products, and most importantly, yourself.

Just like the restaurant, you too will make mistakes. You will order the wrong product, something will arrive damaged, a product will get lost in the mail, or if it's delivered, the customer won't like it. When those things happen, use them as opportunities to show your customer that you have amazing customer service, are dedicated to making them happy, and can confidently and easily find a solution to their problem.

You also never want to get involved in gossip. If one of your team members is having a problem, help them find a solution without worsening the situation or getting involved in the negativity. Discussing their situation with others breaks down the trust — and therefore, in many cases, productivity. Instead, show them your positive attitude and help get them back on track.

Overcoming Self-Doubt

The truth is, none of us ever fully overcomes self-doubt. Even top athletes, musicians, actors, and political leaders are often crippled by self-doubt. The trick is to recognize it, because the sooner you recognize it, the sooner you will come out of it. If you recognize what causes you to doubt yourself, you are more likely to avoid those feelings and maintain a positive attitude about your business and your skills.

Don't beat yourself up over self-doubt. Just remember that the sooner you recognize it, the sooner you can work on overcoming it.

Many people doubt themselves in the direct sales industry. They doubt whether they're suited for the business or they doubt their abilities when sales and recruiting go down. They convince themselves that it wasn't meant to be and they actually start talking themselves out of their business.

To help yourself and your team members overcome self-doubt, it's important to look at the four cornerstones of belief.

The four cornerstones of belief

The four cornerstones of belief are the four main areas of your business that you must remain positive about and remind yourself of when you are experiencing self-doubt:

- ✔ **Belief in the industry:** Do you believe that the direct sales industry is a good model that offers a flexible schedule and fair compensation for your work? Do you believe it's a great way for people to supplement their income, make their dreams come true, meet different and like-minded people, and do something fun? Remind yourself of all the reasons you believe in direct sales.

- ✔ **Belief in your company:** Do you believe that your company has your back, provides you good, quality products, and has programs in place for you to be successful? Can you count on your company to provide you with the support you need to achieve your goals? Look at your company, at both corporate and field leaders, and remind yourself of all the amazing things they do every day to help you succeed.

- ✔ **Belief in the product:** Can people benefit from your product? Is it easily marketable? Do people want it and enjoy it? Will people buy it? Ask yourself: Do I love the product because I sell it? Or do I sell it because I love it? Remind yourself of what drew you to the products in the first place.

- ✔ **Belief in yourself:** Do you believe you deserve to be successful? Do you believe that you can reach your goals and achieve your dream? Do you believe that you can earn the money you desire if you work hard enough? Remind yourself that your dreams matter and that you can achieve anything.

Starting with self-talk

Believing in yourself starts with self-talk. What do you say to yourself during the day? I hope you don't say things like this:

✔ "I'm not very good at this."

✔ "I'm not organized."

✔ "I'm so stressed out."

The more you have this type of self-talk and repeat those same words day in and day out, the more you will eventually begin to believe them.

Instead, say things that encourage belief in yourself. Instead of saying how stressed you are, say, "I'm a little overwhelmed right now with what I have going on. What can I do to fix this? What can I get off my plate?" To keep myself from being stressed, I learned to take things in bite-sized chunks instead of looking at everything I had to do. Doing so allows me to focus on a few things at a time and lets me feel accomplished about what I do complete.

It's also up to you to know how you feel about your business and your life. For example, I have a very busy schedule with travelling. I can say, "I can't believe I have to leave again. I am so tired. I am so sick of living in hotels and spending all of my time flying," or I can say, "I am so excited I get to do what I love! I love sharing my passion and knowledge of this industry with so many people."

You have control over your self-talk and have the power to remain positive. It all starts with you. If you say no one wants to buy this, or no one wants to book a party with me, then no one will. It's important to believe in yourself and talk positive about yourself and your business, because if you remain positive, you will work towards positive results.

Building confidence and self-esteem

The following sections were inspired by Pat Pearson's *Stop Self Sabotage* (McGraw-Hill, 2008).

A lot of people think that confidence and self-esteem are one and the same. They are actually very different.

Confidence comes from knowledge and practice. The more experience you have, the more confident you will become. The more parties you hold, the more you will learn, and the better you will be at them. Your bookings will increase, you will maintain high sales every month, and you will welcome new team members to your team. Even if you have an unsuccessful party, you will still learn from your mistakes and pinpoint the things you want to change. Having a student mentality for your business and always striving to learn more and be better will help you increase your confidence.

Self-esteem, on the other hand, is established based on the relationships you have and the people you surround yourself with. Surrounding yourself with people who are extremely positive helps build your self-esteem and your belief in yourself. Your self-esteem gives you the push you need to learn more, seek new opportunities, and network with others.

Don't keep going back to people who are going to talk negative to you. Find inspirational people within your industry and follow them. Surround yourself with successful people who are positive and who motivate you to want to achieve greater success with your business.

Your confidence and your self-esteem combined are the perfect recipe for success.

Getting Out of Your Own Way

As I've tried to make clear so far in this chapter, the main force that limits your success is likely to be yourself. It's important to discover what things are holding you back from achieving the success you want. Each of us deals with many reasons why we hold ourselves back. For each person, some reasons may be stronger or more dominant than others.

The sooner you recognize what your Achilles heel is, the sooner you can correct it. This section covers some of the more common ways people hold themselves back from achieving everything they could achieve.

Settling for less

This happens when you are going along and you almost get to your goal but you decide this is good enough. For example, say you want to book six parties next month. You call up past hosts and leads from your booking lead notebook (See Chapter 7 for more information on creating a lead notebook) and do effective booking talks at your party. Doing all of this gets you five parties on your calendar. You decide to stop at five parties because you have convinced yourself you have done good enough. Those five parties are *almost* six, so you give yourself a break from getting that last one booked.

Why? Why are you settling for less when you wanted six parties? That sixth party might help you get the income you want for that month, earn an incentive, or achieve a promotion.

Instead of being satisfied by less than what you really wanted, work to push through and achieve the goals you initially set out for yourself.

Avoiding resignation

Avoiding resignation is when you convince yourself that whatever you were trying to achieve wasn't going to happen anyway. You decide that it won't make a difference even if you put your best effort forward. You say things like the following to yourself:

> "I'm not going to bother calling these leads. They weren't that good anyway."

> "I might as well not go. No one I know is going to be there."

> "I'm going to skip that event, I'm sure no one will be interested in my services."

> "Even if I get that fundraiser, it will be too much work for me right now."

It's important to have confidence in your skills and in your business that things will work out and that you will find success.

Managing perfectionism and procrastination

Another thing that inhibits people from achieving true success is being a perfectionist. This is *my* Achilles heel. I decide I want to do something, but before I jump into it, I think of all the things I need to do first to make it perfect.

I have thought about writing a book for many years and have started the process over a dozen times. But I never completed it because I got too wrapped up in what the cover would look like, what the title would be, which chapters I would include, and so on. I got to the point where there were so many details in my way, I never got started. But when it came time to write this book, with the help of my editor at Wiley, we set small, achievable, and deadline-oriented goals. So instead of feeling overwhelmed by writing an entire book, I focused only on writing a chapter at a time and then editing a chapter at a time. (And voila! Here it is!)

You may decide to make booking calls, for example, but before you do that you need to make files first, then you need to make a spreadsheet, then you need to run to the store to get highlighters instead of sitting down, digging in, and just making calls.

Other people suffer from procrastination. They think, "Well, I still have a day and a half to get this done. I will just wait. If I wait until later to call, more people will be home; I'm really tired right now. I'm going to wait until tomorrow when I'm feeling more up to it."

It took me a long time to realize that perfectionism and procrastination go hand in hand. Even though I had never considered myself to be a procrastinator, my perfectionism caused me to procrastinate. When I finally came to that realization, I had to let it go, because I did not want to be a procrastinator or feel that I had the inability to stay on task.

I have not overcome this shortcoming completely, but now when I catch myself saying, "I first need to do this," I analyze what I'm doing and force myself to start digging into the project.

Staying away from denial and blame

It's in our nature to want everything to be fine, so denial functions as a gloss over the harsh realities of life. When we ignore or refuse to believe what's going on around and within us, denial creeps into our lives. Denial is refusing to accept reality or a situation for what it is. As a self-sabotage strategy, denial operates very much to our detriment. The more you fear you don't deserve something you want, the more denial you have to use.

Here are some examples of denial:

> I eat pretty healthy most of the time — I don't know why I can't lose the weight.
>
> I didn't want to win that trip. We're going to be going on a really great family vacation anyway.
>
> It's okay if I don't make my promotion next month. If it's meant to be, it will happen.

People who suffer from denial convince themselves they have done everything they could to get a good or positive outcome, when in fact they may be too afraid to try everything. They also deny that they ever wanted something in the first place, so they can try to avoid the feeling of disappointment.

Blaming, or *projecting*, is maintaining that the responsibility for the behavior lies somewhere else, not with you. You don't deny the behavior, but you place its cause "out there," not within yourself. I see this all the time in direct sales. People are so quick to blame anyone else they can for the mistakes and actions they've made themselves:

> If my upline were more supportive, I would be better.
>
> If my husband supported me, I would succeed.
>
> If my job was more structured, I would have more time to focus on my business.
>
> I don't live in a good neighborhood.
>
> My friends don't make enough money to purchase the product.
>
> I don't have people to watch my kids so I can go do a party.
>
> If the company could get the promotions out faster, I could get more bookings.
>
> I was never trained properly.

You are in charge of your business. You need to decide to take the steps to achieving your goals and not let your fears get in the way of your success.

Taking risks: Getting past the fear

Fear is usually fear of the unknown. People get paralyzed if they don't know the outcome. Part of getting over fear is realizing that you aren't going to know the outcome, and the only way is to jump in and try.

Again, this is where being solution oriented comes into play. The more solution oriented you are, the more likely you are to take risks because you know at the end of the day, you will be able to find a solution. You need to tell yourself, "No matter what happens, I am going to figure out a way."

One of the things I always do if I really find myself in fear of moving forward or taking a risk is make a list of pros and cons. I look at what would be the absolute worst thing possible that could happen, and what would be the best thing possible. Most of the time, the best thing far outweighs the worst. But if I look at the worst and ask myself, "Can I live with that? Can I change that?" and my answer is *yes*, I move forward.

Comparing yourself to others

Many people sabotage their success by comparing themselves to others. Does that person have what you really want? Do they live where you really want to live? Do you want that type of house? Do you want to work the same amount?

Remind yourself that *you* define what success looks like and do what it takes to get you there. You cannot compare your success to someone else's, just like you can't compare the beginning of your journey in direct sales to that of someone who has been in the industry for years.

Another way not to compare yourself to others and keep a positive attitude is to have an attitude of gratitude. Always stay focused on what you have and what you are capable of. Write down all the good things in your life. List the things you are grateful for. Starting a journal is a great way to accomplish this.

Chapter 5

Creating a Vision, Setting Goals, and Boosting Your Productivity

In This Chapter

▶ Understanding the difference between vision and goals

▶ Participating in company incentive programs

▶ Exploring my proven productivity system: the Power Hour

▶ Developing other helpful skills

*S*uccess is measured in different ways for different people. What success means to you is personal to you. Success is a journey, and it is your journey, so you shouldn't compare your journey to someone else's.

Whatever success looks like for you, there are certain components that are almost guaranteed to get you where you want to go. This chapter aims to offer suggestions on how to improve them in your business:

✔ **Vision** is the big picture of where you see yourself and what motivates you. Keeping your vision front and center can help set you apart — very few people develop a vision.

✔ **Goals** are the actionable and measurable steps that get you to your vision.

✔ **Incentive programs** are programs created by direct sales companies to increase productivity. You can use them to boost your own sales and earn more income.

✔ **Productivity:** Creating and staying on a consistent schedule is one of the hardest things for most people, especially those who have never been self-employed before. Learning how to set the right schedule to manage your time will contribute to a large portion of your success. I call my system the Power Hour, and I believe you will find it very useful.

✔ **Practical skill sets:** Working on your focus, commitment, consistency, and organization can help you take your business to the next level.

Before I explore these components in detail, I want to mention two more very quickly: Healthy habits and positive thinking.

Anyone who has ever achieved success in anything — whether that be personal finances, health and wellness, relationships, or running a business — does it by creating healthy habits. Your habits are the things you do day in and day out, over and over again, that in some ways define you. Bad habits, of course, can prevent you from achieving success. Good habits help you on your way to success. It's important to develop healthy habits so that they become natural things that you do, that you will not waver from.

Having the right frame of mind and a positive attitude are vital to your success. You attract what you put out into the world. Always see your glass as half full and find the silver lining in every situation. That may sound a little cheesy, but I promise you, positive thinking will help you become a successful business owner by developing your critical thinking and problem-solving skills. Having a positive attitude is also imperative when you are trying to lead others and build a team.

Vision: Your Big Picture of Why

Your *vision* is the big picture of what you want in life. A large part of what I do as a direct selling consultant is conduct surveys and reports to learn more about the field and gather statistics to help develop my training. Through conducting surveys and focus groups, I have found that only about 3 percent of people have a vision for their lives. According to Brian Tracy, expert on goal setting and author of *Flight Plan* (Berrett-Koehler, 2009), this statistic is true for people in general.

To succeed in direct sales, you *must* have a very clear vision of what you want. That's because you'll face frequent challenges, and if you're like all the most successful direct sellers, you'll become discouraged. That's right. Every single person who has succeeded at direct selling has questioned themselves, and most will tell you they've been tempted to give up. Having a vision to strive for can keep you going.

Picture what you really want in life. Make that picture very clear. Don't just envision more free time and more money. Add detail. Paint the picture of what you really want the time and money *for*. Perhaps you would like to buy a new home, become debt-free, or help your spouse retire. Writing your vision down and placing it prominently on a bulletin board is a good way to keep your vision alive.

My vision in direct sales

I have made tens of thousands of dollars a month in direct selling (which was a big deal in the 1980s), and I know dozens of people who have earned that much and even more. But if I hadn't had a very strong vision of what I wanted and why I wanted to succeed, I would have given up. If you don't have a clear vision why you should continue to work through the challenges, you'll be tempted to quit, too.

When I first began a career in direct sales, selling crystal, my vision was to be a rock and roll star. I know that sounds funny, but it's absolutely true. I was a drummer in a rock band, and our gigs weren't paying my bills. So I needed to earn money in a job with a flexible schedule that didn't interfere with drumming and that also let me sleep in a bit on mornings after I played. Direct selling fit the bill — and paid the bills.

A few years later, I traded in my dream of being a rock star for the dream of staying home with my new baby girl. I began to take my direct sales business more seriously so I could still contribute to our household income and afford some luxuries like tiny cute outfits for her. Once again, direct selling fit in with my schedule and helped me earn money during hours that my husband could be home with our daughter. It allowed us to save substantial money for things like family trips, groceries, and yes — tiny cute outfits.

After having two children, my vision for myself and my business was to reach the top of my company's career plan, earning a six-figure income by the time I was 30. When I was 28, I changed companies and had to start my business completely over. My goals changed (more on goals in the next section) — but my vision never did. And three months before my 30th birthday, I was promoted to the top of my company, earning $10,000 a month.

My vision now for my business is to make my training and consulting company, Step Into Success, a one-stop-shop for corporate offices, direct selling leaders, and representatives for all their direct selling and marketing needs. My vision is to continue to build my already successful business, so I can spend more time with my husband, children, and grandchildren.

Your vision will change

Your vision will change. So don't worry about trying to create a vision that will address every possible detour your life might take. In fact, your vision will continue to change throughout your life as you reach important milestones. Once you reach one milestone, you set a new vision for what you want in life and in business.

I've always updated my vision in ten-year increments — when I was 20, 30, 40, and so on. I didn't always reach every goal, and I didn't always get there the way I thought I would. I definitely had some bumps and detours along the way. But almost every time, I ended up where I wanted to be.

To succeed in direct selling, you must have a vision of why you want to succeed in this business.

Being a leader and helping others with their vision

According to my focus groups and industry surveys, only about 1 percent of people are born with the natural ability to help others create a vision. The rest have to develop the ability to mentor through practice.

When you join your company, your leader will sit down with you and discuss the career plan and ranks within your company, as well as the qualifications to achieve them. According to your company's career plan, you technically become a leader when you start to bring other people into the business and achieve a leadership rank within the career/compensation plan.

But being a leader doesn't happen automatically when you hit a leader rank in your company's career plan. Part of what it means to be a leader is the ability to inspire others to discover their vision and their success story. You must become a student of it and help others find their why. Find the fire in your belly and then help others find the fire in *their* bellies. See Chapter 17 for more on what it means to be a leader.

The real gift when it comes to vision is when you master helping others achieve their vision. When you begin to see results in people's lives that you touch and truly inspire, it is the most rewarding feeling in the world — far beyond any financial measure.

Building vision in others is important because it helps them remember why the challenges are worth going through. As a leader, you know that whether it's a busy personal schedule, an unorganized calendar, or personal situations, there will be challenges to building your business!

When those challenges come, your representatives will need to be able to focus on the vision they're working toward, so the challenges are in perspective. The majority of your team members may not have a clear vision of what they want in life, so when the challenges come, they focus on the challenges. By helping them build vision, you give them *staying power*.

Goals: Milestones to Success

Vision and goals both contribute to success, but they are not the same thing. Success is achieving your vision by reaching the goals you set. Goals are the milestones on the way to your success.

Whenever I ask people what success looks like to them, most respond with "I don't know." Most representatives are fine just going with the flow and taking whatever business they receive. That is because for the most part people don't know what success looks like for them. If you don't know what it looks like then how do you know what you are striving for? If you don't know what you are striving for, how are you going to know when you've gotten there? If you don't know that you've gotten there, how are you going to feel successful? And if you don't feel it, how are you going to project it?

For as far back as I can remember, I have been setting goals. It's hard for me to even go through a regular day without setting a goal and achieving it — whether that be getting on the phone with a client, getting in a workout, or writing ten pages of this book.

When I was young, my goals were things like how fast I could ride my bike around the block or how many records I could collect. When I started playing drums at ten, a goal might be trying to master a technique or playing along to a particular song. Everything was always about hitting a target. Now as an adult, this habit has carried over into my life without any thought. No matter how big or small my vision is, I always set mini-goals to help get myself where I want to be.

Goals don't have to be scary

Maybe you are afraid to set goals because you fear they are too daunting or challenging. Nonsense! For one thing, goals don't have to be stupendous. People think goals need to be life-changing. That couldn't be further from the truth.

Goals are exactly what you need them to be. A goal could be creating an Instagram account, calling five people, or recruiting a new team member. You may be in this industry as a hobbyist or for some part-time income to help pay for the everyday things in your life like dance lessons, gas, groceries, and so on. That is your vision for your business, and your goals will align with that.

If you don't hit a goal, that doesn't mean you've failed. To my way of thinking, there are no failures in business or in life, until you fail to try again. If you are driving and miss a turn, for example, or go the wrong way, you don't just give up on reaching your destination. If you're using GPS, it will take a moment and say, "Recalculating route." It doesn't say, "Okay, you're a loser, you went the wrong way, just turn around and go home." You follow the recalculations and get yourself back on the route.

Goals are not scary. Fear paralyzes people, and most of the time, it is fear that stops them from setting goals. Fear they will fail and what others will think. Now, if I said I've never been afraid, well, that simply wouldn't be true. But I don't let it stop me. I ask myself, what's the best thing that could happen? And what's the worst thing that could happen? If I can live with the worst, then I move forward and strive for the best. And most of the time, I land somewhere in between. Everything in life is either a blessing or a lesson, as they say.

Goals don't need to be life-changing. They can be simple, actionable, measurable steps that will keep you on the road to your vision. And you can always reset your goals depending on your personal situations. Don't let other people's opinions worry you, especially if you don't reach a goal. Most people will actually admire you for doing something because they are still usually sitting in the same place.

Setting intentional goals: The five Ds

Your goals may change over time. You may need to do things differently, or your goals may not work anymore, or you may find better ways to get to the end of the race. Goals help you measure your success on your way to your vision.

I believe that when you put your vision out there, or even just say it out loud to yourself, that is when things actually begin to happen. Some call this the Law of Attraction — the idea that like attracts like, and positive thoughts bring positive things.

Regardless of whether the Law of Attraction has an effect or not, when you are more aware of what you want, you're more purposefully pursuing it. So, really knowing what you want from your life and from your business can only help you develop your commitment to your business and your success story.

Goals are a way to break down your vision into manageable steps. Look closely at your vision. What steps, or goals, will it take to get there? For example, if you want to take your loved ones to Disneyworld, you need to determine how much that trip will cost. Once you know the dollar amount, you can easily plan how you are going to achieve that in commission.

Think how many parties do you need to book, how many tradeshow events you need to do, how many more products you need to sell, and how many one-on-one appointments do you need to schedule. Those can become goals.

Random acts get random results. Be intentional. If you're specific about your goals, you are being intentional. Make things happen instead of waiting for things to happen.

Follow my Five Ds of Setting Intentional goals to help you create the steps that will lead to your vision and develop your success story.

Decision

First, you need to make a decision about what you want. For example, should you put your children in public school, private school, or home school them? Do you want to move to a new neighborhood or a bigger house? Facing tough choices can make you waver between the two options. How do you feel when you're indecisive? Anxious, frustrated, overwhelmed? Who would choose to live there on a regular basis? But by not making decisions, isn't that what you're doing? When you make a clear-cut decision — even one with consequences — you feel relief, like that huge weight has been lifted off your shoulders. That is a much better place to live, and it's the only way you're going to get what you want.

Often, if you're feeling anxious, think about what it is that you need to make a decision about. Once you have that decision or clarity, you'll begin to feel excitement. You'll create a desire for action and you'll get in the mode of action. You'll feel empowered and in control. You are now back in the driver's seat of your life!

Desire

Once you've made a decision, the desire to act on it will build. Many people put off a decision and tell themselves they will feel an overwhelming desire to get moving in the right direction when they wake up in the morning. If you wait for desire to overwhelm you, you're going to be waiting a very long time. You'll *never* wake up one morning and suddenly be overcome with the desire to get moving with your business without ever setting goals. But once you've made a clear decision, the desire will follow. Almost always, action is side by side with desire. When you decide, *Okay, we're going to move*, you get excited. You call a real-estate agent and you start making your home ready to sell.

Details

Details are better known as *daily lists of things to do*. Most people make regular to-do lists. You need to know what the list is for. You need to know where you're going. Ask yourself, *What are the four to six things I can do that will move me closer to my goals?* The details are the work you do to get there.

Keep your daily list limited to what can realistically be achieved. Then, when you cross all the items off the list, don't just turn the page and start another list, *celebrate*. Put your feet up and relax with a cup of coffee or glass of wine.

Destination

Let's recap: When you make a decision, the desire builds, you follow through with the details, and you reach your destination. You may need to pull over and get directions to your destination (meaning you may need to get help from your upline or an accountability partner), but you don't ever give up.

Success is a journey, a road traveled. You will have speed bumps, road-blocks, and detours crop up along the way. If you don't know where you're going, the detours that you come across in life will take you off in different directions. By having the destination in your mind, plus written down and posted around your home or office as reminders, you'll be able to get through the detours and challenges and still be headed in the direction you want.

Determination

All this requires determination. Tell yourself that you are not giving up. And then don't. When a party cancels, don't just think, *Oh well, I guess I have the night off,* and then hang out watching TV. Instead, make some calls and get another party (or two) booked. If you are short on your sales goals for a trip, don't hang out watching TV — instead make up the sales with more bookings, one-on-ones, or re-servicing orders.

Be Rewarded: Strive for Company Incentive Programs

Many companies offer programs and incentives to help motivate you and keep you consistent in running your business. It is important for your success and momentum, especially at the beginning of your business, to set your sights on earning these incentives and programs.

Most companies offer programs within your first 90 days of starting (typically called Fast Start, Quick Start, Fast Track, and so on). The fast-track type program is a great way for you to earn additional products for your kit, gain items for your own personal use, and of course, establish good business habits and patterns. From my experience as a trainer and coach, I have found that what you start with is what you are likely to continue with. So, if you get your business off to a healthy and successful start by pushing yourself in both sales and recruiting, you will most likely enjoy long-term success.

Company incentive trips

Now that I am a full-time speaker and trainer, people ask me all the time if I miss being in the field. My answer is always no, because I'm still getting to do what I love and train thousands of people on making their direct sales businesses successful. But what I do miss are incentive trips. There is really nothing like taking an incentive trip with your company.

Most companies offer *incentive trips,* where you can earn free vacations around the world just for hitting certain qualifications with your business. Company incentive trips keep you focused for a long period of time. Some programs run six months up to a year. Striving for so long for something teaches you to be consistent each and every single month and to stretch yourself to keep your business growing.

Not only do you receive a paid vacation for yourself, you get to be with others who have earned it as well. Being around like-minded people where you can brainstorm, immerse yourself in the company culture, and get the bigger picture of what's involved are all great motivators. There is nothing like being at a cocktail party with 300 other people who are excited about exactly the same thing you are.

When you earn incentive trips, there's a huge sense of recognition. And recognition is one of the main reasons people join this industry. You are able to say you earned an all-expenses-paid vacation for you and your spouse, and people will be drawn to that. This will help you develop your success story with your business, which will increase results in your recruiting efforts.

It's important to familiarize yourself with the program and the exact requirements and qualifications you need to hit to earn it. Not only will earning this program get you off to a great start and land you a nice reward from the company, but you will be getting paid at the same time.

Companies offer ongoing incentives because they want to keep you focused, excited, and engaged in your business. So, anytime your company is running a program or incentive, make it a priority to earn it.

Productivity and the Power Hour

Do you have an hour to spare? Of course not. No one does. But could you spare 15 minutes here and there? My system, called the Power Hour, uses one simple hour to produce results. The Power Hour means taking an hour in your day and breaking it down into four income-producing activities, or key things, that you want to accomplish in that hour.

Using the Power Hour, you take small blocks of time and get extraordinary results from them. Once you've mastered the concept for your direct selling business, you'll find you can apply the Power Hour concept to almost every area of your life. Even fitness. Did you know that three 15-minute increments of cardio exercise gives the same benefit to your heart as one 45-minute session? It's true.

Have you ever had plenty to do, but felt like you really couldn't achieve anything because you didn't have a day, an afternoon, or even an hour available? Then you're going to love Power Hours.

A Power Hour means you only spend 15 minutes on a single task and then move on to another one. The idea is that, because you're focusing solely on that one thing, you actually accomplish more than if you attempted to spend a full hour on it while being distracted by other things.

For direct selling, you'll need to spend a Power Hour on four activities: booking parties or appointments, host coaching, recruiting, and customer follow-up. But you can also use the Power Hour concept to achieve everything from working on your finances to cleaning your house.

To ensure you're able to focus on your direct selling Power Hour, it's a good idea to remove distractions. You may want to turn off your social media alerts, or even silence the ringer on your phone.

In the Power Hour system, you create four folders, either on your computer or using actual cardboard folders. Label them as follows:

- ✔ Host Coaching
- ✔ Booking Leads
- ✔ Recruiting Leads
- ✔ Customer Follow-Up

If you're like most people, you have piles on your desk — sticky notes, and scraps of paper with notes scribbled on them. During your Power Hour, you put your information in one of these folders, so it's always easy to find. When you're out and about and get questions because you have on logo wear, or you happen to talk about a product or the opportunity, put these leads into the appropriate folder. Any lead you get will live in one of these folders.

In doing the Power Hour, you don't have to do it seven days a week to get results. Four days will get amazing results; three days will get great results; two days will get good results; and one day will still get results.

If you're looking to build your business, 15 minutes of phone calls is less daunting than spending hours on the phone trying to get bookings or repeat sales. Even if you only get a few orders, by the end of the week you have 10-15 additional orders. Not bad for 15 minutes and a little consistency!

You don't have to wait until you have an hour to become entrenched in what you're doing so that you're successful at creating a habit. Take 15 minutes with each task and it can turn into results and rewards quickly. And over time, it will become a habit of reward and success.

Your 15 minutes on host coaching

Often hosts complain that they booked a party and the representative didn't touch base until two days before the party. So spend 15 minutes touching base to make sure you're keeping your host excited, engaged, and informed.

I use a ten-contact time system for host coaching (see Chapter 10) which can be utilized with the Power Hour. Use folders to help you organize your pending hosts, so you can always keep an eye on who you're reaching out to. When you have multiple books, it's easy to forget who and when you've reached out to your hosts. And that's how people fall through the cracks.

Your 15 minutes on booking

Now you're ready to spend 15 minutes solely focused on contacting people to schedule a party with you. By booking during your Power Hour, you'll soon sharpen your skills speaking the language of booking by doing multiple booking calls during a single short block of time.

Whenever you add a name to the Booking Leads (or Recruiting Leads) folders, be sure to make a note of the circumstances. For example, if your lead told you she wanted to have a party when her kitchen remodel finishes in six weeks, then make a note of those details — and mention them during your call. Your call to her would sound something like this:

> "Hi, Mary! This is Belinda. Have I caught you at a good time? Great! The last time we chatted you were remodelling your kitchen. How's that coming along? Wonderful! I'll be so excited to see it. The reason I'm calling is you asked me to give you a call when the work on your kitchen was finished so that we could go ahead and set a date for your party. What do you think would work better, a weekday or a weekend?"

When you follow up with a lead, make a reference to why she wanted to delay. This shows her that not only do you remember her, but that you care about her. Then it will come off as a friendly call and not a sales call. And remember, the key is to build relationships with our customers and leads.

When you get a booking, immediately make another booking call. It's not time to celebrate yet! The excitement from the previous *yes* will still be with you, and you will discover that the language you used from the last call will come easier to you. This will build your confidence, and people will notice that. People will always mirror the energy you give to them — if you sound hesitant, nervous, or desperate, they will pick up on that too. In fact, you can reference the prior call to show your new lead that you are busy, energetic, and in high demand. You can say something like this:

> "I just spoke with my last host and she is going to do a margaritas and manicures party. Do you think that's something your friends would enjoy also?"

Your 15 minutes on recruiting

Recruiting is the one area of your business where timing is everything. When someone has expressed interest but then says no, that doesn't mean no forever or that they don't like you. It just means right now isn't the right time.

People's lives change. This is why follow-up is so important. Previous leads showed interest about your opportunity, which is why they're in your lead notebook. But just because the timing wasn't right at that time doesn't mean it won't be right sometime in the future. If you get a *no* or a *not right now,* don't just say, "Okay" and forget about it. Ask her if you can keep her informed with specials, especially those to do with the kit. Say something like this:

> I *totally* understand, Sarah. I want you to feel confident in this business when you start. Is it okay for the time being that I keep you on my list? I would love to keep you informed on upcoming specials we have, especially starter kit specials.

When you talk to recruit leads in a friendly and casual way, just as you do when you're doing a customer service call, you build a relationship. And that means they'll come to know and trust you, rather than feel like you're bugging them.

Your 15 minutes on customer service

During this 15 minutes, you simply contact people who have previously ordered from you and ask if they're enjoying the products they purchased. After they say *yes,* ask if they would like to add another specific product to their collection. Tell them about a current sale or special or ask if they need to reorder more of their original purchase. It's a good idea to know what they ordered last, and you should be prepared to tell them what the specials are this month.

> "With Mother's Day right around the corner, I wanted to find out if I could help you with any special ladies in your life, including yourself."

Direct sales companies say that only one to three percent of direct sellers do re-servicing calls. When you don't make these calls, you're leaving money on the table. Someone, either another representative or competitor, will pick that money up. Great customer service is incredibly important not only to your sales, but also to your bookings and recruiting. So be sure to make these calls. The results we have documented is that it can increase your business as much as 50%.

My 2+2+2 program (discussed in Chapter 13) teaches that you should follow up two days after a purchase to thank the customer, two weeks after that to ask how they are enjoying the product, and two months after that to see if they would like to re-order. It's important to follow up with your clients and continue to keep in contact with them. It helps create loyal customers.

However, don't overdo it either! You want your customers to feel like when you call, that it is a service to them — one that they appreciate.

Developing Important Skills

There are four more skill sets I want you to develop for your direct selling business. You can use each of these skills during a Power Hour to create exciting results:

- ✔ Focus
- ✔ Commitment
- ✔ Consistency
- ✔ Organization

The power of focus

For a lot of people, the idea of *focusing* on something with undivided attention seems almost impossible. There is just too much to do and there are too many interruptions.

In business, you normally find yourself in one of two situations:

- ✔ **Situation 1:** "Omigosh, I need to call this recruit lead, put this order in, and make coaching calls to my three hosts." You have so much going on that you can't focus on completing any one project. In this case, you're not focusing on anything, and you're not producing any results.

- ✔ **Situation 2:** "I have no business. I don't know where to begin. I'm feeling so bad. I don't even have any good leads." You have let fear paralyze you. Instead of feeling overwhelmed by all the tasks you have to do, the end result is so stressful that you don't even know where to begin — so you don't.

With the Power Hour, you learn to take each task and break it down, making it easy and well prioritized, and giving you a starting point.

There's no way around it: Focus takes focus. Everything else in your life needs to be put away for 15 minutes, so you can focus your undivided attention on the priority at hand. It is easier than it sounds. You can do *anything* for 15 minutes! Do it with the prize in mind — at the end, you'll have achieved what you wanted. You'll have results, and the next block of 15 minutes will be even easier.

What you focus on is what you get

Most people tend to spend their days focused on what they *don't* want:

"I don't like the way I look in this. I don't want to go to work today. I hate dealing with this person. I don't like making phone calls. People aren't open to me. The kids don't listen to me. I don't want my relationship to be this way."

In life, and business, you are guaranteed to get whatever you focus on. If you focus on the fact that you're not feeling good, you're going to continue to not feel good. If you focus on how bad your business is, your business is going to continue to be bad. But if you focus on what a great product you have and what an awesome family you have, you're going to be excited and your business is likely to do well. You have a choice every day to look at the glass as half full or half empty. Choose well.

When your strength is focus

Create a habit, practice your focus, and you will be rewarded with results you never expected.

Some people's greatest asset is truly their ability to focus. These people are good at *doing;* deciding their goals and getting it done. In this asset, there is also a slight weakness. Sometimes, they get so hyper-focused that they miss the bigger picture. For this reason, they miss the details and planning. *Does this sound like someone in your life?*

Usually these peoples' tasks go something like this. On a Saturday morning, they think, *Okay, I am going to clean out the garage.* They're excited about it and spend the whole day on it. By the time they finish a full eight hours later, it is spotless and looks like a showroom. The tools are hung, screws, bolts, and nails are all in their own little jars, and gardening tools have their own area. A place has been made for everything, and everything is in its place.

Of course, they will have gone to the hardware store 3–4 times that day because they didn't look forward and plan what they would need. But to them, that isn't the point. The point is the garage looks spectacular.

When you think your strength is multitasking

Many people feel their greatest asset is multitasking. But it can be more of a weakness than a strength. Some people can plan their whole day out, but many times they lose sight of the one thing that they want to accomplish.

Often they start their day by thinking, *I need to make booking calls.*

But before they get on the phone to make booking calls, they make coffee, clean the kitchen, and start a load of laundry. Then they sit down to make the calls, but it's almost time to pick up the kids and they don't want to get started on this important task until they get back. Once they get the kids, they decide to visit a few stores and runs errands. Now it's time for dinner and they never really get started on what they wanted to do in the first place. The biggest problem is that people like this delude themselves into thinking they had a great day. . . but they never did the one thing they set out to do.

Some can multitask like no one else — and many times it can be a strength and work in their favor. But sometimes it's hard for them to stop focusing on the big picture so they get lost with the small important details.

The power of commitment

Commitment is one of the most important promises you make to everything and everyone in your life and business. You need commitment to get anywhere, and you absolutely need commitment to succeed with your direct selling business.

Commitment means saying what you're going to do — and doing it. It means respecting your relationship with yourself, and with others, enough to follow through with what you have promised. There will be days when you'll be tired, and perhaps even wishing the host would call and cancel the party. You will even be tempted to cancel it yourself.

Your reputation as a businessperson is always on the line. Honoring your commitment means your customers never have to question whether they can rely on you to provide the products and services they want to purchase.

Be in it to win it. Your commitment to your vision is a powerful thing. Your commitment to show up when you really want to give up is the secret to achieving your vision and making it a reality. Success doesn't happen overnight in direct sales, so continue to see the people, fill in your pipeline, and keep making calls. You need to stay committed to achieving those goals.

You're going to have bad parties. Your host may not invite people. Your best recruit may quit. Are these reasons to give up on your dreams? Not a chance. You need to stay committed to your vision of why you got in direct selling to begin with. Don't let circumstances discourage you and steal your commitment. You come back and make the next day better. Don't talk about it for days on end. The longer you talk about it, the longer you live in that place. Remember, what you focus on is what you will get.

The power of consistency

Consistency is doing something again and again. It is making your effort a habit. Consistency can help make your business successful.

Habits are consistent. Habits are just the things that you do continually. Once, probably a long time ago, you made the choice to do it consciously, liked the reward enough to do it again, and continued to do until it became part of your natural flow. Whether it's a good or a bad habit, if you practice it consistently, you become successful at it.

Direct selling is a simple business, and you can be very successful just by learning and practicing a few basic skills and repeating them over and over until they become habits. (One of the very best habits you can form is the Power Hour.)

Whether your goal is to work your business part-time or full-time, you will have to schedule time to make phone calls, follow up with leads, and do your parties. One of the most important things you can do is set a work schedule and stick to it. Set aside the appropriate time in your calendar to work your business. Schedule your work time and write it in your calendar, just as you would a doctor or dentist appointment.

One reason I was so successful as a direct seller is that I had a regular schedule and I stuck to it just as if a boss set it for me. On Mondays I coached my team. On Tuesdays I made follow-up calls. On Wednesdays I ran errands and handled personal business. On Thursdays, Fridays, and Saturdays I held parties. My schedule was always consistent, and it helped prevent procrastination.

Don't forget the Power Hour, discussed earlier. It helps you concentrate 15 minutes at a time on building your business. Consistency is easier when you realize you don't have to do it for the entire day. In short bursts, something can become a habit. Every time, begin with your vision and goal in mind, see the reward ahead, and give it your full focus . . . *consistently*.

I've had moments — even whole days — when I just didn't feel like doing something. On those days, I have to get flat-out honest with myself. I have to ask myself: What if I gave up today? And: Do I want to stay where I am, getting what I've always gotten — or would I rather power through and keep myself consistent so that I reach my goals and realize my vision?

It's important to accept that you will have days like this. You're human, and your brain wants to stay with the pathways it has always taken. But you've already decided on a new course, you have the roadmap, and you are headed to your destination — if only you can stay consistent.

Here are some things you can do to be more consistent:

- **Call an accountability buddy.** Your best bet is to call your friend who is great at *tough love* and have them whip you into shape. They're the one that will make sure you're not listening to the part of your brain that's trying to talk you out of doing something.

- **Understand the implications of your choice:** You can not do it today, and have to start fresh tomorrow without the reward you'd receive today — or you can power through your inconsistent feeling and just get it done, and get the reward.

- **Ask yourself some questions:** What would someone you admire do in this situation? What would happen if the Olympic athletes skipped their training on the days when they didn't feel like it? Think about who admires you. Will your kids be getting a good role model if they see that you decide you "just don't feel like it" today?

- **Review:** Look back at your goals and vision, and at your progress so far. Are they worth putting on the shelf because you don't feel like getting results today?

You can pay the price of discipline, or you can pay the price of regret. Yes, it's about being consistent, and doing it today and every day. But it's not about what you get today. It's about what you're becoming: successful.

The power of organization, or lack thereof

Many people dread hearing this, but organization is also vital to your success in direct selling. Your lack of organization will rob you of more time than any other single thing. The good news is that organization doesn't have to come naturally to you, and it doesn't require sophisticated methods to work well.

How organized is organized enough? You are sufficiently organized when you have a method for tracking what needs to be done, and what has been done. You should also know what supplies you currently have, what you're running low on, and what you need to get. And you need to be able to quickly and easily access the records of your lead contacts, your previous sales, and your previous hosts and customers.

Organization does more than help you keep track of what needs to be done. It also allows you to fully enjoy whatever you're doing, without feeling the pull of other tasks.

If there is one thing I suggest you organize first, it's your calendar. For at least the upcoming three months, have your family commitments and the days you plan to hold parties marked in your calendar. I also suggest that you always know what your next three available dates are. This way, if you're chatting with a friend, and she mentions (as some definitely will) that she might be interested in having a party or hearing about the opportunity, you can say, "That sounds great. I have Thursday the 3rd, Saturday the 5th, and Friday the 11th available. Which one works best for you?"

Always have Host and Recruiting packages pre-made or in a folder on your computer so you're not running around trying to put one together when you have a hot lead. (See Chapter 6.)

Direct selling is a high-touch business. While you use technology to place orders and track your business systems, your customers value the personal service and product knowledge you have. You provide much more excellent service when your office area and files are neatly organized.

Having an organized home office space will make working on your direct selling business more enjoyable. I have a simple (and it's pretty common, I didn't dream it up on my own) system for decluttering an area. I simply sort everything into three piles:

- ✔ Keep pile
- ✔ Throw Away pile
- ✔ Donate pile

I actually have a rule that I can only touch an item once, so I don't allow myself to have a Decide Later pile — that's how the clutter happened in the first place.

In your home office space, you should have a strict policy on organization. Phone numbers, host files, and customer records should always be in reliable, easy-to-reach places. This is information you'll frequently need, so it's important that you can put your hands on it quickly.

Your lack of organization will rob you of more time than any other single thing.

What if I don't have office space?

A nice, fully furnished office would be a great thing to have and is everyone's dream. But often, a large corner office in our home isn't in the cards for us. Don't worry — you don't need an office to be successful. Improvise!

When I got started, my office space was my dining room table and two shelves out of my linen closet. Be creative. Try putting all your files and supplies in a storage ottoman, and taking them to the kitchen table when it's time to work. Or maybe you can put a corner shelf at desk height in your living room.

A home office is definitely nice, but it's not absolutely necessary. You don't have to have a fully furnished home office to start creating success with your direct selling business.

Chapter 6

Always Be Ready for Business

In This Chapter

▶ Understanding best business practices

▶ Being ready for business wherever you go

▶ Learning business etiquette for direct sellers

▶ Securing interest and leads

*I*n direct sales, being *ready* is one of the most important things you can be. Unfortunately, there is sometimes a small hurdle to being ready, and that is not taking it seriously. Your direct sales business is a business, even if you consider it your "part-time" business. And "part-time" can mean big profit, if you take it seriously. This chapter shows you how being and staying ready for business helps you take advantage of opportunities that will occur throughout your day.

Being ready for business doesn't mean you have to be always hunting for the next sale or recruit, or wearing your business hat 100 percent of the time. You're busy with the rest of your life, too — kids, school, another job, social responsibilities, and so on. People constantly tell me that when they are out and about, they just want to relax. They don't want to be all about their business all the time.

But even if you're pursuing this business part-time, it is important to always be *ready* for business because you never know when the opportunity to book or recruit will present itself. Being ready doesn't mean bringing up your business to every person you see at the grocery store. Being ready means that if your business comes up authentically in a casual conversation, you are ready to provide your lead with information on the services and opportunities you offer. And you can do this all without ever feeling burned out.

Often when I'm out and about and I meet someone I want to stay in touch with, I'll ask, "Do you have a business card?" They usually reply with something like, "Oh, they're in my other bag," or, "I just gave my last one out to so and so." Sometimes I'm chatting with a direct sales rep and I say, "I'd love to see a catalog — do you have one with you?" And they reply, "No, but I can send you one, or you can view it online."

Don't be that person! Each and every time you get caught without materials, like your business cards and catalogs, you are not

- ✔ **Physically ready for business:** That means you're not ready to take an order, book an appointment, or share the business opportunity.

- ✔ **Mentally engaged:** It's important to always mentally prepare yourself to leave your house with the expectations that you might meet someone or that you could get some business today.

Opportunities for these conversations can happen at any time. They can happen, yes, while you're at the grocery store — or at the doctor's office or a little league game. They can happen during a PTA meeting or when you're out at a restaurant. You need to be ready at all times to share your business, your products, and your opportunity because you never know when moments like this are going to present themselves. When they do, and you're not ready, you'll miss a sale, booking, or even a new recruit for your team.

You say you *want* business and you wish you *had* more business. You want additional bookings, more recruits, and better sales. You must be able to offer these things to people while you are out and about. Take a minute right now to ask yourself: "How ready am I?"

Use the seven tips for always being ready for business that I discuss in this chapter. I promise you'll feel prepared and confident — and you'll get results.

Always Be Ready to Give Out a Business Card

Not just are they in your purse or wallet, but do you know *exactly* where they are? The last thing you want to do is start searching through your purse saying, "I know I have one in here somewhere" — or worse, start dumping the contents out while searching.

Your business card is an extension of yourself — it's what you leave with people. Always having a business card ready for someone shows professionalism and preparedness. It's something that people expect professional business people to have on them at all times. *Do you always have business cards with you?*

Here are four key tips for business cards to make them more effective:

- **Say what you want to say *before* you extend the card.** When somebody compliments you on your jewelry or bag or the lotion you're wearing, tell them it's part of a line you represent. More than likely, they will ask you if you have a business card.

  Once the card is extended, the conversation is typically over. So before you hand it over, take the time to say, "A great way to really see the products is by getting a few of your friends together for a fun girls night out," or "I love these product so much. They have made my life easier by . . ." or "This business is amazing. I am really excited by the way everyone falls in love with . . . ." Once that card is extended, the person takes it and usually walks away.

  When people ask for your card, let them know what you do and explain the services you offer (home party, online party, one-on-ones, and so on). Tell them why it would be fun for them and their friends. Start an authentic conversation — and then close with your card, and hopefully a booking.

- **Capture their contact information in return.** Always say something like, "Sure, I have a card, but what I would love is to get your information so that I can follow up to answer any questions you might have." Or say something like, "I would love to get your information so I can send you a link to my website where you can view the catalog." If you don't get their contact information, you're likely to never hear from or talk to that person again.

- **Keep them in the same place.** Be in the habit of putting your business cards in the same place all the time. You want to be able to access them immediately, without having to conduct a search. Get in the habit of checking before you go out to see if you need to restock.

  There is nothing worse, I promise you, than when someone asks you for a card and you don't have one. No one cares why you don't, so don't even bother giving them a reason. All they know and care about is that you don't have one for them. End of story. So be prepared.

- **Make sure they're clean.** I keep my business cards in a little plastic bag in the inside pocket of my purse. Otherwise, if they're floating around in the bottom, they may get scuffed and bent, or get make-up on them, or even worse, a cough drop or piece of candy could be stuck to them. That's not the way you want to be remembered.

  And gentlemen, don't put your business cards in your back pocket. No one wants to receive something you have been sitting on all day. Keep them in a shirt or jacket pocket.

If you don't have a business card, and your company doesn't provide them to you for free, get some made right now. Nowadays it's easy and cheap. There are many resources available to you online (many of which offer discounts or for free with purchase), such as Vistaprint.com and Zazzle.com.

Keep Catalogs with You

Your catalog is another great tool for showcasing your business and the products you represent. Without having some sort of catalog, doing business can be difficult. If your catalog is large or very expensive, you may decide to carry a mini catalog or brochure that your company offers. Or you may just decide to carry a larger purse, tote bag, shoulder bag, or whatever. Regardless of what your catalog looks like, it is your store, your inventory, your list of services, and your marketing.

More than having your catalog with you, it's what you do with it that really matters. Here are two important things you just can't miss:

✔ **Your contact information:** Make sure your contact information is on your catalog and that it is clearly visible. Many catalogs have a spot on the back page where you can put a stamp or a label. You want to make sure that your customers, clients, and leads can find your information quickly.

Let me emphasize once again: Stamping your information or placing a label on your catalogs is extremely important. I cannot tell you how many people give me catalogs and then later, when I want to make a purchase, I have no way of reaching them because they didn't put a label on their catalog. Don't let this happen to you. For one, you miss out on opportunities for sales, bookings, and potential recruits. And two, you miss out on your chance at a great first impression because you weren't ready for business.

Label your catalogs as soon as you get them in the mail. Make it a habit!

✔ **Their contact information:** It's important to get your lead's contact information as well. You won't always be able to rely on leads to contact you, and because you're responsible for the income your business creates, you shouldn't rely on their initiative.

I used to stick a note in the upper right-hand corner of my catalogs. Then when I was out and about and gave a catalog to someone, I could say, "And if you wouldn't mind just putting your information on there so that I can follow up with you, that would be wonderful." Make sure you always have a pen handy, too. She gets to keep the catalog and you have her information to add to your lead notebook so you can follow up with her.

Convenience is king. When people have to wait for information, they move on to someone else.

Have Host and Opportunity Packets Handy

Host packets and opportunity (also called recruiting) packets are like the sprinkles on your sundae. Business cards and catalogs may be your ice cream, but having the extra toppings takes your business up a notch. These packets really show a potential lead that you mean business. A host packet is for people who are interested in hosting a party or for people you have already booked as a host. The items in this packet will cover more information about the products, your company's host program, company specials, and host coaching information (Chapter 10). An opportunity packet focuses on sharing the business opportunity with potential leads. These typically consist of items that discuss the benefits of joining the business as well as information about the compensation plan and income structure.

If your company offers these for purchase, that's great! If not, you can easily make them yourself.

Generally, you only need a few things in these packets:

- ✔ Catalog (in both host and opportunity packet)
- ✔ A few business cards (in both host and opportunity packet)
- ✔ Short letter from you (in both host and opportunity packet)
- ✔ Host planner (in host packet)
- ✔ Recruiting brochure (in opportunity packet)
- ✔ A starter kit flyer that shows the contents of what a new team member would receive after joining (in opportunity packet)
- ✔ Monthly specials and maybe a flyer about your company's upcoming incentive (in both host and opportunity packet)

You should be able to print most of these pieces from your virtual office. Keep these materials short and simple so you don't overwhelm your potential lead.

The actual information in these packets is secondary to the real purpose the packets offer: the opportunity for you to schedule one-on-one time to talk to the lead about hosting a party or starting a business.

You should always have at least six packets made up and ready to go. It isn't necessary to have them in your purse/bag at all times, but they should be somewhere handy, like in your car. When I was in the field, I always had six in my briefcase for my parties and six in the trunk of the car that I kept in a container. Keeping it in a container ensured they would stay dry, clean, and ready to give to potential hosts and recruits. When you are out running errands or at a party and the opportunity presents itself for a booking or sharing the opportunity you can say, "I have a packet in my car. Let me go grab it." Or say, "I have them right here." By having the information handy, you are visibly demonstrating *this business is simple* and *hosting a party is simple* to your prospect.

You never want to be caught without your packets. If people have to wait for information, they have already moved on to something or someone else.

Without being prepared, you run the risk of losing *the moment*. For many people, they are interested because something grabbed their attention. Maybe they are looking to buy a gift for someone. Maybe they wish they had a little bit of extra money and you present the perfect opportunity. Or maybe they think a party would be a perfect idea for a bridal shower they are planning. It's the moment when you can be a solution to their problem. And because what you offer fulfills that, they are willing to engage with you — *in that moment*. If you let the moment pass, you may not be able to gain back that interest at a later date.

Plan Your Show-on-the-Go

Your mini show-on-the-go is a huge opportunity for you while you are out and about. An outing with the kids on a play date can quickly turn into a sale, booking, or new recruit for your team. It's an opportunity that, if you are ready for it, can be very successful.

Your show-on-the-go is like a mini kit that you carry with you in a tote bag that contains items you can throw a mini party with. Carrying around your large kit that you take to your parties is unrealistic — but having some items in a small bag is an easy way to show off some of your products while you are out.

Here's what goes in your show-on-the-go:

- Two or three catalogs
- One host packet
- One opportunity packet

✔ Small collection of products

You should always have a small collection of products for your clients to see, experience, and sample. If you represent a skincare line, you might carry the most popular products and a few of the newest, along with a couple applicators for people to apply the product. In cases where your products are too big or you're unable to carry them around, you should always have samples or swatches. You can also carry some of your smaller products to show the quality.

✔ Tablecloth

A tablecloth can make your setup look better and act as a backdrop for your products, especially if you're in a less-than-desirable location. Buy a small black tablecloth, or go to your local fabric store and get something presentable, with a solid color (patterns can be distracting and take away from your products).

Choose a tablecloth or fabric that won't be wrinkled after being rolled up in your tote bag.

Here is an example of how a show-on-the-go might play out:

> While at the pool or the park with your child, you are chatting with someone. Eventually they ask you what you do.
>
> You: I help women select great accessories to stretch their wardrobe.
>
> Woman: That sounds amazing! That's something I could use some help with.
>
> You: I happen to have a few of my favorite and most versatile pieces with me. If you want, I can show them to you now.
>
> You roll out your mini tablecloth and put a few of the pieces on it that are the most versatile.

This kind of thing can happen almost anywhere. I've even had this happen at a family reunion:

> Family member: Hey are you still selling that jewelry?
>
> You: Yeah, I am!
>
> Family member: Oh, I'd love to see a new catalog.
>
> You: Well, actually I happen to have a few of the new pieces with me. Let me go grab it.

These examples give you the opportunity to do a little mini show right then and there. Numerous reps have shared with me that they have had a $400 party poolside in the middle of summer while relaxing on a fun afternoon with their kids.

If you want business, you have to get out and see people. And if you're ready, you will get business.

There is always an opportunity to create a connection, find a lead, or get a sale. When people see the product, they get a chance to touch it, experience it, and hold it. That's when it becomes real for them. That's when people can imagine owning it themselves. That's when they will buy in to your products and buy in to you as an interesting person with integrity, as someone they want to do business with.

It doesn't matter how beautiful a catalog is. It's when they get the actual products in their hands that they see how amazing the quality is or how great the benefits are. And they want it. You can't create that same excitement, spark, or interest for your products through any other medium.

Of course, you can still *use* other mediums. Social media is playing a huge role in the way direct sellers sell, book, and recruit (see Chapter 11). But again, and I can't say this enough, if you want business, you need to get out and see people. People today are becoming more engaged with technology and less engaged with each other. That means face-to-face (F2F) interactions are becoming even more important. If they don't see your product, experience it, or understand it, they're likely to just move on.

If you are in a network marketing or multi-level marketing company (see Chapter 3 for more on these) that doesn't offer catalogs or have easy-to-show products, then have a packet with recruiting literature and samples available. As always, the important step here is to *make sure* your contact information is attached to the sample — whether with a label, business card, or other means that will remain with the sample until after it is used.

Nowadays, people can get *hi-tech* for almost every product or service they want: Amazon.com, major retailers, and even small businesses today have websites and even apps that offer a product similar to yours. What they can't get as easily today is *hi-touch* — that is, the experience of interacting with both the product and a knowledgeable representative. By being ready for business, you provide what other businesses don't.

Whether you are doing a show-on-the-go, a one-on-one appointment, or a home party, it's important to perfect your closing. While you are creating an interest for your product, you want to make sure that you secure the sale. You want to avoid "Best Buy Syndrome" — where people shop around, try your products, then try to find it cheaper somewhere else. To learn more about how to do a successful closing, see Chapter 9.

If you remember nothing else, remember this: When you don't have your materials on hand with you (business cards, catalogs, packets, a mini show-on-the-go), you have lost an opportunity.

Create Your 30-Second Commercial

Often called *elevator pitches,* what I call *30-second commercials* are essential for your business. This is the answer that you give when someone asks what you do, where you're working, or what you've been up to. In reality, it's only a few seconds that you have to get someone to ask more about what it is that you do.

There are two kinds of commercials:

✔ What you say when you are at a networking event or party and people ask you what you do.

✔ What you say when people compliment you on your product or mention something to do with your logo wear, better referred to as wear-to-share apparel.

Your response is something that you really want to perfect. That way when someone asks, you know exactly what you want to say and how you want to say it. In this section, I give you some examples and then offer some guidelines for creating your own.

Many professionals aren't really sure what to say about their business. They want to get it right, but when asked what they do, it's clear they haven't practiced anything to say.

An acquaintance who worked in financial services once heard me speak on having a great 30-second commercial. He later told me that when he was asked what he did for a living, he used to say he worked in financial planning and investments with (company name). The other person in the conversation often either didn't know what that meant or couldn't find anything in it to grab on to and continue talking about, so the conversation moved on to other things. "After you talked about 30-second commercials," he told me, "I changed to: I help people build their savings and save on their yearly taxes. People now respond by asking me to tell them more. I'm getting many more clients just from this simple change!"

Another woman I know, when asked what she does, would simply say that she owned a cupcake shop. Now, after hearing about the importance of the 30-second commercial, she's getting more customers by saying, "I create beautiful and delicious cupcakes for every occasion of your life!"

Then there are people who are clearly very excited about their business but skip over the actual question about the line of work they're in. Their 30-second commercial might sound something like this:

> "Oh my gosh, you'll never believe it. I'm with this fabulous company and as a matter of fact we give over $200 away in free products if you have a few people over to your house. We should do that. Here, I have my calendar in my purse. When are you free?"

The lead was just given a lot of information in a small amount of time, but still isn't sure who this rep represents, what products are involved, or what the experience could mean for her.

Finally, there are the people who have been doing business for a while and have learned to say something intriguing, in just a few short sentences. They would say something like this:

> "I empower women. I change their lives both personally and financially."

That may sound dramatic and impressive, but if there isn't follow-up conversation, it's not very useful. These reps think they're painting a picture of what they do, but are they? If that lead then runs into one of her friends, and she asks, "Hey have you seen Belinda lately? What's she up to?" — they still have no idea.

Your 30-second commercial is what you do, not who you are. The biggest mistake that people make is failing to make it clear what they could do for the prospect.

Another mistake is leading with your title. People don't generally know what your title means, especially if your company has unusual title names, like *double diamond stars.*

Here's what a good 30-second commercial does:

- ✔ **It paints a picture around the product or service.** You show your customers the benefits of your product or services, and they learn what your products do, not just what they are.

- ✔ **It creates a wow factor.** Your 30-second commercial should create interest. It should show off a benefit that makes it appealing.

- ✔ **It supplies a need.** Your 30-second commercial should make people think, *I have to have that.*

Let's look at a few good examples of a 30-second commercial:

- Beauty

    "I show women how to take years off of their face by taking care of their skin."

    "I help women get salon quality nails for a fraction of the price."

- Spa

    "I pamper women and help them create a spa experience in the privacy of their own homes."

- Jewelry

    "I help women share their story and create personalized lockets for themselves and their friends."

    "I can help women completely update their wardrobe with the latest trends in fashion designer jewelry."

- Health

    "I help people achieve the lifestyle they want by sharing products that promote overall health and fitness."

    "I help people achieve their weight-loss goals."

- Home decor

    "I help people update their homes by taking out the frustration of decorating and providing them with the latest and most popular trends."

- Food and beverage

    "I take the stress out of meal planning to achieve simple, easy meals in a matter of minutes."

    "I can teach you how to become a gourmet chef simply by opening a jar."

    "I create a fun wine-tasting experience where we teach you how to pair wines with your favorite foods and take the stress out of selecting the perfect wine for your meal."

- Cookware

    "I can help you get in and out of the kitchen, making amazing meals in under 30 minutes, and make preparation and clean-up a breeze with the most awesome, innovative tools on the market today."

Dress for Success

You've gotten this far and you're thinking, *Okay, I've got everything with me. I've got my business cards in a nice holder. My catalogs are ready to go, all my packets are in my car, I've got my show-on-the-go, and I know exactly what I am going to say. I am ready for business!* And you head out the door.

You get to the grocery store, start shopping, and you run into your daughter's dance instructor. You engage in conversation, you do everything right, she takes your card, says thank you, and walks away. You're left thinking, *What just happened?* or, *That could have gone better.* Then you look down and realize you're wearing sweatpants with sandals, a tee shirt, and your hair is up high in a ponytail and you have no makeup on. No wonder she walked away! Would you want to do business with someone who looked like that? Probably not.

People ask me all the time, "Can I wear jeans?" I always say, "Do you look good in jeans?" Some people look fantastic in jeans with a nice blouse, some jewelry, and their make-up on. If you don't, you might want to think about wearing something else. A lot of times people go to the store dressed just like the scenario just described, and of course that is when they run into someone who is looking to do business with them.

Before you head out of the house, look into the mirror and ask yourself: "Would someone want to invite me into their home?" If your answer is no, you probably should take a moment, change, and look appropriate.

It probably doesn't take that long to get ready. Some can do it in five minutes. Some take longer, of course, but you know how you feel when you look good. You know how you feel when you are looking to impress. Find a nice, professional outfit, put your make-up on, and fix your hair. You probably look fabulous when you're headed out for a party or appointment. Take the same time in your day-to-day life as well. The better you look, the more opportunities you'll have for business.

Getting dressed in the morning is one of the single most important details that can determine the outcome of your day. Not only does it serve you well when you're out running errands, it changes your mentality, even if you stay inside and work from home all day. You might think, *Oh, I'm not leaving the house, I'll just wear my pajamas all day* or *I don't really feel like getting dressed, I have nowhere to go today.*

I can't tell you how many times people tell me that they work from home, wear pajamas all day, yet get nothing done. I tell them, "Get dressed first thing and then see how you feel." Most of the time people come back and tell me that getting dressed has made the difference in their day. They feel better and more professional when they talk on the phone. It makes them want to work harder, and they are able to stay focused.

A representative came to me after hearing my training on dressing for success and shared this story with me:

> "I was doing a fundraiser for a school in my community. I had a meeting where all I was supposed to do was go in and drop off a fundraiser packet with the secretary at the school. That's all it was. So I was driving down the road and I realized I was not dressed appropriately.
>
> "I thought, should I run in there? I'm just dropping it off with the secretary. But then I remembered what you said, so I went home, changed, and drove back up to the school. When I walked in, not only was the principal in the office, but the superintendent as well. I was able to talk to them about the fundraiser I was doing and was able to book a fundraiser for all the schools in the district."

If she *hadn't* gone home to change, this situation could have ended very differently. When you're out and about, you want to be presentable and look professional. When you know you look good, you walk with a pep in your step. You walk with confidence and you feel good.

Although this isn't something that I would typically do, I have a friend who keeps a cute hat, hoop earrings, lipstick, and sunglasses handy at all times. If she has to run to the store in a hurry, or get in a carpool line quickly, she feels confident that she still looks presentable, and that she made an effort with her appearance.

People can respect differences in style, but they rarely respect a total lack of grooming when it comes to who they want to do business with.

Know Your Next Available Dates

Never leave home without knowing your next two available dates to have a party or a one-on-one appointment. Why? Maybe you're thinking, *Can't I just go home and look them up and then call them?* Well, you could, but again, when you have a potential lead, regardless if it is a sale, booking, or recruit, if you have to go home so that you can look at your calendar, you have lost that opportunity.

If you know your next available dates in your schedule, you will be more likely to get the sale or booking, make an appointment, schedule an interview, or sign a new recruit than if you have no clue what's going on in your schedule.

I always make a habit of looking at my calendar first thing in the morning so even when I am on the phone, I always know my next two available dates. When I'm out and about, I know my next two available dates. I trained myself early on in the business. I used to write my available dates on a piece of paper and put it in my pocket before I left the house in case I needed to reference it.

After a while, it became such a habit I had it in my memory. I knew my calendar so I didn't need to carry it anymore. You can do whatever it takes to help you be able to offer people a date to get together and do business with you.

I still use this practice when I am trying to fill my speaking calendar. Every morning before I leave the house, I always look at my calendar so I know when my next available dates are. If I run into someone or talk to someone that day who has an interest in booking me, I can quickly secure them and get them on the calendar while they are excited. Then I keep them excited during the follow-up process (see Chapter 13 for more on following up).

Here's a great example of what it can mean to know your next available dates. I was speaking at a leadership event, and during lunch, one of the leaders came up to me. Our conversation went something like this:

> Leader: We didn't know we could hire you ourselves!
>
> Me: Oh, absolutely! Other than conventions and corporate events, I do regional meetings, product launches, and workshops throughout the year.
>
> Leader: Well, we want to have you at our next one for sure.
>
> Me: Do you require a Saturday?
>
> Leader: Yes. We are going to have people coming in from a variety of different areas.
>
> (This was in February and I knew my calendar very well.)
>
> Me: Well the only Saturday I have available between now and September 23 is April 16.
>
> Leader: Are you kidding me?
>
> Me: No, I'm sorry, that's all I have available.
>
> (The woman left the line and returned a few minutes later.)
>
> Leader: We'll take it.

And that was that. A booking in a buffet line.

Knowing your next available dates also means deciding when you are open for business. If you want to book parties on Tuesdays and Thursdays, then you need to look at those holes in your calendar and aim to fill them. When you're out and about and you talk to someone, you will have those holes in mind and will be able to quickly offer them and secure the booking by acting with intention. Circling days when you want to work also helps because it eliminates having to remember every single day. You will start to become so familiar with your calendar that you'll soon know every single availability for longer and longer periods of time.

Being ready for business is really about having the will to *want* to do business. It's about getting up and saying to yourself, *I want business today!* All the power is in your hands. The great thing about direct sales is that you can decide how and when you work your business. If you are mentally prepared and have all of your materials ready to go, you will be ready for business.

Part III
Putting Sales Strategies into Practice

The Four Segments of Your Power Hour

- ✔ Host coaching
- ✔ Booking leads
- ✔ Recruiting leads
- ✔ Customer follow-up

Check out ways to get involved with trade shows at www.dummies.com/extras/directsales.

In this part . . .

- ✔ Booking, booking, and more booking — plus booking
- ✔ Launching your business with a party or show
- ✔ Discovering how to host successful parties
- ✔ Helping your hosts be successful
- ✔ Selling online and on social media
- ✔ Selling one-on-one
- ✔ Following up with great customer service

Chapter 7

Building Your Business on Bookings

In This Chapter

▶ Maintaining your calendar, hours, and schedule

▶ Securing and dating bookings

▶ Overcoming common objections

▶ More tips on getting bookings and more business

*I*n today's direct selling world, there are many ways in which you can conduct your business. The most efficient and strongest way is through live presentations or *parties*. These are most often held by *hosts* in their homes. However, getting bookings for shows in offices and cafés and a variety of other locations is popular now, too.

Bookings are the heartbeat of your business, and without them your business *will die.*

Okay, maybe your business won't *die,* but it certainly won't be living up to its full potential. One of the most important goals of a direct sales or Network Marketing representative is to *see the people.* You want to try to get your product and business in front of as many people as you possibly can. And the way you do this, of course, is through scheduling home parties, online parties, and one-on-one appointments. (I always equate three one-on-ones to equal one home party.)

As long as you have bookings or appointments scheduled and secured, you have the ingredients to create a successful and lasting business.

By booking a party (or show, demo, tasting, jewelry bar, Facebook party, and so on), you are able to see lots of people in one setting. You present your product and show them how fun and easy your job is. Online parties are great because you can connect to potentially a lot more people at one time, especially with people who don't live in your local area (see Chapter 11 for more on online parties). Being able to connect with people face-to-face is an important aspect of direct sales — if you do it right, people will buy in to your personality just as much as your product. Home parties and appointments are also important because your guests get to experience the product first-hand.

When people interact with you face-to-face, it builds trust and likeability, and people do business with people they know, like, and trust.

This chapter takes you through the importance of bookings, controlling your calendar, ways to get bookings, how to overcome objections, and other odds and ends.

Understanding the Importance of Bookings

If you hit your booking goals (see Chapter 5 for more on goals), you will have the income you want. It's as simple as that. And I'm guessing you went into business to make money (at least it was one of the reasons), so what could be more important than striving for your goals?

Collecting orders through friends, coworkers, and social media contacts is a great way to top off your monthly orders and get you closer to your monthly sales goal. But *bookings,* whether accomplished online or in-person, are a sure way to generate the income you want and desire.

Just why are bookings so important? Well, bookings give you the opportunity to do all of the following:

- **Earn an income by selling product.** You will be able to present the product to your clients, and they will be able to experience the benefits first-hand. By being able to see and interact with more people at one time, you'll have a greater amount of sales in one setting, thus earning a larger income.

- **Build a client base for re-servicing.** Re-servicing is an important part of your business and will give you an extra stream of income. By holding more bookings, you will reach more people quickly, thus creating a larger pool of customers and clients to sell to on an on-going basis.

- **Schedule new bookings from attending guests.** Customers from parties make the best hosts because they have already seen a party first-hand. People are more inclined to book their own party that night while they are enjoying their time with friends, which is better than waiting to call to book with them at a later date.

✔ **Find potential team members.** Some of your best recruit leads are at the party because they see your job in action and understand the job description, so make sure your job seems fun, easy, and manageable. You will find that the people you meet from your parties are more productive because they tend to do the business in the manner in which they met you.

You get to kill four birds with one stone. How important (and awesome) is that?

Keeping Control of Your Calendar

It's important that you are the one who controls your calendar — not your clients.

Decide when your business is open. Will you work weekends? Weeknights? It is completely up to you. One of the amazing benefits of direct sales is the ability to create your own schedule and work your business around your existing priorities. Be intentional. Make a clear-cut decision on when you are open for business and then lead clients towards those dates.

Managing your calendar is one of the most important factors to your continued success. It all begins with scheduling your first six parties (online or home party) within a 30-day period of time. (See the section "Practice, practice, practice" for more on why six parties is the magic number.)

When you're starting your business, getting those six parties scheduled within a three-week period (21 days) is even better! The first one or two could be your launch party (see Chapter 8 for much more on launch parties). You want to create momentum and build a firm foundation for your new business. When you start with just one or two parties, most people never really get going and their business continues to limp along.

Think two parties per week for those first few weeks, and you'll set yourself up for success right away. You'll usually reach the end of your first month with your investment paid, money in your pocket, an increase in confidence, and a healthy number of bookings to begin setting your own schedule.

Setting a schedule

First things first. Decide how many parties a week you want to hold. If you only want to hold one party a week, open your calendar and clearly mark the day or night you want to work. If you want to hold two parties each week, decide which two days or evenings you want and then mark those dates in your calendar. For three parties, mark three days, and so on.

When you have some idea of when you want to work, it's much easier to book than just randomly filling dates as you go. Be proactive, not reactive. Creating a set schedule will also create consistency and help form habits that will make your business more successful.

Booking for sooner, not later

Always try to book within the next four weeks (or sooner if your party is online), unless your calendar is already full. When you book too far ahead, people have a tendency to cancel or they lose their excitement for the party. Keep in mind that people book parties because they had a fun experience. They are excited about the products and enthusiastic about offering them to their friends, and they have the drive and desire to get free and discounted products for themselves.

When you book too far out, the host's excitement begins to wane, and the host may lose the desire to have the party. The booking may not hold, and then you'll have to scramble to fill the hole in your calendar left by that cancelled party. And of course, parties are often cancelled at the last minute.

When I got a cancellation, I would immediately replace it with three one-on-ones.

So it's really important to keep your bookings within a four-week time-frame to capitalize on your host's excitement and build momentum for your business.

Setting goals for your calendar

When I was holding parties, I used to challenge myself to make my night "equal three." My goal was to get three bookings from every party I held. When that didn't happen, I would get on the phone the next day and make calls from my booking lead list. If I got two bookings from the party, I would be determined to get one more on the phone. If I only got one booking from the party, I would challenge myself to secure two more by phone the next day. This strategy resulted in an overflow of bookings and allowed me to maintain my desired three-party-a-week schedule. It also helped me get the job done while I was at work.

If your goal is to hold two parties every week, challenge yourself to make your night "equal two." That way, you'll never feel overwhelmed.

It's much easier to make one phone call to close the gap after a party than it is to make six calls in a panic because your calendar is empty. When you're doing follow-up calls, you will sound much more enthusiastic when your calendar is full. When your calendar is empty, you may sound desperate.

As a business owner, it's up to you (not your clients) to take control of your time and your calendar. Create your own business hours and offer choices of appointments for your clients, customers, and hosts. When you meet someone, *only* offer the dates you want to offer. Don't ask them when they want to book. Think about your hair stylist, doctor, or dentist — they are in complete control of their calendars. When you call for an appointment, they offer you dates and times to choose from, and you select what works best for you. What if they told you to come in for your appointment whenever you wanted? I'm sure you'd think the business probably wasn't doing well. It's the same with your business.

Knowing your next available dates

To offer dates, you need to know them, of course. Make it a habit each day to look at your calendar. Mentally, you should always be moving towards a target and know your next available dates. Always know where you stand, how many bookings you need within the next four weeks, and your available dates. If you know your next available dates at all times, you're more likely to be able to offer a date, without hesitation, and get someone to date on the spot while you're out and about. Be intentional! Random acts get random results. If you act with intention, you will get your desired results.

Weave dating your calendar

Industry surveys show that almost 20 percent of hosts move their dates or cancel, so to ensure calendar control, try *weave dating*. If you want to consistently hold one party a week, "weave" by booking one party one week and two the next. If you want to consistently hold two parties a week, book two one week and three the next — and so on. That way, if a party from the week with three parties has to reschedule, you still have two parties left. You'll still be able to meet your monthly goal of eight parties (or whatever your personal goal may be), and if you end up with an extra party, you'll make some additional income.

Scheduling Appointments and Bookings

Whether you are a new representative or someone who has been doing the business for a long time, it is never too late to start over and take control of your calendar and bookings. This section dives a little deeper into bookings and schedules.

Jump-starting your bookings

As I've mentioned, your first objective in starting your new business (or re-launching your business) is to book six parties (home or online) in a 30-day period. I call this *jump-starting your business*.

Another way to jump-start is to book three parties in a row. That can bring big benefits: The average representative who does three parties back-to-back generates seven new bookings to schedule in their calendar. That creates momentum, builds confidence, and makes instant money. Plus your enthusiasm grows and you feel great about your business. As a bonus, you'll be able to reference the previous party at your new party by saying something like this:

> "Okay ladies, last night our [product] was the most popular of the night! This is definitely something you cannot leave this party without. Everyone was so excited about it because. . . . I had so many people booking last night, just so they could get this item at half-price."

Being able to say something like that implies a few things:

- ✔ **Your business is booming with bookings.** They'll see that everyone wants to host a party with you and that it must be fun and enjoyable. They'll start to consider whether their friends would love it too.

- ✔ **The product is amazing.** People will see that it is in high demand. And people want what other people want.

- ✔ **The concept works.** People will notice that your calendar is full and assume your business must be doing very well. It looks like fun and, most importantly, appears to be easy and fun to do. Many will consider it as an opportunity and possibly want to join your team.

You may say, "Well, I came into this business to do only one party a week," or, "I came into this to do it part-time." That's fine. It is your own business, after all. But to really establish yourself in the very beginning, it is very important that you hold six parties in a three-to-four-week period. The closer you can make that time frame, the better off you will be. There is no substitute for getting off to a strong start.

Practice, practice, practice

The only way to get really good in this business is to practice — whether online, in person, or in one-on-ones. The more bookings you hold, the better you get, and the more comfortable you become. You can build mastery quickly, but it involves repetition. Usually, out of your first six parties, a couple of them are fantastic, a couple don't work out so well, and a couple are just average. Once you get through those first six parties, you'll be able to look back and honestly evaluate the entire experience.

The more targets you aim at, the more you hit. In the early days of direct sales, when I was in the field, it was *mandatory* to have six scheduled parties in a *two-week* time frame in order to receive your kit. At that time, the average representative held eight parties a month. Many years later, it was a requirement on most contracts to list the six parties you had scheduled in a 30-day period of time. The average representative at that time held about five parties per month. Today, there are typically *no* requirements in order to enroll and receive your kit, and the average representative today in the industry holds . . . just 2.3 parties per month.

What you start with is usually what you will easily maintain. So, if someone starts with two to three parties in their first month, that is what they will likely maintain. Two to three parties per month will not generate a significant amount of income, and with that, most new starts are left not feeling excited about their business or their success. If you started with six, you will usually be able to maintain that. Six gives you more income and will create a success story for you. When you feel you have a success story, you will share it with others more readily, thus attracting more people to you and your business opportunity.

A concentrated "training" period like this helps you really get the hang of this business and gain confidence. With each party, you'll have something to compare to the last party — what you liked, what you didn't, and how you would do it differently.

If you don't have another party scheduled for four weeks after you have a less-than-stellar party, you have nothing to help you recover and fill your calendar. That can create a lack of confidence, which can snowball into diminished success because it becomes harder to get on the phone to secure more bookings. So, give yourself the best chance of success by getting out there and lining up those first six parties from the very beginning.

Making some money right away will leave you feeling good about yourself and your new business. If after doing those first parties, you decide it isn't for you, what have you lost? Absolutely nothing! You can walk away from the business saying, "It was a very positive experience, it just wasn't for me." You also are in a position to evaluate your business from a position of strength.

Building momentum for your future business

Having several parties in a month builds momentum. Those first six parties will provide new business for the future, and you can schedule those new bookings however you like on your calendar: one party a week, two parties a week, or even three parties a week.

When you reach the end of your first month — your training or trial period, if you will — you'll have more bookings and can plan your business to fit your desires and goals. It's much easier to keep things going and continue to make money when you reach the end of the month with new bookings on your calendar. Your new skills will make you more confident, and you'll enjoy a feeling of success.

Most companies have some sort of incentive program (usually called "Fast Start" or "Quick Start" or something similar) that help you earn products, rewards, or business aids during your first 90 days. They do this to help you establish good business habits. Find out what the program is and set your sights on hitting those goals. People who are fast-start achievers usually have a greater retention and climb the career plan quicker.

Building your Booking Lead Notebook

When you're new, you're also very excited; it's human nature to want to jump on the phone, call everybody you know, and try to explain everything about your business to them. But because you're brand new, the best thing to do is make a list of everyone you know and put them in your Booking Lead Notebook. You can keep your notebook on a physical pad of paper, on a document in your computer, or in an organizational application like Evernote (check out www.evernote.com for more on this popular tool). You know a lot of people. And they probably divide into more categories than you may have considered. Here are some ideas for your list:

- ✔ **All the places you've ever lived:** Think of current and past neighbors, acquaintances, people in the communities, landlords, realtors you have worked with, and so on.

- ✔ **All the places you've ever worked:** Consider coworkers, associates, past bosses, past employees, employees of other firms with whom you've done business, clients, and vendors.

- ✔ **All the places you've ever gone to school:** This can include grade school, middle school, high school, community college, university. Think of old friends from classes or seminars you've attended, people you met at swimming, yoga, scrapbooking, or cake decorating classes. Don't forget past teachers, administrators, and staff.

- ✔ **Friends and family:** This is the category that's the easiest to think of, but ironically, these are the people who may not be as eager to assist you. So, when your lifelong best friend decides not to have a party for you, get over it and move on to the next one. I have found that those who make the best hosts are your second and third level of friends. (The people you don't see often but who are on your holiday card list.)

✔ **Organizations, committees, and affiliations:** This could be comprised of acquaintances or members of your church, folks from recreational activities like bowling and/or softball leagues, and people at the gym or fitness center where you work out. You may know people from children's sports activities, such as soccer, Little League, dance, or gymnastics. Think about committees or groups you've belonged to, like Scouts, political organizations, ladies' groups, leads clubs, or women's business groups.

✔ **Children-related contacts:** Kids' friends' parents, coaches, teachers, doctors, tutors, and so on.

There are a couple of ways to organize your list. Beside each name, you can categorize them as 1s, 2s, or 3s — the 1s being the people you think are most likely to have a party (what you usually classify as your friends and family), and the 3s being those that you think may be least interested. Your inclination would be to start with the 1s because you think they are most likely to help, but this is not always true. Sometimes your best friends feel more comfortable shutting you down and giving you a no.

I find that the 2s and 3s are actually better candidates. These are your second tier friends, old friends from high school and so on. This group of people is actually happy to hear from you and are more likely to say yes. So think about starting with those first.

When we start with our friends and family, and if we start to get no's from them, we often feel discouraged and never move on to our 2's and 3's. This is why I think it is important to start your list with your 2's and 3's then move on to your 1's.

Another way to organize your list is to write C, H, or R beside each name. C is for those likely to be customers, H is for those most likely to host, and R is for recruits, those who could potentially be right for the business. This list will help you be more intentional in your conversations when you're reaching out to your list.

However you categorize your leads, your goal is to get them to see the product in person — or if you run your business completely online (see Chapter 11), to send them a video or share photos of the product. After that, your goal is to secure a date for a party within your first 30 days.

For those first parties, it's important to create several *chains* of business — this means having people from as many different categories as possible. Doing so exposes you to many different circles and areas, which makes for a healthy and diversified start to your new business.

Think of a wheel. The spokes on a wheel represent the different categories of people you know. If your first parties are done with your sister, mom, aunt, and cousin, that may sound like a lot, but all of those still only represent one spoke on the wheel (the "family" spoke). With only one spoke, a wheel collapses.

Instead, if your first parties include a family member, a friend from church, a neighbor, and a coworker, you will expose yourself to a larger group of people. Your spokes are spread out, and your wheel will continue to roll along successfully.

Once you get your six bookings secured and dated on your calendar you should continue to refer back to your original list in your Booking Lead Notebook for ongoing bookings. Don't forget to add to this list with the people you meet moving forward.

Securing Bookings or Appointments

When you're trying to secure bookings, you need to talk about your business. You can't just hope that people will want to book with you or that people will approach you on their own. You need to talk about what you offer — parties, products, and the business opportunity — wherever you go.

Learning to be sociable and confident with your customers is important. But you don't want to become an actor. Honing your sales techniques is about using the personality you already have. You want to be authentic with your customers and you want to seem likeable and approachable. People want to do business with people they like and people they want to be friends with. Being pushy or sales-y with your customers is a sure way to get a no.

This section talks about a few of the many ways to present your booking opportunity.

The casual approach

Make it casual when you're in casual conversations. You don't even need to use the term *home party*. You can offer your customers "a fun night to get together with friends." It's as simple as that.

I was out and about at the mall one day when a woman complimented me on my necklace. I thanked her and said that it was part of a line of jewelry that I represented. She said, "Oh, I am a jewelry nut." I enthusiastically explained to her what I did and asked her if she would be interested in hosting a party. She replied with, "No, I don't like home parties."

Now, many representatives would have taken this as a no and walked away feeling discouraged. But I knew that there was still an opportunity to gain this woman as a customer. Instead of accepting defeat, I let her know that I also offered one-on-one appointments where I would come to her house, bring my jewelry, and help her match them to her outfits. The woman loved this idea and can you guess what she asked next? "Would you mind if I invite my daughter and some of her friends?" And what are we doing now? You guessed it — a party! Sometimes people have their own ideas of what this industry is, and what it means to host a party, or even be a representative.

You do not only offer home parties. You offer a magnitude of ways that clients and customers can purchase from you. (See Chapter 3 for more ways to touch, or interact with, your business.)

Make sure you are always talking to potential hosts about the benefits for her friends.

One of the best skills you will ever learn as an entrepreneur is to listen. Listen to what your customers, leads, clients, and team are telling you. They may still be interested in what you have to offer, just maybe not in the exact manner that you are offering it. So be sure to listen and start conversations. You have to know and understand your customer in order to sell to them effectively.

See the people

In this business it is important to *see the people* — meaning you want to get you and your products in front of as many eyes as possible. You want your friends, family, and customers to experience the product first-hand. That creates a bigger desire for the product and a sense of ownership.

Think about how realtors take you through a home you are looking to buy. They always refer to it as *your* master bedroom, *your* kitchen, *your* patio. They want you to feel a sense of ownership over the home, so that you start to imagine what it would be like to live there and have your things there. It is the same in direct sales. Having clients hold your product in their hands is better than showing them a photo on Facebook.

Using your Booking Lead Notebook discussed earlier, you will want to start to call some of your friends, family, and acquaintances to set up a time for them to see the products. When you call them initially, you may want to start with something like this:

> "Hi Jessica, this is Belinda. I was wondering if you're going to be home this weekend (or evening or afternoon). (Wait for response.) Great! I'd love to come over for a quick visit. I have something really exciting to show you!"

Or maybe something like this:

> "Hi Jessica, it's Belinda. I can't wait to show you the new business I've decided to do." (Wait for a response.) "Terrific! I'd love to stop by for a few minutes to show you some awesome products. I know you're going to love them."

Or even:

> "I've started my own business and I would really value your opinion. Could I practice by speaking with you about the business? Is there a day this week that I could swing by?"

If they ask, "What kind of product is it?" just say, "Oh, it's an awesome line of _____. And I know you're going to love it!" After you show it to them, it also creates excitement for those who end up having parties because they've already seen your fabulous product and they have first-hand knowledge to share with the guests they will be inviting.

It's especially important to get out and personally show the product as much as possible when booking your first six shows. Creating enthusiasm only over the phone or online is very difficult, so get out and *see the people.* Show them what's got you so energized! Allowing your friends and family to see the product for themselves and how excited you are about it also reduces any need for you to "sell" them on the idea.

Once you get there, take a few minutes to relax and engage in small talk about common friends, family, and so on. When you're ready to talk about your new business, begin by saying something like this:

> "I wanted to stop by to tell you about my new business and show you some of the products."

Show her some of your favorite products and your current catalog. Get her involved and let her know that hosting a party would be a great way to get you started in your new business. In return, she will earn a wonderful shopping spree and have the opportunity to shop at a discount.

> "Melissa, that's one of my favorites, too. You know, you could get that absolutely free just for having a few friends over. You would be a great host! And it would really mean a lot to me if you would help me by hosting one of my very first parties."

Let her know the dates you need to fill with your first parties and ask her to help you with one of them. People like to be part of the success of those around them. You'll be surprised by how much your friends will want to help you, if you ask. When she says "Yes!" proceed to coach her for a great party (see Chapter 10 for more on host coaching):

> "Bridgette, I would love to get my business off to the best start possible. Would you be willing to help me get things going?" (Wait for a response.) "Thank you so much! I know your friends will love it and will appreciate learning about these great products. I have a couple of days to fill with parties on my calendar — which day will work best for you? Thursday or Saturday?"

Enlist your friends

When you're starting your business, don't hesitate to ask people for their help. Friends will often surprise you with their willingness to help you get a great start in your business.

Let them know what you need to be successful and that you need the practice; you'll typically find them eager to know exactly how they can help you:

> "Hi, Sarah. This is Melanie. Do you have a couple minutes? I'm just getting started in a new business and I was wondering if you could pull a few friends together for a fun evening and help me out by hosting one of my first parties?"

Or you could say:

> "Hi, Sarah. How are you? I'm calling to tell you about my new business. I just started and I can't wait to share our incredible products with you. Sarah, you are a great friend. I promise a fun night for your friends, and there are some great perks in it for you. Can I count on you to get a few friends together for a fun night out?"

Sometimes people are hesitant about having enough time to host a party for you. They don't fully understand that there really isn't that much work involved in having a party. You can alleviate their concerns and overcome their objections (more on objections later in this chapter) by saying something like this:

> "Hi, Katie. Is now a bad time? No? Great. I was wondering if you could help me out by having a party to help me get started in my new business. I need to hold three large parties and three small ones. Could you help me out with one of these? You will benefit from getting a few selections free and getting to shop at 50% off."

Ultimately, for you, a party is a party, but the choice helps people feel that the commitment isn't as large as it would be to have a large party. They feel like it is okay if they only have three to five friends.

Regardless of what approach you take, it's your friends and family who help you get your business started by having parties for you early on. Their willingness to help you simply because they care so much about you is a great advantage at the beginning of your business, so don't overlook it.

But it isn't just your family and friends that will help you grow your business. That is why it's important, even at these parties with friends, to do a good job and get *their* friends booked in your calendar (see Chapter 9 for more training on how to book a party).

So make your list, contact them all, and allow them to feel good about being able to do something for you. Those early parties help you get some practice, get those initial sales, and meet new people. The more parties you book in the first few weeks of your business, the better. So, get on the phone!

Host your own party

This is the perfect opportunity to show your friends and family what you're doing, so it's preferable that your launch party (see Chapter 8 for more on launch parties) be one of your very first parties. This way, when you're creating interest by seeing the people and getting on the phone to enlist the help of your friends, you'll have something fun to invite them to if they don't immediately opt to book a party with you.

People you call who can't or won't book their own party with you are still often quite willing to attend a party at your home. When one of your contacts says they can't host one of your first parties, for whatever reason, be gracious. They may have really good reasons! It's just no for now. They may have a party in the future. You might say this:

> "Lisa, I totally understand. It is a really busy time." (Say something that validates their reason.) "I'll be hosting my own 'grand opening' for my business next Sunday and would love to have you attend and let me know what you think. It's going to be a lot of fun, and I'd really like you to be a part of it."

Make your invitations sincere and make sure they highlight how much you'd like to see them there:

> "I'd love to have you come to my party next Friday to launch my new business. You'll have a lot of fun and get to try our wonderful products. I am confident that there are a few items that you're going to fall in love with. Do you think you can make it?"

And send reminder texts like this for those who've said they'll come:

> "Hi, Lisa! I really appreciate your support as I start my business. I'm looking forward to seeing you Saturday night at 7 p.m. for my business launch. It's going to be so much fun! If you have any questions or need directions, give me a quick call."

Your launch party is a great chance for your friends and family to see the products and experience the fun and excitement of a party. Plus, it's also a really natural and effective way for you to secure future bookings. You may find that you'll want to host more than one party: to provide people who weren't able to attend your first party a chance to attend and learn about what you're doing, or if you have several distinct groups of friends.

Your launch party is a kick-off for your new business. You'll want to include all your family and friends in the celebration.

Why People Book — Or Don't

Your parties are the best place for you to get new bookings. It's easier and more efficient to get bookings at the party than it is to try to obtain them later.

A good goal is to secure at least two to three bookings from every party:

- ✔ 1 booking to replace the one you just did
- ✔ 1 booking to grow your business on
- ✔ 1 booking for insurance (in case one of your previous bookings cancels)

There are three main reasons that people book and three reasons why they don't. First, let's talk about why they *would* want to have a party:

- ✔ **Fun:** Guests love a fun night out with their friends to shop. At your parties, it's crucial that you make sure all guests have a great time. This will get them to start to consider hosting one of their own, with their friends.

  Always put an emphasis on having a good time — this is the number one reason people book.

- ✔ **Free and discounted products:** People book because of the amazing host incentives that they will receive, including free credit and half-priced items. Studies show that most hosts get just as excited about discounted products as they do the items they will receive for free.

✔ **Willingness to help a friend:** Some companies offer a gift to a host if a guest from her party books as well. Guests at the party want their friend (the host) to receive the gift, so they will consider having their own party. If you remind them how much their own friends will appreciate you for getting them together, this will usually tip the scale. They will usually agree to having the party.

Here are the three biggest reasons people *don't* book:

✔ **You haven't asked:** This one is so simple, but is often overlooked. People think that asking is simply saying, "Hey, if you'd like to have a party, let me know." But asking is more about doing an effective booking talk (see the section "The Booking Talk" later in this chapter). You always want to showcase your parties as something people will want to host. You should always ask, "Why wouldn't you want to host? You will have an amazing time with your friends and will be able to enjoy some free and discounted products."

The "ask" also comes at checkout time. This is where you sit with a customer while they're making their decision on what products they want. What we find so often is that people are in deep thought during this time. They are contemplating their choices and how much money they want to spend. The left side of their brains, the analytical and computing side, is in full swing.

While they are thinking, you might say, "So, Lauren, would you like to have a party?" Because she is so deep into her analytical thinking, she will most likely look at you and say, "No." She might also say something like, "No, I'm good," or "No, I'm all set." After this, your typical response is, "Okay, well if you should get home and change your mind, let me know."

What you want to do is get people to use the right side of their brains, and you get them to do that by complimenting them on their selections and by making them feel good. "Oh, Lauren, you made a great choice. I know you're really going to fall in love with it."

People start to feel validated for their purchase, like they made a good choice. This leaves them feeling good and more likely to consider hosting a party.

✔ **People are busy and can't make a decision:** This is the second reason people say no to having a party. They say no because no comes easy to them. To overcome this, you want to offer three power questions that will get three quick yes answers in a row: "Did you have fun? Are there any products that you want but couldn't get tonight? Do you think your friends would enjoy this experience?" The next section goes into these questions in detail.

✔ **Fear that people won't come:** The third reason why people say no to hosting is the fear that their friends won't come. What we know from focus groups is that it really isn't the fear that no one will come, but the fear that they won't *want to.*

They also fear the feeling of getting something for free at the expense of their friends. That is why you never want to focus too much on the free and discounted products. The way you overcome this fear is to remind guests throughout the party that their friends would love it and would appreciate them for having the party. Remind guests that their friends are going to enjoy a night out, shopping and learning about (whatever your product offers).

Make sure you're always ready to book. Aim high and you will receive greater success.

Three Power Questions to Get the Reluctant to Say Yes

If someone seems unsure about booking, you should ask a series of three power questions that will get them to say yes. These three yesses will remind your guest how much they enjoyed the party and help lead them toward saying yes to booking a party:

✔ Did you have fun?

✔ Are there any products that you want but couldn't get tonight?

✔ Do you think your friends would enjoy this experience?

When they have answered yes to these questions, we want to help them make a decision by offering choices. For example, ask your customer what works best for them — weekends or weeknights? And continue to narrow down a date from there. Aim to get three confirmations:

"Okay Michelle, if you were to have a party what would work better — a weekday or a weekend?

"Weekends are perfect. Would you prefer a Friday night, a Saturday morning, or a Sunday afternoon?

"Sunday afternoon? Would you prefer 1 p.m., 2 p.m., or 3 p.m.?

"3 p.m.? Great! I have Sunday, January 25th and Sunday, February 8th. Which works best for you?

"Okay, it sounds like the 25th at 3 p.m. sounds good for you. I will do the majority of the work, so why don't we go ahead and book it? It will help Kim" — the current host (say this is if your company offers booking gifts for hosts whose guests book a party) — "and your friends will love it."

By following this process of choices, customers come to their own conclusions with a little bit of help from you.

All these suggestions will prove helpful in maintaining your calendar and controlling your business . . . and your paycheck.

Planting Booking Seeds

Booking seeds are a subtle way to plant the ideas of why a guest would want to have a party, without actually saying it.

The following are booking seeds:

"I have more clients choose this item for free than any other product."

"This is our most popular half-price selection."

"Right now, I have so many people booking parties just to get this product. It is a really popular item right now."

"I just did a party in a teacher's lounge after school and this was the best selling item at the party."

"I did an office party the other day, and the ladies went crazy over this product."

"These items are always best-sellers at my bridal/baby shower parties."

"This is one of my favorite products and it's actually the most popular in our fundraising package."

Sprinkling your booking seeds throughout your parties, one-on-ones, and even social media posts is a great way to get people thinking about hosting a party with you.

Show customers that by being a host they can get some of your most coveted products free and have fun with friends. You can also show them that parties don't have to be in the home and that there are multiple ways that they can host a party, including starting a fundraiser with you (see Chapter 3).

You want to create relationships with your customers. You never want to come off as a salesperson. Salespeople think about themselves — what they can get from a party, how much money they can make, and so on. *You* want to be authentic and build your sales techniques into casual conversations.

You always want to come from a place of service. Like, "Let me help you. This is how I will help your guests." You don't always need to actually ask for the party. Subtly include these seeds into your conversations and let booking be their idea.

The Booking Talk

Throughout the evening you have planted the idea of hosting a party. But a booking talk is one of the most important aspects of your party for encouraging people to host a party,

Your booking talk is usually at the end of presenting the products, before you start your shopping experience. It is a small commercial and really a call to action for them to book the party. It shouldn't last more than 90 seconds. See Chapter 9 for more information on perfecting this.

When you deliver an effective booking talk, combined with sprinkling booking seeds throughout your presentation, you will get multiple bookings from your parties. Particularly at the beginning of your business, that is your primary goal: to get more bookings. Too many new representatives — or their *sponsors* (someone who welcomes someone else to the business) — focus on only achieving sales, so they bring far too many products to show and sometimes skip the booking talk altogether.

I'll say it again: Your bookings are the heartbeat of your business.

Your goal at your first few parties is to get practice and get comfortable — and yes, to get bookings. These bookings will replace and add to your business and lead to much higher sales as you continue.

When you're new, you often think to yourself: "I'm running out of time. I'm sure if they want to book, they'll let me know." So, your booking talk consists of something like:

> "We have a wonderful hostess plan, and I'd love to do a party for you. If you want to book, please let me know."

That's not a booking talk!

At the other end of the spectrum are those who go on and on with a booking talk that's a lengthy bullet-point presentation on the host plan, complete with percentages and half-price and free items. Don't do that either. One of the biggest mistakes you can make is to start giving every single detail about your host plan. Why? Because it goes right over their heads and you lose them. You're host coaching before you even have a host.

Your booking talk is not about what a host is going to get; it's about why they would want to book a party. Your booking message should leave your guests thinking that booking a party is going to be fun. Why in the world wouldn't they want to do it? They'd be crazy not to take advantage of this.

One way to initiate your booking talk is to do your opening talk where you thank the hostess and mention her generous shopping spree and discounted products. Then do your presentation showing groupings and a variety of products.

Now, as you're showing your products, they're wondering how they can get that shopping spree. After you are finished showing your products, continue with your booking talk:

> "Ladies, I know you all have fallen in love with many of the wonderful products this evening, and you're probably thinking to yourself that you aren't able to get everything tonight, and that generous shopping spree sure would be nice. Well, let me tell you how easy it is for you to get that. It takes one night out of your busy life and a handful of friends.

> "And really, ladies, why in the world wouldn't you want to have a party? I'm going to do all the work for you; it takes no more time than the time you've spent here tonight. It's easy and fun! Haven't you had fun this evening? That's how much fun we're going to have with your friends.

> "I'm going to come in, entertain your friends, give them some great ideas" (feed them, size them, teach them, and so on). "Your friends are going to appreciate you and absolutely love it. And again, why in the world wouldn't you want to have a party? I can't imagine! So, I'm encouraging each and every one of you to say yes, and I will work with you on a date that is suitable for you and your schedule."

It's got to be the why factor and the wow factor that you share with your guests: "You would be crazy not to" and "This is what you're going to be able to get. This is what you're going to be able to experience." And so on.

Learning how to deliver an effective booking talk is going to make a huge difference in your business. For more on booking talks, see Chapter 9.

Tips for Securing More Bookings

If you do all the following things, you greatly increase your chances of getting new bookings at your parties:

✔ **Do a booking talk.** Don't skip it. When you include an effective booking talk at your party with a strong opening that references the benefits of booking, you create interest in hosting a party long before you get to speak with each guest directly. You want your guests to start thinking about why *they* should have their own party while they're having fun with their friends. Your other techniques (such as asking everyone, playing booking games, or booking bonus dates — all covered in upcoming bullets) are so much more effective when you have already explained the benefits of hosting and created a desire.

✔ **Ask everyone.** Yes, I'm saying it again. Make it a personal goal to speak about the opportunity to host with every single guest at the party. "Adriana, you had such a great time tonight and you were so excited about our products. Can you see why it would be fun to host a party of your own? I know your friends would love the experience as much as you did."

✔ **Don't leave without a date.** Even if it is only a tentative date. Do your job while you're at work — going over the details while you're there with your potential new host will save you a lot of time and energy later on.

In this business, the rule of thumb is: *It's not a booking until it's dated.* When people say they will book without setting a date, it creates a false sense of security. You may think you have six or seven bookings, but unless they are scheduled on the calendar, they are meaningless.

✔ **Set bonus booking dates.** This encourages people to book to receive an extra gift from you. Your *bonus booking dates* are always your two closest dates. You don't have to offer gifts for booking other nights because your company's host program is usually rewarding enough.

✔ **Show your booking tree.** Individually display your next available dates. This allows people to look at the dates while you are assisting other customers. Let guests know that they can take a look at the available dates and choose one to bring up during the checkout process. I have seen representatives use photo holders to display these.

✔ **Play booking games.** I have never been a fan of games, but I have played booking games if my calendar was lower than I needed it to be. For some people, a game makes it easier to incorporate the booking talk into their party script. There are a variety of different booking games — some are during the party, some are before the booking talk and sometimes your booking talk is incorporated into the game. Some companies encourage a particular game or leaders will recommend one that they find is successful. I have never trained on booking games, because they are not something that I personally liked, but if your leader has found success with a particular one and you feel more comfortable incorporating it, go for it!

The studies I have conducted throughout the years show that about half of the participants like games at parties and half don't. So, decide what works best for you. If you are going to do a game, make sure it gets the results you want — in other words, it should bring in bookings.

Don't give away something for nothing. An example of a booking game would be having a customer choose a box for a prize. And to receive that prize, they have to complete the action on the card — which is book a party, of course. Whatever you do, keep it simple and short.

✔ **Know your dates.** Know the dates you want to work and offer those dates, and only those dates, to your clients. As I've mentioned, don't leave things open-ended. Ask them, "Would you like Friday the 14th or Tuesday the 18th?"

Overcoming Common Objections

Choosing the most compelling words and knowing when to use them is a must for overcoming common objections and keeping your calendar full.

"Let me check with my friends first"

This is the most common objection to booking a party. But what they are really saying is, "I don't want to pick a night that no one will come." This is people's greatest fear. Nobody wants to host a party where no one shows up. But the reality of it is, they can't check with their friends without a date.

In response to this objection you would say something like this:

"I totally get where you're coming from — but I gotta be honest, if you go to your friends with an uncommitted question, you're going to get an uncommitted answer. Like, hey you guys do you want to come to a jewelry party? And they will say when is it? And you'll say, well, I don't know. If you give them a date, like the 21st, they will say yes or no.

And Amy, if too many people can't come that day, we can definitely move it. So why don't we go ahead and select the 21st as the option you offer your friends."

"My friends are partied out"

This is a very positive hesitation because it means that she and her neighbors are very receptive to home party shopping, and they love to do this kind of entertaining. In response to this objection you would say something like this:

> "Great! It sounds like your friends love this type of entertainment. Maybe I could do something special at your party." Or: "We're fairly new in this area, and most people haven't been to a _____ party yet." Or: "Let's date your party as soon as possible before someone in the neighborhood books something else."

"My house isn't big enough"

You may get this response if the home where the current party is being held is quite large. Your prospect may feel inadequate, so it's important to make her feel like what she has to offer is exactly what you want.

> "It doesn't take much space, Mary. I can adapt to whatever setting you have. And I have found that when you're having a great time with friends, no place is too small. Plus it makes the party intimate and cozy!"

"I don't have any time — I'm too busy"

This is another very common objection. The first response would definitely be to help them weed through the busyness in their head. You may want to make a little small talk to find out what your prospect is "too busy" doing. For example, perhaps he/she normally works part-time and for the next week or so is putting in full-time (or overtime) hours and, therefore, is feeling over-whelmed. If she knows she doesn't have to date for this immediate week, she may be more receptive:

> "I would love to have you as a host! Busy people actually make the best hosts because they get things done, are more organized, and typically know more people. But don't worry, I'll do the majority of the work. All I ask is that you get a few of your friends together to have a good time. And honestly, it takes no more time than the time you spent here this evening."

"I think I just want to do a catalog party"

A catalog party is when a host collects orders from her friends using your catalog, instead of hosting a party at her home. The majority of the time, the host will leave catalogs at her place of work and other places like the dance studio, karate, baseball and so on. Her friends will look through the catalogs, try any samples you have given your host and place orders that way.

Catalog parties typically won't result in the party totals that a home party will. If a guest at a party asks for a catalog party, your goal is to turn it into a mini party for her:

> "Oh Melissa, that's a great idea! I have a lot of people who do catalog parties. Do you have a lot of people at work who would like to order?"

I always want to agree with my customer, but help steer them in a different direction:

> "Why don't we set a date where I can come out and collect the orders, and you can select your free products. While I'm there, why don't you invite a few neighbors or friends over to see the collection?"

Once you frame it like this they will most likely choose a date. This gives a close date to the party as well as the opportunity for you to get additional orders through a party. People who want to host catalog parties are usually afraid no one will come. So when they hear that they only need to invite a few friends, they feel better about saying yes to hosting.

This is a win/win for you both. The host will enjoy getting together with her friends, and you will receive additional sales through a home party. Even with a smaller group in person, the home party is still typically higher than the orders your host collects from her catalog party.

I once had a host who lived in the country. She didn't want to host because she didn't think she could get a lot of people there, but she did have people at work who were interested. I used the preceding scripting on her, and she agreed to have a few friends over a couple weeks later. She only had four guests the night of the party, but her party with four guests had higher party sales than the eight outside orders she collected from the catalog. The biggest bonus was that I was able to use my booking talk to book two out of the four guests for parties of their own. The result was that the party was double what it would have been if she had only hosted a catalog party.

Tips on Finding New Business

New business is everywhere. There are many different places where you can connect with new people, expand your network, find referrals, and obtain host and recruiting leads. This section offers some more ideas on drumming up new business.

Using your social network for referrals

The first step to finding new business is to use your social network. Reach out to your social media network and ask who they know in that area. Don't be afraid to ask for help and referrals. Be sure to use your Booking Lead Notebook. As soon as someone gives you a referral or a lead, put it in the notebook.

I have found the best way to build a business is to use five simple words: *Who do you know who?* As in, "Who do you know who might like this product?" I built not only my direct sales business on this model, but my speaking career as well. Another strategy is to offer a referral gift. If someone that person knows books a party or joins the business because of their referral, I would always be sure to give them a special gift to thank them.

When you are reaching out to your referrals, always be sure to mention who referred you to them:

> "Hi, Mary! We have a mutual friend, Kathy, and she gave me your number. I have recently relocated here, and Kathy thought you would be interested in helping me establish myself in this new area. Kathy was very confident that you would love our products."

Use my tips on how to secure a booking in the earlier section "Securing Bookings or Appointments."

Getting leads from leads

If your lead seems hesitant, let her know that you appreciate her time and that you understand this isn't the best time right now for her to host a party for you. But before you get off the phone, ask her who she knows who might be interested in hosting a party or who might really love the product.

Always ask for leads from leads.

Let people know that you are looking to build a team and a business in that area, so if they have anyone in mind who might be interested, you would love an introduction. I have found that the third-party approach really works best, especially in the areas of recruiting (see Chapter 14 for more on recruiting).

Continue to follow this trail of *who do you know who* and work on this daily.

Go where your customers are

Another great way to find new business is to frequent places where your clients would most likely be. Most of the direct selling, especially party plan, is directed towards women. So ask yourself, *Where do women hang out?*

✔ **Salons:** Salon owners and hair stylists are amazing resources. They know a lot of people and have close relationships with most of their regular clients. I used to own a couple Curves franchises, and I was opening one in an area where I knew no one. When I drove to the town, my first stop was at the hair salon. I introduced myself, let the owner know I was opening a Curves, and asked if they knew an amazing person who could run and manage the facility. She immediately gave me the number of three people. And the best part about these three leads? It only took me 15 minutes. So, always ask *who do they know who* might be interested in hosting a party. And I did end up hiring one of those three!

You can also suggest that the hair salon have a party. If they hesitate, ask if you can at least leave behind some of your catalogs for the lobby. But this is the last-case scenario. Use your best booking talk and share how fun the party could be for the salon's guests and clients.

I had a very good friend who had an established direct sales business, but needed to suddenly relocate. As soon as she moved, she began going to get her nails done and her hair cut every two weeks at a different place each time, just so she could meet new people. Her goal was to reestablish herself through this chain of engagement.

With social media, you have so many options, but there is nothing more effective than selling your personality, in person.

✔ **Gyms:** Talk to local gyms, especially those that offer a women's center, and ask if you can set up a booth and pass out information.

✔ **Mom groups/play groups:** Depending on the age of your kids, look for local mom groups or play groups to be a part of. This is a great way to make new friends and find potential hosts, customers, and recruits.

✔ **Networking groups:** Networking groups are a great way to establish yourself as a business owner in your local community. People in networking groups are also always willing to share leads and referrals.

✔ **Clubs:** Clubs like book clubs, women's clubs, running clubs, and so on, are other great places to meet women.

✔ **Local restaurants:** Attend local restaurants and let them know you have a new business in the area. Develop relationships. If you become a frequent customer, they will be more likely to help you as well.

- **Malls:** One of the ways I built my business was by going to the mall. I would have a small tote bag, equipped with my show-on-the-go (see Chapter 6 if you don't know what that means) and I would head out for the day. I always made sure that I looked professional and presentable. I would go into stores, and when asked if I needed help, I would tell them that I needed an outfit for things like a convention, business meeting, or gala. I always made sure my answer had to do with my business. Naturally, they are trying to get a sale, so they also probed for more information. This gave me an excellent opportunity to let them know what I do, and mention I was looking to develop my business in that area and if they knew anyone who might be interested.

  Often, the salesperson *herself* would want more information on the hosting or business opportunity. I would then ask what time her break was and would meet with her in the food court to grab something to drink. I would then talk about my three Ps: products, profits, and programs (see Chapter 2). I would lay out a couple of product samples, a host packet, and a recruiting packet.

- **Church:** Often, church groups and small groups are more like a community and are more eager to help, especially if you have gone to the church for a while and have started to build relationships. If you are new to an area, finding a new church is often a really good place to start. After you have gone several times, you will begin to make new relationships and bonds.

- **School:** If you have children, school can be a great way to meet other parents and teachers. See how you can get involved at school and build friendships with some of the other parents.

- **Realtors:** If you are looking for new business because you have moved, ask the realtor who sold you your house if they are interested in helping launch your business or know of anyone who might be interested. Because realtors are salespeople too working off commission, they also usually know of the best networking groups in the city. Be sure to ask them for leads and groups you can join.

- **New neighbors:** Your new neighbors are also potential hosts, customers, and recruits. Introduce yourself to people on the street and (I can't say it enough) build relationships. Let them know you are looking to start your business in the area and ask if they would be interested in holding a party to help you get started.

I know in today's busy world, with all the technology available at our fingertips, some of the preceding suggestions may seem dated or old. But remember, there are multiple ways to touch your business (Chapter 1). Social media can certainly provide great resources for you that you may have never met otherwise, but know that these tried-and-true strategies will help you find quality leads. Even though the process may be more time-consuming, the leads are usually more concrete and give people the chance to connect with you on a more personal level than they did online. People are also more likely to refer a friend if they have met you in person and established a connection.

The most important thing to remember is that you can't build a business overnight. Take it one day at a time and stay positive. Use the third-party approach of *who do you know who*. People are more likely to refer someone instead of feeling the pressure of making a decision themselves. But if you follow my training and deliver your commercials with passion and enthusiasm, most times they will recommend *themselves*.

Finding business after relocating

Once you have built a team and a large list of customers, relocating can be very challenging. You are dealing with a lot of emotions and the feeling that you have to start over.

The key is to stay positive and look at it as a new opportunity in a different area. You actually have the opportunity to *expand* your business. But no matter what, relocating can be difficult. So you will need some reassuring to happen:

✔ **Reassure your team.** An important first step you will want to take when you decide to relocate is to reassure your team that you will still be there for them and will not abandon them. Let them know everything is going to be fine and put in place some concrete systems for staying in contact. The best thing you can do is find someone who is either a leader or close to promoting and give them some ownership of that area. Train them on what it means to be a leader and instruct them on how to handle your monthly meetings. A lot of times when someone is suddenly given this responsibility, they rise to the occasion and become the leader you always knew they could be. Make sure you choose wisely and talk with them so that everyone on your team is clear of the change and expectations.

Phone and video conferencing — for example, Skype — are good ways to stay in touch with your team. If you don't have one already, creating a Facebook Group for everyone in your downline is something you will want to start. Posting training tips, news, and recognition in your Facebook Group will build confidence in your team that you have not abandoned them or have lost interest.

✔ **Reassure yourself.** I hear from most people that they go through a feeling of depression, and have a tendency to feel like they don't even know where to begin. This is and can be daunting, so first things first. Take it in small steps. Reassure yourself that you can continue to grow your team back home and expand your business in this new area.

Try to set simple daily goals, like meeting one new person per day or making five phone calls a day. Don't feel like you have to build a new business in a new location overnight. Also, depending on the level of leadership you are at and the size of your team, you may have been more in the leadership or managing mindset — meaning less personal business.

✔ **Pretend you're new.** Perhaps the easiest way to start over is to start from the beginning. This can be challenging to wrap your head around, but acting as if you are a new representative is the easiest way to start your business in a new location. Pretend you are a new representative and continue to re-promote yourself through the ranks of your company. Aside from needing to do it because of your relocation, this exercise can challenge you and get you excited about your business again. This time around, you will find yourself achieving promotions much faster than you did when you actually started your business.

✔ **Provide excellent customer care to existing clients.** With the Internet and social media, running a business far away from your clients is very doable. And not only doable, but can still be very successful. The key is to maintain your relationships with your customers through phone, email and social media. Continue to service them as you would in your previous local area and they will order from you again and again. (See Chapter 11 for more on running an online business.) And don't forget to ask your existing clients if they know anyone in the area you are moving to who would be interested in your product or service.

✔ **Find new business.** The above tips under Tips on Finding New Business is a great resource for you while re-building a business.

Chapter 8

Planning a Launch Party or Show

∙ ∙

In This Chapter

▶ Understanding the importance of a launch party

▶ Planning and executing a successful launch

▶ Having a back-up launch party

▶ Scheduling your parties with the two-booking method

∙ ∙

A *launch party* is an in-person event where you launch your new business to your friends and family. The launch party sets the tone and creates momentum for your business. Some companies may call it a *grand opening, debut, kick-off,* or *introductory party.* Whatever you want to call it, it is the best way to introduce your new business to a large group of people.

The people at your launch party are what we call your *warm market.* Your friends and family are likely to be your first customers as well as your first hosts.

Keep in mind that even though it is your friends and family that will help you with your first parties, it is the bookings that you get *from* those parties that will help you grow your business.

A launch party shows your friends and family exactly what you're doing and lets them experience your products first-hand.

Being able to share your new business with as many people as possible at the same time creates excitement, saves time, and helps you build a customer base quickly. This is one piece of your business you honestly don't want to leave out.

You should set a date for your launch as soon as you purchase your kit. Having a date set helps prepare you both mentally and physically.

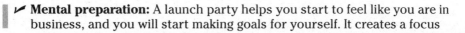

✔ **Mental preparation:** A launch party helps you start to feel like you are in business, and you will start making goals for yourself. It creates a focus for you in the first stages of your business. Your excitement will build as you are telling people about your new business, and you will have somewhere to invite them to so that they can become familiar with what you're doing.

✔ **Physical preparation:** When you have a "start date" set for your business, you work toward that date. You start to learn as much as you can about your products and plan how to do a presentation. You start inviting people to your event and lining up your next set of parties/appointments. You are in a *make-things-happen* frame of mind rather than *wait-and-see.*

I recommend throwing a regular home party for your launch, if possible. Home parties typically result in higher sales, bookings, and recruit leads. But there are a couple of other kinds you may consider. There are four main types of launch party:

✔ **Home party (recommended):** You run this party like a regular party, except in this case you act as both the host and the representative (see Chapter 9 on how to run a successful party). You greet guests, do an opening talk, give a presentation, give a booking talk, plant recruiting seeds, and help guests with their shopping experience. Your guests will have the opportunity to socialize with each other, and you are able to do a presentation in a group setting for the first time. Home parties start at a specific time and are well-structured — yet still fun for your guests. You can talk to each guest one-on-one during the checkout process.

✔ **Open house:** An open house is where you have your kit set up for people to view and experience. This type of launch is more flexible than a home party. You work with people one-on-one rather than doing a full presentation to a group. Typically you have a time frame set up, and people stop by at their convenience — like an open house a realtor sets up when you are selling your home.

When you give an open time to people, they may not be as committed to attending, and this lack of commitment can lower overall attendance. However, it does allow for someone to stop by who may not have been able to attend a home party that starts at a set time.

✔ **Online party:** Representatives who run their businesses almost exclusively online may opt to have an online party. It is important to note that when doing an online party, you will want to follow the same basic principles as a home party. For your online party, follow the format laid out in Chapter 11. Be sure to invite friends and family to an online event, where you will showcase the products and your new business. I suggest posting some videos of you demonstrating the product online.

- ✔ **Business opportunity:** This event is most utilized by Network Marketing companies. A business opportunity launch is where you talk about the products in a group setting, often accompanied with a video, but you focus on sharing the opportunity and the income potential for those who become reps. This type of launch often leads to more recruits, but may not generate as many sales or future appointments. However, many successful Network Marketers still encourage guests who aren't yet interested in the business to become customers, which can lead to immediate sales. Perhaps those customers will later refer more business or join the team.

If your leader lives in the area, he or she may want to assist you with your launch party, answer any questions, and help out with bookings and recruit leads.

Understanding Why Your Launch Party Is So Important

Your launch party can accomplish the following things:

- ✔ **Introduces your business to your market:** Your party launches your business to your friends and family and lets them experience your products first-hand. This will help increase product sales, party (online or home) bookings, as well as recruit leads.

- ✔ **Builds your confidence:** Your launch party gives you the practice and confidence you will need going forward, for the next parties you book. The only way to get good at this business is simply by doing it. Practice, practice, practice. As mentioned in Chapter 7, I always suggest booking six parties on your calendar within your first 30–45 days. This will give you the momentum you need to keep your calendar full every month.

- ✔ **Earns back your investment:** During your launch party, you act as both representative and host. So, not only do you receive commission from the party to help pay back the cost of your kit, you may also receive free and discounted products that you can use to add more products to your kit to show at future parties.

- ✔ **Leads to more bookings:** Your launch party can also help get more bookings on your calendar. When people at the launch party are having fun and seeing the reaction of the other guests, they become more inclined to book with you right then, rather than later over the phone. Be sure to practice your booking talk as discussed in Chapters 7 and 9. It's important to try to book your family and friends right out of the gate, so that you can build bookings off of those parties. Even though your friends and family aren't the most likely group to help you in the long run, those first parties will help you expand your network and reach, and you'll book people at their parties that you might not have otherwise met.

It's always your goal to turn a party guest into your next host or new recruit.

✔ **Aids in recruiting:** Your launch party is also a great place for you to find some additional team members. Statistics show that representatives have more fun and earn more money when two friends start their businesses at roughly the same time. So invite your friends to learn more and join you on this exciting new venture. Chapter 14 talks more about recruiting.

✔ **Builds your client base:** Being in front of a large number of people allows you to build your client base and begin enjoying the benefits of re-servicing your customers. Check out my "2+2+2 follow-up" method in Chapter 13.

✔ **Earns your fast start:** The sales, bookings, and recruits you gain from your launch party will also help you in achieving your company's Fast Start (or Quick Start or something similar — most Party Plan companies have a program that propels you with incentives during your first 90–100 days of your business. Network Marketing companies often have shorter timelines for their Fast Start programs, often with deadlines that occur in the first 30–45 days). These Fast Start programs help you create healthy habits for your business, give you the momentum to reach sales and recruiting goals, and are designed to get you making money quickly — see Chapter 5 for more details.

Preparing for Your Launch

Your launch party will set the tone for your business and will show your friends and family what it means to host a party, attend a party, and do business with you. Even though you're still new, and your launch party might not be perfect (it's okay! it's your first one!), it's important to prepare as thoroughly as possible. That way, you can generate excitement and fill your calendar with bookings, your team with recruits, and your pocket with sales.

As mentioned earlier, now is a great time to reach out to your leader or sponsor. They will assist you in planning for your launch party, give you tips on how to best utilize your business starter kit, and help you with your booking and sponsoring efforts.

Here are some tips for planning your launch:

- ✔ **Choose a date and time as soon as you can.** You have ordered your kit and are excited about your new venture. Within the next two to three days, get the date for your launch party on your calendar, as well as the date for your second (back-up) launch — see the next section for more on this back-up launch party.

- ✔ **Over-invite.** One key to a successful launch is to *have as many attendees as possible*. Only about a third of those invited will typically be able to attend. Ideally, you would love to have 10–15 guests. Start making your guest list using your cellphone address book and your Facebook friend list.

    Probably the best way to invite is with a personal phone call. On the phone, the person on the other end can feel your excitement, which leads to increased attendance. Follow up with the 1-2-3s of inviting (see the next section).

- ✔ **Build desire and create an interest.** Social media is a great way to build excitement for your new business. Be sure to announce to your family and friends that you've started a new business and have created a Facebook Business Page where you share information about the products (Chapter 11). Begin exposing your market to your products through photo posts, statuses, blog posts, and videos well before your launch party.

- ✔ **Explore your starter kit.** The kit you purchased when you signed up contains everything you need to conduct a successful party, appointment, or presentation. Become familiar with the products in your kit as well as the benefits to using your products. You will use this kit for your launch party, so it's important for you to learn as much as you can about the products you will show. But don't worry, your leader will be able to assist you with questions your guests have about the products that you are unable to answer.

- ✔ **Study your catalog.** Even though you will focus on demonstrating the products that are available to you through your starter kit, it's important to familiarize yourself with your catalog. Your party guests will be able to shop through the catalog for additional items that you didn't cover specifically in your presentation. If there is an item you know that your guests will love, be sure to let them know that they can see the item in the catalog. Make it a priority to also shop the catalog yourself — you will be able to get many other products for your starter kit through the host benefits you receive at your launch party. If there is a particular item you don't have that a customer is interested in but wants to see in person first, let her know that you'll be selecting that as one of your items from your host benefits and encourage her to host her own party where you can share that product with her friends.

✔ **Practice, practice, practice.** Read through Chapter 9 and practice. In that chapter, I go through all the key elements of a successful party as well as scripting. Use that chapter to learn how to conduct a party, create your own talks, and then practice, practice, practice.

✔ **Attend a party with your leader.** Another great way to get practice before your launch party and after reading Chapter 9 is attending a party with your leader. Chances are you became interested in joining your company after attending a party yourself. However, you had a different perspective on the evening as a guest or host. Go to one of your leader's parties and watch how she gives her opening talk, demonstrates the products, shares the hosting and business opportunity, and completes a full-service checkout.

✔ **Learn from your leader:** It is great if your leader can attend your launch. That way she can help you with your booking and recruiting talk, answer any questions you might not have the answer to yet, and give you assistance during the checkout process (see Chapter 9 for more). However, if that's not possible, let your leader guide you and offer expertise and wisdom before and after the party. Beforehand, you'll practice what to say so that you're familiar with demonstrating the products and presenting the three parts of the party: opening, booking, and recruiting.

✔ **Review company training.** I want you to succeed. Your leader wants you to succeed. And your company wants you to succeed. Your company has made training information available to you, usually online or in the form of a guide that may have came in your starter kit. Be sure to review this information — especially the training specific to launch parties, home parties, and online parties.

The 1-2-3s of Inviting

Inviting guests to your launch party is as easy as 1-2-3. Follow these three easy tips to increase attendance at your launch party:

1. **Pick up your phone and invite each person personally.** Let them know how important it is to you that they come. Encourage them to save the date and bring a friend. Think of a friend they may know, and suggest they bring that friend. People are more likely to attend a party if they know a friend will be there.

2. **Send an invitation seven to ten days before the launch party.** You can send e-vites, Facebook invitations, or even mail postcards. There are many resources for this, including RedStamp, Canva, MarGo, and Pic Collage. Chapter 22 talks about these and other resources.

3. **Make reminder calls.** A few days before the party, call or text guests to remind them that you're looking forward to seeing them. You might say something like this: "I'm really looking forward to having you at my launch party! You're going to love the products, and it's going to be a fun time. Are you bringing a friend?"

Having a Back-Up Launch

One of the best things you can do for your business is to have *two* launch parties within three days of each other. The second party acts as a back-up. Having two parties allows you to accommodate more guests and get your products in front of more people. Because only about a third of those you invite will be able to attend your first launch party, being able to offer a back-up date immediately is essential to making sure that a particular guest or client is able to see your product.

Scheduling two launch parties very close together also gives you immediate practice, boosts your confidence, and helps you become more familiar with the product line. Plus seeing the reactions of your guests creates excitement.

If any guest tells you they can't make it to the first party, simply say, "That's okay, Michelle! I'm having a second one on _____ for those who can't make it to the first. Does that work better for you?"

For best results, don't mention the back-up launch unless and until a guest says they can't attend the first one.

Depending on the sales, you can combine both parties into one order or split them up for two great parties. These two parties will put you on track toward earning the rewards of your company's Fast Start program.

After the Launch: Introducing My Two-Booking Method

This section outlines what I call my *two-booking method* for scheduling your first six parties.

Your first two parties

Your first two parties are — no surprise here — going to be your launch party and the back-up launch party already discussed. These launch parties create the foundation for generating interest and desire for your products and getting sales, bookings, and recruits.

Your second two parties

Do you wait until after your launch party and back-up to schedule your third party? No. You should book two additional parties on your calendar even before you hold your launch parties. Doing so begins to fill your calendar and continue your successful start.

If someone is unable to make it to either of your two launch parties, simply say something like this:

> "Amy, how I could really use your help is by hosting one of my first parties! Your friends will love it. It's a lot of fun and they will get to experience some of our amazing products. You'll be helping me get established in my new business while getting the practice I need. In return, you will be treated to a very generous shopping spree of free and discounted products! Do you think you could help me out?"

By scheduling two additional parties, you can also quickly implement what you discovered in the first two parties regarding the techniques that worked best, which products guests were excited about, and what were the most popular items purchased. It also gets you on your way to hitting the first level of your Fast Start!

Your third two parties

Your launch party and back-up are also excellent places to acquire two or more additional bookings. (Remember, you likely got your other two bookings from people who couldn't attend your launch parties.)

One of the keys to your guests wanting to host a party is your enthusiasm and excitement. People enjoy being around people who are excited to share your passion for your new business.

While everyone is enjoying your party, you will have an opportunity to ask each guest to host their own party to help your business get off to a great start and get some great products absolutely free. As you spend time with each guest, you can say something like the following:

> "Karen, wasn't this a lot of fun? Would you consider hosting a party of your own? I'm sure your friends would really love it, and it would really help me get off to a great start in my new business. We treat our hosts so special — the rewards are really amazing."

You can also invite them to look at the business opportunity:

> "Karen, I've learned that friends who go into the business together actually have more fun and greater success. You should think about doing this with me — you're someone I would love to work with!"

Always make sure at your launch that you are offering all of your services to buy, host, or join. Many people put all their emphasis on sales, and as much as that is exciting, getting bookings and having someone join you is going to create a sustainable business. Even though the goal I've given you in this chapter is to get at least two bookings, your ultimate goal is always to book as many parties or one-on-ones as possible.

The greatest benefit of holding six parties within your first 30 days is that you are starting your business on a firm foundation. You earn money right away, get the practice you need, and create momentum. You'll feel good about yourself and your new business. Your friends, family, and potential leads will see first-hand that this business is fun, easy, and financially rewarding. You can typically earn back the cost of your start-up kit within your first 30 days, if not by the end of your launch parties.

You may say, "Well, I came into this business to do only one party a week," or "I came into this to do it part-time." That's fine. It is your own business after all. But once you're trained and comfortable with what you're doing, you can schedule your parties to fit your needs.

With any job, especially a sales position, comes a training period. Often, the training happens with no commission. With direct sales, you will be training and earning an income at the same time.

These first six parties will provide new business for you and help you fill your calendar for the upcoming months. It will be much easier to keep things going and continue to earn money when you reach the end of the 30 days with parties or appointments on your calendar, the confidence provided by new skills, and a feeling of success.

Booking one-on-ones instead of parties

I always equate three one-on-ones to one party, so you could book three one-on-ones in place of one of your first six parties.

Chapter 12 talks more about one-on-ones. This is where you make an appointment with a potential customer or team member to discuss your business and share your products. One-on-ones are popular with Network Marketing companies and are sometimes necessary when establishing your business or deepening your relationship with a new contact.

All in all, a home-run launch party is where you have above average sales, two to four additional parties scheduled, and find someone interested in joining the business opportunity. You won't achieve that every time, but if you go in with that expectation, you are much more likely to achieve it. Not only for yourself, but when you're working with new team members and helping them get their businesses off to successful starts.

Chapter 9

Hosting Successful Parties

. . . .

In This Chapter

▶ Exploring the six key elements of a successful party

▶ Giving your talks at parties, with scripting examples

▶ Building desire for products, hosting, and the opportunity

. . . .

*I*n my many years of experience in direct sales, I have participated in thousands of home parties and have had the privilege of being a part of several surveys and focus groups. In that time I have discovered why people want to host and attend home parties, and the best ways to go about doing so. This chapter contains my distilled wisdom on this important topic.

Contrary to what some may think, the home party is alive and well. People enjoy it as a form of entertainment. A home party is a good reason to get together with friends and socialize. In today's busy and stressed-out world, it's a good opportunity for people to get together and relax.

Except for your launch party, when you're doing a home party (also known as a *show, workshop, class, herbal hours, trunk show,* and so on, depending on your company), you typically need someone else to host this event. Whether in their home, workplace, or another type of service establishment, these people are usually referred as the host. *Hosts* are individuals who are willing to invite a group of people to see or try your products.

Your host can be regarded as your business partner for the evening. They are generally given some type of reward by the company for taking the time to introduce the product line or business opportunity to a new group of people. This relationship is important, and it is therefore a must that you treat your hosts with professionalism and kindness. It is also very important to understand why someone would choose to have an event with you.

A Brief History of Home Parties

Going back to the early days of Tupperware, the product wasn't very successful sitting on the shelf of a retail store. It needed some show and tell.

Once the product was part of a demonstration, it started selling like crazy — and thus began the popularity of the home party, or show.

Back in the 1950s, 60s, and 70s, the home party was all about socializing. It was a way for a housewife to get out of the house for a fun time with her friends and neighbors — and to see what the hostess would serve for dessert. And because most of the women didn't have jobs or independent income, the idea of getting products for free was appealing. In a nutshell, they enjoyed visiting with their friends, seeing the products, and shopping.

In the 80s, 90s, and early 2000s, the home party focused more on education and learning more about the products. The increase in the number of products distributed by direct sales was amazing. You could get almost anything you wanted for your home, especially with regard to health and beauty and your wardrobe. This was a time when people still wanted to socialize, but were very interested in getting things for their home for free or at a good discount.

Home parties were very popular. The presentations grew longer, and hosts (yes, nonsexist language took hold) were encouraged to go very light on refreshments. You didn't want it to be too much work for them. Hosts wanted to be the first in their circle of friends to introduce a new company and its products.

In the past ten years, home parties have completely come full circle. With the hustle and bustle of life, friends rarely get to catch up with one another today. They want the experience of mingling with each other, as well as the feasibility of shopping in one location. Home parties give them both.

Understanding the Appeal of Home Parties

What do people say they want in a home party? They want to socialize. They enjoy getting something to eat and drink and they want to catch up with those they care about. They also want your presentation to be very short, no more than 20–25 minutes in length.

They don't want extensive details about all the products. They would rather get highlights of the benefits and features of the most popular items and then get to the shopping experience. They don't want to be lectured the entire time. They want to participate, to interact in the experience. They want to be serviced or assisted in their shopping experience, and they expect representatives to be experienced and professional in the way they conduct themselves.

Hosts want to provide their friends with a fun night out. They want to entertain and offer light refreshments for their guests. They do this first so that people can spend time catching up with one another. They want to give their friends a convenient shopping experience where they can all try the products before they buy them. Hosts don't want their friends to sit through a long presentation either. They too just want you to hit the highlights of the company and benefits of the product so their friends can stay engaged and interact with you.

Whatever you can do to involve the guests is going to be a hit.

There are three main reasons people will decide to host a party:

- ✔ **Fun:** People like to be entertained and educated at the same time. Hosts like to be able to interact with their guests and try the product.

- ✔ **Free and discounted products:** People enjoy free, of course. But they also say they don't want to have the party at the expense of their friends. They really want to enjoy the free and discounted products *without* the emphasis placed on what they are going to get free or the fact that they are having the party in order to get free products.

- ✔ **Help a friend:** People like to help their own friends, and most people say they would host a party so that their friends can have a good time. When you are talking about booking a party, you need to say things like this:

   "Your friends are going to love it. They are going to appreciate you for introducing them to these fabulous products, and you'll have lots of great customer specials for them."

It's important to have some goals in mind for your parties. Just as a host has goals, like their friends having fun, you too need to set goals so you can measure the success of your party. Your goals should include generating sales, bookings, and recruit leads.

Fun is definitely the top priority for your host and her friends. But you have goals for building your business. A party is considered a home run when you get average to above average sales, two to three bookings, and two to three people taking home information about the opportunity. This is what you should always be striving for.

Whether it be a home party or launch party (Chapter 8) or an appointment (Chapter 12), six key elements are needed, and the rest of this chapter covers these in detail:

- ✔ Creating desire
- ✔ Giving your opening talk
- ✔ Giving your presentation

> ✔ Giving your booking talk
> ✔ Giving your recruiting talk
> ✔ Checking out customers

Creating Desire

Your true objective at a party is to *create desire*. If you create desire for the product, you will get sales. If you create desire for hosting, you will get bookings. And if you make your job desirable, you will get recruit leads.

Keep your focus on your host. The host is the most important person in the room. Everything is riding on the host. If she is having a good time and she knows her friends are having a good time, she will be able to drive sales, help get bookings, and suggest one or two people who would love the opportunity.

Creating desire starts right at the beginning. The fun begins the minute the guests walk in the door, so it is very, very important for you to have your entire display and all your paperwork set up and ready to go before the first doorbell rings. You are creating the fun environment, so it's important for you to meet and greet your host's guests. Don't miss this part of the party, because it will set the tone for the rest of evening. Let your host focus on entertaining.

While your guests are mingling, that's the perfect time for you to walk around and get to know everyone. Tell them what they can expect from the evening and find out their experience with the product.

As you approach people, extend your hand, make good eye contact, and smile. A conversation like the following will work for any type of party:

You: Hi my name is Mary, and you are?

Melissa: I'm Melissa.

You: Melissa, is this your first time at a spa party?

Melissa: Yes, I've never been to one before.

You: Well, thank you so much for coming. Tonight we're going to pamper you, and I can't wait to show you our all-natural spa and bath products. How does that sound?

Melissa: Sounds great!

You: We're going to start shortly. Feel free to take a peek at the table.

If they have been to a party before, you could say something like this:

> You: Well, Melissa, you'll be happy to know we've just launched our new catalog and have some amazing new products. I have them with me tonight, and you'll be one of the first to preview them. I know you're going to love it.
>
> Melissa: Okay, great!

Remember to focus on your host. You might also ask Melissa how she knows her.

For an open-house format, you might say something like the following:

> "Hi, Sarah. Is this your first time at a jewelry show? Wonderful! What I would love you to do is start making your way around the table to check out some of these beautiful pieces of jewelry. I suggest going around about three times, because it can be hard to see everything the first time. Please feel free to try on anything you want because it will look better on you than it does on the table. I'll be here mingling if you have any questions. How does that sound?"

If guests haven't been to a party before, they came because their friends invited them and because they have some interest in the product. If they have been to the same party multiple times, it's because they not only enjoy the product, they love the party. And that is the number one criterion for anybody deciding to try out your business.

Your meet and greet should engage people and pull them in. It also develops a relationship and likeability. It should make them think *she's really nice* or *I think this is going to be a lot of fun.* If they think you're nice, they'll like you. And if they like you, they're more likely to introduce you to their group of friends.

People do business with people they *know, like,* and *trust.*

Giving Your Opening Talk

The opening talk is one of the most significant and important parts of having a successful party. It's where you create first impressions and you have the guests' full and undivided attention.

Your opening shouldn't take very long — only a few minutes. You are giving the guests an overview of the evening and telling them what to expect and what's in it for them.

Your opening should really pack a punch, though. You need to know exactly what you're going to say. If there is one part of your script that you want to memorize, it is this portion. Of course, you want to want to be comfortable with your entire party presentation, but you really want to be sure of the opening.

Eventually when you start showing the products, you want your guests to engage, laugh, and make comments — but now is when you want them to pay attention and say to themselves, "Wow, I'm glad I'm here. This is going to be a lot of fun!"

What not to do

When you know exactly what you're going to say, you come off very confident. But if you don't know and haven't taken the time to memorize, you tend to make mistakes, give misinformation, and can even forget to thank your host. You come off very nervous.

When men are nervous or haven't thought about what they want to say, they have a tendency to clear their throats and stammer:

> "Uh, yeah, uh, my name is Bob, and, uh, thanks, Tom, for having me here tonight, uh. . . ."

That probably won't go over very well with your guests.

Nervous or unprepared women often add a high pitch to the end of their phrases, almost sing-song. I like to call it *winging it:*

> Hi, my name is Mary . . . I will be doing the party . . . I want to thank Martha . . . for having the party . . . and *wing, wing, wing.*

Here's another way that people waste this precious real estate of time, by saying something like this:

> "Hi, I'm Mary and I would like to begin by telling you a little bit about the company," or, "Hi, I'm Mary and I want to begin by telling you a little bit about myself."

In the opening, you want to grab their attention with something about *them.* See the upcoming example for how to introduce yourself and your company.

Creating a powerful opening talk

Here are some tips for creating a powerful opening:

- **Practice your name.** This might sound silly but practice saying your name before the party. You want to sound confident when you are introducing yourself.

- **Give positive affirmation.** Always give your guests positive affirmations. Depending on your product line, you may say things like, "You're in for a real treat," or, "You're going to be so glad you came," or, "We're going to have so much fun tonight." This sets the tone for how your guests are going to enjoy the rest of the night.

- **Share what you're going to do for them.** Punch it with at least three things they're going to learn:

  "I'm going to show you how to make simple, easy meals in under 30 minutes."

  "I'm going to show you how you can create meals your entire family will love."

  "I'm going to help cut your grocery list in half with these four ingredient recipes."

  And so on. You can also mention how the party will run — that you'll be doing a short presentation, passing out catalogs, and then assisting them one-on-one during the checkout process.

- **Plant booking seeds.** Bookings are among the most valuable things you can get from your parties. You'll give your booking talk a little later, but in your intro you can start planting seeds.

  "Having a party is so much fun, and I hope you will think about how much fun your friends will have in your own home."

  You don't need to go into too much detail here, just plant a seed and create the desire. Be sure to plant seeds five times throughout your entire presentation.

- **Plant recruiting seeds.** The three most important services you can offer are shopping as a customer, saving as a host, and earning as a representative. You want to make sure that you plant these seeds at the beginning of the party, as well, so they can consider it throughout the rest of the night. Again, don't go into too much detail here, just paint a picture of what additional income could look like for them and their family.

- **Thank the host.** You always want to acknowledge the host and thank her for having you in her home, as well as thank the guests for coming.

Example opening talk

Your opening talk might sound something like this, which can be modified for any type of party:

> "Hi, my name is Mary, and I am going to be doing the party this evening. Quick show of hands, how many of you have been to a jewelry party before?

> "Great! You're in for a real treat because I have a wide range of beautiful designer jewelry to share with you this evening. I have a little something for everyone depending on style, personality, and budget. You're going to fall in love with so many of our beautiful pieces and styles that your biggest challenge this evening is going to be what to choose. If you find you're unable to get everything you want tonight, the best way to take care of this is simply by hosting your own party like Sarah is doing here this evening.

> "We really appreciate our hosts and we like to treat them to a very generous shopping spree of free and discounted items, as well as a fun night out with their friends.

> "As you watch me do the party this evening, you'll see that it is fun and pretty simple. If any one of you is looking for a way to add an extra stream of income to your household budget, you'll be happy to know that on average we make about $150 to $200 in an evening." (Or whatever your company average is.) "If you would like some information, I'd be more than happy to send it home with you.

> "With that, I would like to thank Sarah for having me in her home and I would like to thank each and every one of you for coming. Now I would like to introduce you to the wonderful world of _____ (your company)."

As you can see, the opening talk is very short and simple. If you can perfect this part of the party, you will breeze through the rest.

Giving Your Presentation

You want your entire product presentation to be short, simple, enthusiastic, and solid. In fact, it should be entertaining and educational at the same time. You don't want to get too detailed into your product line. And you want to stay away from going into a lot of detail about the history of the company. You could end up losing the guests' attention.

Presentation tips

Here are some tips for creating a winning presentation:

- **Keep it short.** In order to keep your presentation to 20–25 minutes, you are going to want to show your products in groupings or sets. It appears you are showing one product, but in reality you are showing four. This could ultimately help with increasing your party average.

- **Use testimonials because they sell.** The more stories and testimonials you can use in your party, the better. They show that your products are loved and used by many. If the host already has some products or if there are guests who've attended before, you can ask them to talk about their favorite product. Testimonials are the single most powerful ingredient that prompts people to take action.

- **Sell the benefits, not the details.** Stick to the benefits of the product and what it can do for them. Don't go into details about how or where the products are made and so on. If your company has a lot of factual content, you can put together a binder and let your guests know that you have more details for them to look at while they are shopping if they want.

  Show value by sharing the benefits. Your customers need to understand how your products are going to impact them and how they're going to make a difference for them. *How is this going to make my life easier? How is it going to save me time and money?* Value also means showing versatility if your products can be used in multiple ways. "Ladies, no wardrobe is complete without _____. No kitchen is complete without _____."

- **Plant more booking and recruiting seeds.** You need to be planting seeds throughout your party. You want to plant three in your presentation. For bookings, "This is something you might choose as your half-price item when you host your own party." With recruiting you can share why you started with the company and what your business has done for you and your family. Again, you don't want to go into too much detail. Remember that you want to keep your presentation going at a smooth pace.

Your presentation is going to primarily focus on the product, sprinkled with some information on booking and recruiting, and topped with value. Remember, if people see the product and like it, they are likely to buy it.

Building more desire for the product

You want to build up the product so that anyone listening to you will be compelled to buy. They will have a desire, a want, and a need. Avoid being descriptive about the products. If you hold up a blue purse, don't describe the color and size. They can obviously see what it looks like. Instead, sell the benefits. Tell what the purse can do for them. How functional is it? Is it perfect to go with their casual wear or for a dress occasion?

Here are two examples of selling candle holders. First, how not to do it:

> "This next item, ladies, is from our vintage collection. And this is our beautiful vintage bowl. And you could put flowers in it. You could put candles in it. You could put fruit in it."

Instead, paint a picture:

> "This next item, ladies, is our vintage collection. And it has the bowl with the matching candlesticks. I walked into one of my host's homes the other day and she had our beautiful bowl sitting on the center of her mantelpiece with a gorgeous bouquet of flowers spilling out onto the mantel. On either side she had accented it with our gorgeous matching candlesticks. I have to tell you, it was breathtaking."

You have to share stories.

Make sure you're using many adjectives instead of just one. One idea is to make a list of all your products and next to them write a descriptive word for each. That way during your presentation you won't use the words *my favorite* or *so awesome* or *special* for every product that you feature.

Giving Your Booking Talk

A booking talk is vital to keeping your business going. In Chapter 7 I refer to bookings as being *the heartbeat of your business*. Bookings help you keep your calendar full, help you see more people, and of course, help you get the commission you desire.

Choosing what to say

Most consultants either don't have a strong booking talk, or they don't practice it. You have to do both. Again, it is important to memorize your script. Otherwise, you're likely to be all over the place, and it's difficult to get to the point. You need to have a strong booking talk without going into too much detail. Go light on what the host gets, and balance it with what her friends get.

I have seen and heard many examples. Here are two of the most popular. Some merely say something like this:

> "So ladies, if you would like to have a party, please let me know."

Does that make you want to have a party? Probably not. You haven't shared the benefits of hosting or created the desire. You are putting the ball completely in their court to make a decision, which probably won't get you a date on your calendar.

The other booking talk I hear often is the exact opposite and goes something like this:

> "Ladies, I'd like to tell you a bit about what Sarah's doing tonight. As a host, Sarah is going to walk away with a tremendous amount of free product. Let me give you an example of how this works. First of all, she can earn 20 percent of her sales in free product. Now, the average show is about $700 in sales, so that will give her about $140 to spend how she would like. That's not all. Sarah is also entitled to four half-priced items, which can be anything in our line. Actually, she can also get the hostess bonus. Then for every booking she gets, she will receive this item. With three bookings, she could get that. That's not all! Hosts also get to take advantage of our host-exclusive products."

And so on. This type of booking talk doesn't work either. It is overwhelming, gives too much information, and makes being a host sound complicated. You don't want to host coach before you have a host.

The key is to make your parties sound fun for their friends as well as easy to host. You should be speaking to the people in the room and not to the current host. Just like with products, the focus is on benefits versus description. You want to people to think, *Why on earth wouldn't I want to host a party?*

Here are some things you can work into your booking talk:

- ✔ It's easy to have a party.
- ✔ Your friends are going to love you for having it.
- ✔ It's a lot of fun.
- ✔ I will do most of the work.
- ✔ As a thank-you from me and the company, hosts get to take advantage of free and discounted products.
- ✔ Your friends will get to take advantage of our customer specials.
- ✔ Guests will appreciate learning about our products.

Here is an example of an effective booking talk:

> "Ladies, I'm sure you've all had a wonderful time tonight, and possibly you're not able to get everything that you want this evening. You're thinking, *Wow, a $100 shopping spree sure sounds nice.* Let me tell you how simple and easy it is, and really, it takes no more than the time you spent here this evening.

> "Haven't you all had fun here tonight? That's how much fun we're going to have at your house with your friends. They're going to love you for having them over for a girls' night while introducing them to these amazing products.

> "I will do most of the work, and all you have to do is get some friends together and have a great night socializing and shopping. So, honestly, why in the world wouldn't you want to host your own party?

> "That's why I'm encouraging each and every one of you tonight to just say yes, and I'll work with you on a date that's suitable for you and your calendar."

If you come out of the gate with confidence and enthusiasm about your business and your products, your guests will mirror that same energy.

Building desire for hosting

There are a couple of ways that you can create desire for hosting during your presentation and in your booking talk. The most important thing to remember is that *stories sell.* Also, when you're talking about your product, you can sprinkle in some things about booking. It's planting those seeds again. Here are a couple of examples:

> "This next item, ladies, is a very popular item in our line, and I tend to give it away free more than any other item. I find that more of my hosts select this item with their host credit than any other item in our line. This is one of our most popularly chosen half-price selections."

Here's another idea where I'm planting a booking seed even though I'm talking about a product:

> "This next item, ladies, is one of our single most popular items. In fact, I just did a show in the teachers' lounge after school last week and I sold six of them."

Now, I'm talking about the product, but what am I really saying? "I did a show in the teachers' lounge after school." There's an idea. It gives people other options, other than a home, to have a party.

The Recruiting Talk

Your recruiting talk is going to be short and sweet. You don't want to push people, but rather mention what the business can do for them. If there are any recruiting benefits or specials with your company, you can mention those as well. Here is an example of a recruiting talk:

> "Ladies, you've seen me do the party tonight and you've been able to see how easy it is. You're probably thinking that an extra $600 per month sure would be great. Well, let me tell you how easy it is to get started with our company."

You can make that brief. Then:

> "If you are interested or know of someone who is interested in the business and would like an information packet, I'd be happy to send you home with one."

There is much more to it than that. And you're going to plant seeds throughout your presentation. Chapter 14 covers recruiting in great detail. The main idea is to show people that your job is easy. You didn't come in with a lot of bags, you didn't spend a lot of time on the presentation, and you're making them feel like your job is also fun.

When people watch your job in action, and they start to fall in love with many of the products, it becomes easy for them to see themselves selling it to their friends.

As I mentioned before, your main objective at the party is to create desire. Half the people at a party have some level of interest. It's your job to create a safe, relaxed atmosphere where people can show interest without feeling pressure to join.

Upselling, Checkout, and Closing

You've done a fabulous party presentation, and everybody is engaged and having fun. You've planted some booking and recruiting seeds and are ready to start the closing process. Remain engaged during the closing. It's important to be present and in the room while your guests are looking at your table of products and through the catalog. You say something like this:

> "Okay everyone, why don't you come up to the table. You can try out some of the products I talked about this evening, as well as some others I didn't. Don't be afraid to mess the table up!"

Stay by the table to answer questions. This gives you the opportunity to cover more products than what was in your presentation. Once the guests start to head back to their seats to check out the catalog, say something like this:

> "Okay, ladies, here is your catalog, and before you begin shopping, I'll let you know this month's specials." (Name them and place flyers around, if you haven't already.) "I will be walking around to assist with your purchases today so feel free to ask any questions."

When people are ready, you are ready to begin a full-service checkout. If they don't have their order form filled in, begin by helping them do so. Also figure out the best pricing for them if your company offers a customer savings plan. If they already have the order form filled out, go through their products with them to make sure they have everything they need. Don't focus on the total. Look at the products they ordered. Are they missing any products that would make their experience better? For example, if they have everything to make a pizza, but not a pizza cutter, ask if they would like to add one to their order.

Often, it's easy to get excited about the total. But it is your responsibility to service your customers to make sure they have everything they need. The more you service your customers and create positive experiences for them, the more they will continue to do business with you and refer you to others.

A few years ago I was invited to a candle party a friend of mine was hosting. My son, who had just recently moved into his own apartment, asked me to pick up some candles for his new place. I ended up ordering three candleholders for my son, as well as one for my kitchen. My order total came to approximately $168. The representative was very happy and thanked me excitedly.

When my son came over to pick up his order, he opened the bag and said, "These are nice — but where are the candles?" I was so focused on choosing candleholders that I'd forgotten about candles. The rep had missed this detail, because she was too excited about the large order total. If she had made sure I had everything I needed, she would have noticed — and that would have tacked on an additional $40 to my order.

Up-selling enhances your relationships with your customers by offering them additional products. Here are two ways to up-sell:

✔ **Benefit selling versus descriptive selling:** *Descriptive selling* explains what the product is without focusing on the benefits. Always share with your customers the benefits of your products. How will it make them feel? How will it make their life easier? Show your customers the value they will receive from your products.

✔ **Always showing in groupings:** If you show one product, you will sell one product, so always show your products in groupings. If you're a nail representative, when showing the nail wraps, always complement them by showing your application kit, mini heater, and hand cream. That way, when people look at buying one item, they associate it with buying three others. Learning to put groupings together and having a price ready for them is crucial to helping increase your party averages. Some people buy what's on the mannequin because they don't have the creativity to put things together. Show items in groupings to provide some creativity.

You also always want to compliment people on their product choices. People want to feel like they made good choices and received good value for their money spent. This will put people in a more positive frame of mind to consider booking a party of their own with you.

Once you've totaled the order, thank her and ask whether she had fun at the party. This is also where you will want to ask if she would consider having her own party with her friends. (I talk about this in detail in Chapter 7.) Then, as a full-service checkout, ask if she's interested in taking home some information about the business opportunity and what the company has to offer.

Chapter 10

Coaching Your Host

In This Chapter

▶ Understanding the key role hosts play in your business

▶ Figuring out why hosts do what they do

▶ Coaching on attendance

▶ Maintaining excitement and engagement

▶ Keeping your host informed

▶ Coaching online

*W*hen you want to reach new people with your products, services, and opportunity, the most efficient way is to do a party (also sometimes called a *show, workshop, class, herbal hours,* or *trunk show*). When people host your event, whether in their home, workplace, or service establishment, they are lending their excitement and circle of friends to you for the evening. That means they become your business partner for the evening. The company usually gives them rewards for taking the time and introducing the product line to a new group of people.

Your host wants to have a successful evening even more than you do — after all, you're investing your working hours in them, but they're investing their very limited recreational hours in you. Plus she's trusting you to help her create a fun evening for her friends. That's an important fact, which I come back to later in this chapter.

To help your hosts have successful evenings, in their eyes and your own, you need to give them some encouragement and instruction. *Host coaching* is an integral part of your business. It can literally make or break what happens at your party. It is your responsibility to coach your host on how to achieve success at her party. You don't have to spend a *lot* of time coaching your host, but it is important to connect with them and pay close attention to the details.

A host who has a great experience with you is your best prospective team member. She likes the sales method, she is enthusiastic about the products, and most importantly, she likes you.

Understanding the Host's Motivation

The main reason people book parties today is to have fun. If guests are having fun, they will be more likely to book parties themselves, and if you mention, "When you have your party your friends will appreciate it, and I will make sure they all have a fun time," you are more likely to pique someone's interest.

Hosts like free and discounted products, but they prefer to offer their guests a benefit. Because Hosts are interested in making the party a fun and beneficial experience for their friends, be sure to talk about those benefits. Make sure your host knows what the customer specials for that month are and coach her to tell her guests what they will learn that evening and the value they will receive just for going.

Some companies have booking programs in which a host receives a gift if a certain number of people from her party also book a party. People want to help their friends, so if they know the host will receive something extra, they may be more inclined to set a date with you.

But really, the most important aspect to selling your parties is all the fun her guests will have.

In all my years of experience, and my participation in many parties, surveys, and focus groups, I have been able to gather valuable information that will help you understand why someone would host with you, and what does and does not motivate them. In the past few years I've interviewed groups of independent representatives on what their greatest challenge was with their business. They often quickly respond with, "I can't get bookings." Then they amend their answer: "Actually, I get them booked but I can't get them to hold."

I asked a number of hosts why they would book a party and then cancel. Here is a typical answer:

> When I booked it, I was at my friend's, and we were having a lot of fun and the representative said it would be easy and fun and my friends would love it. I thought, *Okay, I'll do it.* The very next day the rep called and told me I needed to make a list of 40 people. I needed to work on five outside orders. If someone can't come, try to get her to book for an

advanced booking. She wanted me to make a list of everything I wanted and she wanted to make sure we got enough people there in order for me to get everything I wanted. I decided then it was just too much work. I was having the party for a fun time with my friends, not just so I could get free stuff.

Although the requests this person mentions have been effective techniques for successful parties in the past, the sheer number of steps and volume of work can easily become overwhelming to today's host.

In my focus group research, the number one reason why people *don't* want to book is they don't want to have the party and earn rewards at the expense of their friends. They are more concerned about what their friends will get.

When you're host coaching, emphasize the benefits for the host's friends, not just what the host will receive.

Coaching on Attendance and Outside Orders

Getting a booking is great, but of course, it's just the beginning. Most of the work happens after you get the booking, and a good part of that work is in helping the host understand what she should do to have a successful party.

Regardless of how simple the process is, if you don't talk to your host between the time you booked and the night of the party, attendance will be low, and there will be few, if any, *outside orders* (orders from those who weren't able to attend).

When it comes to making a party fun, remember, *the more the merrier*. To help her succeed with inviting her friends, make sure you give her a few things she can say — scripts about what's in store for her guests. That way, when she's inviting friends, she'll feel good about telling them what is in it for them.

When asking her to invite a friend and encouraging that guest to bring a friend, tell her to think of a person that she knows is a good friend to her friend and suggest them by name: "Hey, Carol, you should ask Debbie to come with you." This makes people feel special, gives them an idea to act on, and will likely increase attendance.

Another way to boost attendance is to give her samples of texts she can send out to her friends, as well as letting her know when to send them. Have her send a text the day after booking, mentioning *Save the date for a great Girl's Night In.*

Next, give her a sample text she can send one week before, reminding guests *I'm looking forward to seeing you next week at my party! Bring a friend.*

Then, on the day before or the day of the party, have her send one that says *Don't forget! Tonight is our fun night! Hope to see you there.*

The host should text friends one at a time. Ask your host to use the copy and paste feature on her phone to easily send these texts in individual messages. Sending a group text or a group Facebook message is a sure turn-off, because potential guests will undoubtedly get multiple replies meant solely for the host. Group texts also make her guests feel like she only cares about the quantity of guests and not necessarily who is there.

In addition to helping her get great attendance, coach her on how to get outside orders — orders from those who aren't able to attend the party. This can include coworkers or friends and relatives out of state. Your host can send non-attendees a link to your online catalog and personal website. These outside orders can be your connection to repeat orders, and even new bookings and team members.

Let your host know she can get outside orders:

> "There is never a perfect night for everyone, so if someone is unable to make it or you would like to include out-of-town guests, please send them to my website where they'll find a link to your event. Any orders they place will count towards your party sales. And if you need any extra catalogs for your workplace, just let me know."

By telling her this, you are emphasizing convenience rather than appearing to be requiring more work for her to do.

Keeping Your Host Excited, Engaged, and Informed

Host coaching is an integral ingredient in the recipe for a successful party. In fact, it may be the single most important contributor to the success of your business.

The most important reasons to coach your hosts is to keep them excited and engaged. They also want to be informed so they know what to expect. This builds trust and a strong partnership with your hosts, which typically leads to increased bookings and sales as well as repeat business.

The more excited they are, the more their guests will be excited, and the better the attendance will be. The more engaged your hosts become, the more motivated they'll be to make the party a success. The more information your hosts have, the more they can prepare and the more they feel included in the process.

Building excitement

It's important to build excitement for your host. Why? Because excitement is contagious. If you are excited, your host will be excited, and her guests will be excited.

Here are some examples of what to say to your host:

> "I can't wait to meet your friends!"

> "Your friends are going to love you for having everyone over for a fun night of shopping."

> "There's nothing better than a night in with your friends shopping for amazing products."

The number one reason people book parties is to have fun — fun for themselves and fun for their friends. So always lead with this. The more fun your hosts and their guests have, the more likely you are to gain additional bookings and recruits.

You can also get the host excited by talking about the products. Remember, your hosts fell in love with the products enough to host a party of their own. If your hosts are excited about the products, they will talk about them with their friends. This will get their guests excited about catching up with friends and sampling your line of products.

Giving your hosts some ideas about what to say to her friends can help ensure the excitement builds:

> "This is going to be so much fun, you're going to love it."

> "Mary, you won't believe the quality of these products. I just know you will fall in love with their mascara and lip stain. I thought of you right away!"

"I'm having all the girls over for a spa afternoon! I think it's about time we all get a little bit of pampering."

"I'm having a food tasting at my house tonight! We're going to learn how to make quick, easy, and delicious meals in under 15 minutes. The company has some amazing deals happening this month that I just knew you wouldn't want to pass up."

Hosts will sell that excited feeling, as long as you continue to drive excitement for them.

Keeping your host engaged

Keep your host engaged and committed to moving her party forward. Encourage her to post and create an event on Facebook, bring catalogs to work, collect outside orders, and send out reminder texts. Keep her in the loop and engaged with different things to do throughout the process. By giving her a few, simple responsibilities she will work with you to create a successful party. The more engaged she is, the more likely she is to be committed to trying to create the best party possible.

One game that many representatives find effective is a 50 square raffle. You create a sheet that has 50 squares labeled 1 to 50. Each square is worth $2. Before the party the host sells off these squares. After the party a number is drawn from the squares, and someone wins $100 worth of product credit. This not only increases your party average by $100, but it keeps the host in contact with her friends and talking about the product.

Another game that some representatives play to keep their host engaged is host bingo. The host gets a bingo sheet with multiple tasks (and a free space in the middle), and if she gets a bingo, she receives an additional gift. Some of the tasks are things like get ten guests, get two outside orders, post your event on Facebook, and so on.

Keeping your host informed

You want to keep your hosts informed. Share logistics such as *I'll be arriving a half hour early* and *We're going to do these specific things at the party* and *What area of your home can I set up in?*

Make sure you go over these details with your hosts because without them, they won't know what to tell their guests; they also won't know what they are supposed to do to prepare for the party. If you're not keeping your hosts informed, and if you're not talking to them until the day of or the day before, then you're likely breaking down the trust that they can count on you. They then might feel like they want to cancel, which will not help your future bookings or inspire their help in getting additional bookings.

This section lays out tips that will help you with your host-coaching communications. You won't spend much time on any one of these contacts. Instead you'll focus on trying to reach out and "touch" the host ten times. These ten touches are given here in order from the day you book your host to following up with them after the party.

The day you book your host

If your booking is from a prior party, your host will already know a bit about what to expect during the party. You will also want to have host packets on hand to give to your host (Chapter 6 discusses host packets). So give out a host packet and go over it a little bit that night:

> "Take this home, go over it, and start inviting your friends. I will be making a Facebook Event for you, so make sure you add me to your Facebook friends so I can invite you to it. Once we do that, you will be able to start inviting your friends to the Event page as well."

Let them know that you'll get their party registered with your company and be sure to put all of their contact information in your calendar on the date that you scheduled with them (this is a good example of why it's important to have your calendar with you).

Try to get them a sample of your product and let them know how much you appreciate their help in getting your business started. Be sure to get them a host packet as soon as possible, in person or by email.

The day after the first contact

Making contact with your host this day is critical. There isn't a lot to say yet, but it's important that you say it. All you have to do is send a quick email:

Dear Mary,

Thank you so much for booking your party on _____, _____ (day, date). We're going to have a fantastic time. Read through the host packet, and I will be calling you in a couple of days. If you haven't started making your guest list, get started working on that. Also be sure to remind your guests to bring a friend — this will help with attendance. I want this to be a wonderful experience for you and your friends.

If you're texting, you can shorten it:

> *Thank you so much for booking a party. I'm looking forward to your party on _____, _____ (day, date). Don't forget to send out a friendly text to your friends telling them to save the date.*

Again, this contact time is quick. What it does is it tells your host, *Wow, this girl knows what she's doing, she's on top of her game.* Or, *Wow this is serious, I better get with it. We're really doing this thing!*

The first phone call

This call is usually within three to five days after the host books:

> "Hey, Mary, I want to talk to you about your party. It won't take more than a few minutes. I thought this would be a good time to pick out the products that you want to show at your party, and I just wanted to see if you had any questions after going through the packet of information that I gave you. Also, I wanted to make sure you're comfortable and aren't confused about anything."

This is the time to go over a few details. Remember, make this call short and sweet, so your hosts aren't overwhelmed with too much information. It should only take a few minutes. The key thing you want to focus on during this call is inviting people.

> "I put a little sheet in your host packet about inviting people. Let them know that I have some great customer specials going on."

You can briefly mention all the great things you have going on for the guests. Put some information in her host packet about joining. Ask her if she had a chance to look at it and if that's something she would ever consider doing. If she replies no, tell her to please feel free to pass the info on to a friend. If she replies yes, or begins to ask questions, proceed from there. (See Chapter 14 for more on attracting new team members.)

When the invitations are sent

Most companies provide invitations for you to give to your hosts to send. There are postcard invitations that you can mail as well as online invites you can use for Facebook, texts, and email.

The combination of a digital invitation *and* a paper invitation is very effective, especially now when people's email inboxes are so full. People actually appreciate invitations in the mail and are more likely to read them and respond to them.

After the invitations are sent out, let your host know the following:

> "Everyone on your guest list has been invited, but don't expect everyone to RSVP. Make sure you follow up with an enthusiastic phone call asking your guests if they received it. Ask them if they can come, and tell them that you can't wait to show them these amazing products."

You can also give her examples of texts they can send their friends:

"Hey Trish! Just wanted to remind you about my girls' night this Friday! We are going to be sampling some great wine! Don't forget to bring a friend."

"Cooking party at my house Tuesday at 8pm! We will be learning how to make freezer meals!"

"Jill, I can't wait to see you on Sunday for my spa party! You should definitely bring Patricia, she would love it!"

That is going to go a long way in creating some more excitement for your party.

The booster call

This call happens about five days prior to the party — right around when your host will start getting a little panicked. This happens because she has started to hear from some of the guests who can't make it, and she's begun to doubt herself. She's a little nervous, especially if she only has four people coming. If she's been really busy at work, she's started asking herself why she agreed to a party in the first place.

As the coach, you're going to encourage her and let her know she can do this. So when you call up your host, and she's feeling down, you're going to boost her up. If she only has four guests coming, tell her to have every guest bring a friend. Suggest one of her friends that you know, or maybe mention a neighbor. Having your host reach out to her guests will go a long way, especially if your host knows this is the way to be successful.

Assure your host that everyone is going to have a fantastic time, and not to worry. More important, tell her you're going to have fun with everyone who attends.

Your job is to boost her up, make her feel good about having the party, and stir up excitement.

This is also the call where you go over the logistics. Tell your host when you'll be arriving and let her know if she needs to provide anything for the party.

The day of the party

Confirm the directions. Even with a GPS or phone navigation system, bridges have a way of going out, and road construction has a way of popping up when you least expect or want it to. I also like to use this call to get the host pumped up for the party again. Sometimes what happens between the booster call (five days prior) and now is that she originally only had four people coming, but now she has 15! Confirming that number is important. You need to make sure you have enough catalogs and other materials ready to go. Also, now she is excited about the party again.

Make sure you arrive early, with enough time to get everything set up. A half hour is the optimal time, allowing you time to set up, have a chat with your host, and be ready by the time people arrive so you look professional. This also helps you avoid rushing around at the last minute. This is also where the host will often ask you more questions about the business opportunity.

You want to be poised and you want to be able to meet and greet the guests. Tell each guest that you're happy she came. Ask each one if she's familiar with the products and the company. Make sure your interactions here are enthusiastic and sincere.

Closing the party

Closing your party is the process of officially ending the time you can receive orders for a particular host's party. When you close the party may depend on your host. Some want to close the party at the end of the night, but usually the host wants to keep the party *open* for a few days. I recommend choosing a certain day of the week on which you close all your parties. For me, it was always on Friday. If I had a party on Monday, I simply told the host that I would be closing on Friday.

Regardless of when you close the party, make sure that before you leave you give them a *goal*. Tell your host what the sales are right now and what she's earned so far. Let her know how far away she is from the next level of host rewards and how little effort it would take to get her additional specials, free credit, or half-priced items. If your host says she's expecting two more orders, write those names down so when you're following up with her, you can ask about those remaining outside orders. It makes the closing process more efficient.

If your host wants to close the party that night, tell her ahead of time to make sure she collects the outside orders before the party.

Thank-you note immediately after

Mail your host a hand-written note after each party. You don't *have* to do this, but the gesture goes a long way. Be sure to include a magnet (some companies offer this) or your business card with a reminder for reorders. Let your host know that it was a pleasure meeting her friends and that you had a wonderful time.

Another good idea is to type up a generic letter and put it in with the thank-you note. This letter will be all about the logistics. It should say *Thank you so much for having the party. You still have time to get another booking* (if your company has a booking bonus program). *Your party order should arrive in about ___ business days, and you'll have a packing slip to go with the orders.*

This typed letter is to let her know what to do when her order arrives. That way she's not lost. You can also let her know to call you with any questions she might have while going through the orders.

Two weeks after the party

This is a follow-up call to ask your host if the products arrived, if she's enjoying them, and how her guests like them. Also ask your host if she's heard any feedback. Her guests may feel more comfortable telling her about something that they might not tell you.

Then you can follow up with the guests and let them know you heard that they loved a specific product. You may get more orders this way (if any of the guests or the host has run out of the product or wants to know the current month's specials), and you might even be able to pick up a booking or two. (If you know that the product hasn't arrived yet, adjust the follow-up call date slightly, but keep it relatively within that two-week period.)

The follow-up call demonstrates that you are conscientious and friendly and reminds not only the host but the guests that you are a professional independent representative who cares about them.

Host Coaching Online

Host coaching online happens when your party is conducted on an online platform (Chapter 11 covers online parties in detail). For example, a Facebook party. You coach your host in pretty much the same manner, although most of your contact will be via email, texting, or Facebook messaging.

Choosing which friends to invite and knowing how to invite them are two big considerations. First, you don't want your hosts to invite all 467 of their Facebook friends. That is too many, and it's not very inviting when everyone is getting the same pop-up on their computer.

A good rule of thumb is to stick to around 50 friends.

Regardless of how the party will be set up, everyone the host is inviting should receive a personal message from her. You can help your host type this up, but it should be very personal:

> *Hi, Maureen. I'm having an online party on ____ (day, date) and I would love for you to attend. We are going to _____ and _____ (list a couple of fun things that will happen). I really hope you can join us.*

Do not send this as a group message. A group message to 50 people will turn into an annoying disaster when people begin replying. You can copy and paste the same message to individual text messages.

Finally, have your host gather as many phone numbers as possible. That way she can also follow up with phone calls or texts. And get an address for where to send the thank-you note to the host. You can treat this as a normal, in-home party, but just remember that a lot of your conversation with your host may be online.

Host coaching should be fun. Most of the "ten touches" of contact will happen very quickly, but it is important to do them all. You'll be happy because you will have a successful party, and your host will be happy because she will feel that you care about her.

Chapter 11

Social Selling: Direct Selling on Social Media

- -

In This Chapter

▶ Choosing the right social media for you

▶ Starting a Facebook page

▶ Sharing photos on Instagram and Pinterest

▶ Creating content on Twitter and blogs

▶ Exploring the best apps for your business

- -

*O*ver the past few years, a new term in direct sales has been circulating: *social selling.* It can refer to someone who just wants to sell socially to friends and family, but it is most often used to describe people who sell mainly through social networking. *Social selling* is the use of social media networks to interact directly with customers, leads, and clients. Platforms like Facebook and Instagram give independent representatives the opportunity to interact with their customers, build friendships, answer questions, and offer interesting and engaging content — all online.

New technologies and social media apps are constantly emerging and are changing the way you grow your brand. Social networks and apps like Facebook, Instagram, and Pinterest are changing the way we socialize, buy, sell, make money, do business, bank, and so on. I really could go on forever, because social media is changing the way we do *everything.*

So, if the business landscape is changing, we have to change. It's as simple as that. Social media is becoming an integral part of direct sales, from the way you communicate with your company and teams to your customers and clients. But it doesn't end there. It's not enough anymore just to have an account. You have to be current and consistent and flood your walls with interesting information for your audience. Your fans are watching you and what you're saying. They're deciding who you are as a company and as a brand and can decide based on one post whether or not they want to do business with you.

And not only that, social media networks like Facebook are deciding whether *they* want to do business with you. Facebook's algorithm (don't worry, we're not going to get technical) determines whether your content gets into your fans' newsfeeds depending on how interesting and engaging your posts are.

The way my team explains social media is by comparing it to a highway. Let's say on that highway is a billboard for a soap company. Any marketer will tell you that the billboard needs a strong call-to-action. As you're driving past the billboard, you might glance at it, barely catch it out of the corner of your eye, or not notice it at all. A strong call-to-action means that when you see that ad, you know exactly what that soap company wants you to do — and that's to buy their soap.

The thing with the highway is that the highway doesn't monitor how many people actually look at the billboard. The highway has no clear deliverables to give to the soap company, other than telling them how many people use that particular highway on a typical day. And not only can't the highway tell you how many people look at the billboard, they don't care. The highway will not take down your billboard and replace it with another because not enough eyes are looking at it or buying your soap.

That's where social media is completely different. Social media platforms absolutely care who is looking at your post. They can tell you how many people are seeing your content and will remove your post from your fans if they don't find it interesting enough.

So how do social media platforms measure engagement? Through likes, comments, and shares. That means you need to offer interesting and unique content that is easily sharable, links to fun articles, videos, and eye-catching photos.

The key is to be consistent. One good post will not get the attention of thousands of people. You need to continue to post every day, creating a habit with yourself and for your fans. This will ensure that they keep coming back to check out what you offer as well as recommending you and your business to their friends.

While you are learning your new business, I don't want you to feel overwhelmed with figuring out social media. Follow the tips in this chapter and for the most part, run your direct sales business online the same way you would offline. Throughout this book, I give excellent examples on how you can increase sales, bookings, and recruiting. Apply those same techniques to these platforms, and you will start to see success.

This chapter teaches you how to utilize social media for your business, increase your reach, grow your fans, and drive people to the place that matters most: your business.

Choosing the Right Social Media for Your Business

New social media platforms are emerging all of the time, so it can be hard to decide where to spend your time. The fact is, you can't successfully master every single platform for your business.

Choose one or two social media platforms to use at the beginning of your business. Find out as much as you can about those platforms, test your business on them, and then decide whether you are getting a return on the time you are spending.

For some, your direct sales businesses may not be your full-time job. It may be a part-time job, a way to supplement income every month, or maybe just a fun hobby. Of course, if you're like most people, it's important to spend time on income-producing activities. *Income-producing activities* are things you do for your business that make you money.

Focus your time on the platforms that you get the most results from. Not getting interest on Twitter? Move on to Instagram. Facebook page failing? Try Pinterest. Don't get stuck doing something that doesn't work for you and your business.

Social media platforms don't all operate the same way or for the same purposes. Some platforms are better for communication, some are better for sales, and others are better for connecting with the community.

So before you select which is right for you, determine what your goal is. Are you trying to increase sales every month? Find new customers and leads? Increase your brand recognition? Build an email/newsletter list? Nab a fundraiser? Stop for a second and write down your goals.

Remember to create a healthy list of goals for yourself. Every business owner wants to be successful in every part of their business, but it's important to start off with one or two social media goals. Once you have mastered them and have created a system to maintain them everyday, you can add another to the mix. Here, try to write down two goals for your social media efforts:

1. _____

2. _____

The Five Cs of Social Media

My digital team's "Five Cs of Social Media" are important to discovering what social media networks you should be on and for what reason. Of course there are many more out there, but I prefer to focus on these five main areas for direct sellers (later sections discuss each of these in more detail):

- **Conversation and communication on Facebook:** Facebook is a great way to communicate engaging and interesting content with your customers. The ability for fans to share your business page posts is very powerful. You want to get in front of their friends to turn them into leads and customers. Facebook works much like a home party does. When you book a home party with a host, one of your objectives is to turn one of her guests into your next host. This is the same with Facebook. Your intention is to turn one of your fan's friends into your next customer.

  But you want to have genuine conversations. Stay away from sales pitches and the hard sell. On Facebook, you need to erase "Buy my product" or "Putting in an order tonight and need $___ to reach my goal! Please help me out!" from your vocabulary. Instead, try offering tips, tricks, recipes, reviews, articles, and so on that relate to the type of business you're in. Sell jewelry? Post the latest fashion trends and designer tips. Sell cookware or food products? Post mouthwatering recipes that everyone will want to share with their family and friends. Sell health products? Share articles, workout videos, and before-and-after photos. You don't have to share your *products*. Share your products' benefits and your company's lifestyle. People want to do business with people they want to be friends with. Position yourself as someone who is knowledgeable and in the know with what the latest and greatest is. This will help dramatically with your sales and recruiting efforts, as well as building an overall brand awareness.

- **Consumer sales on Pinterest:** I often explain Pinterest as a place where people go to dream. They dream about the houses they want to live in, the clothes they want to wear, and the food they wish they could cook. But Pinterest is becoming much more than that. People are now going to Pinterest to shop and it is time you take advantage of that. Pin photos of your products to your Pinterest boards with a link directly to your online website and shopping cart.

  Your company provides you with a personal website with a shopping cart for online orders and customers. Your company and leader will provide you with training information on how to utilize your website.

- **Creating a desire on Instagram:** The power of photos and short video cannot be ignored. Instagram lets you create a desire for your product by showing off photos and short demo videos. Do you sell make-up? Try a 15-second make-up tutorial. What about home products? Snap a photo and show off your product in your living room. If you post eye-catching, engaging photos, people will be more likely to buy into you, your brand, and your product.

✔ **Community building on Twitter:** Interact and get involved with your local community. Twitter is great for fundraising opportunities as well as for finding out about local trade shows and vendor events. Many communities use hashtags to brand their community (such as `#Nashville`), so find these out and start a conversation! Twitter is great for quick conversations with like-minded people. I find that community-focused programs and events (like local networking groups, restaurant events, fairs, charities, and so on) do best on this platform. But be authentic: Offer your services to solve a problem, not to spam.

✔ **Content through blogs:** A blog gives you the opportunity to create relevant and interesting content for your customers. It is also a great way to increase your search engine optimization (how easy you are to find on Google) all while driving more traffic to your website. Blogs are an inexpensive way to attract more customers, build relationships with them, position you as an industry expert, and create opportunities for sharing.

Share your blog on your other social media platforms, like Facebook. Blog posts can include product reviews, training, information, and the hottest trends in your industry.

Knowing your company's policies and procedures

Understanding your company's policies and procedures is important when it comes to your online marketing strategies. Companies have different policies when it comes to creating Facebook pages, advertising, use of images, and so on.

Be sure to read through your company documents before you plan your social selling strategy. Always be sure to check with your sponsor or corporate office if you have any questions about what you are and are not allowed to do.

Here are some questions you may ask your corporate office or leader:

✔ Am I allowed to use the corporate logo? Is there an independent logo available for me?

✔ Am I allowed to create my own photos and use the company's name in the images?

✔ Do I have to get all images approved by the company?

✔ Am I allowed to have a Business Facebook Page?

✔ Am I allowed to advertise on social media?

✔ Am I allowed to have a blog where I sell my company products?

✔ Are there any restrictions to URL names (such as www.MyName-CompanyName.com)?

✔ Are there any specific claims I am not allowed to make?

✔ Are there any trademarked phrases I am not allowed to use in my marketing?

✔ Am I allowed to use photos, videos, articles, and other posts made by corporate on its social media pages?

Now take a look at your two goals and the 5 Cs and choose one or two platforms to start your business on. Remember, all of these can look appealing and can help drive your business forward. But for now, stick to just one or two so you don't overwhelm yourself. It is better to do one or two things really well than do many things mediocre.

Facebook for Direct Sellers

The majority of customers in direct sales are women. The majority of Facebook users are women. What an amazing combination for success.

I said go where your customers are, and you guessed it — your customers are on Facebook (www.facebook.com). In this day and age, *not* harnessing the power of Facebook is unthinkable. Today many direct sellers rely on Facebook as a way to transform their direct sales business into an online, money-making machine. The powerhouse platform gives you the ability to increase brand visibility, sales, training, and recruiting, and establish strong customer relationships.

 But the key to reaping Facebook's sweet, sweet success? Engagement. In the land of Facebook, engagement is king. Your goal is to always serve your customers and clients with custom content that will generate the three golden actions: likes, comments and shares.

This section discusses why you should be on Facebook and what to do once you're there. So ready, set, go!

Reviewing Facebook's strengths

Being visible on Facebook is important for a variety of reasons. The following advantages and strengths will help you further decide whether Facebook is the right fit for you and your business.

Authenticity: Knowing your audience

Facebook promotes authenticity. Where many social media platforms allow users to sign up with a user name — for example, on Twitter you may be @stepintosuccess, @sarahscookware, @jenthenailgirl, and so on, Facebook users are identified by their real names. This gives a realness to the people that you connect with on Facebook. This is especially helpful when you are trying to create meaningful conversations and relationships with clients, your teams, and potential recruits. If you create a Business Page, it too will use the real name of your business.

Finding your audience

Whereas some social media platforms only allow you to target your audience by categories or hashtags, Facebook lets you narrow in on your exact customer. Facebook's detailed About sections and personal information allow you to target gender, age, race, sexuality, interests, hobbies, location, education, profession, and so forth.

Building a fan base

Through things like *hypertargeting* (being able to target specific groups of people through social media advertising) and hashtagging, Facebook gives businesses the ability to create loyal fan bases. By sharing content and information that is both relevant and useful to your demographic, you will start to create a community of natural brand ambassadors. *Brand ambassadors* are your elite, top-tier customers. They are the ones who are most likely to recommend your business to their friends, share your products, and promote your overall brand.

Weak-tie relationships

Facebook lets you stay connected with people you otherwise might have lost touch with. Your childhood friend, your roommate from college, even your old hair stylist are now all people you can maintain relationships with. These so-called *weak-tie* relationships are important for your business because you can connect more regularly and easily with your customers.

Creating content

Facebook lets you share a variety of content with a variety of people at the same time. Let's say you are in the food business, and you have multiple interest groups: those who are health conscious, those who enjoy cooking, and those who are looking for convenience. A post that you put on Facebook about the organic and natural ingredients in your products may only intrigue your customers who are health conscious. Delicious recipes in under 10 minutes may only spark the interest of those whose main priority is convenience. If you were with all your customers in one room, in person, it would be hard to share information while fulfilling each of their needs. With your business on Facebook, you still have your customers all in one space, but you can divvy them up into categories and share different content with each category.

Going viral

Word of mouth and recommendations are very powerful when it comes to increasing your sales and overall brand awareness. If you post interesting and engaging content that is easily sharable (photos and videos work best), then you can reach thousands of people quickly.

A consultant in the field that I know posted a short video sharing some of my training and changed it up to fit her company. The video went viral in her company (over 20,000 views), and within three days, she had over 1,000 new friend requests. She reached a new promotion that month with the attention, gained a new customer base, and networked with many other people in her company.

Being insightful

You can review how your fans interact on your page. You are able to measure likes, reach, engagement, and overall page performance. You have the option to view insights once your page reaches 30 Likes. *Insights* are Facebook's analytics for your page, such as how many people your posts are reaching, what day and time people are mostly looking at your page, what demographic your page is most popular among, and so on. Insights are helpful when you're looking at when to post, what posts are doing well, and whether your posts are reaching your target audience.

Watching your competition

When you have a Facebook Business Page (see the section "Setting Up a Facebook Business Page" later in this chapter), Facebook will show you businesses who are similar to you. You'll be able to view these competitors as well as add some of your own to "watch." You'll be able to see whether they are getting a lot of engagement and what posts are doing best on their page. This is a great way to compare what you are doing and see what works best for them.

Enhancing customer service

Facebook allows you to interact with customers on a continuing basis. It makes it easy for you to talk to your customers in real time, follow up with them on their purchases, and reach out to potential leads. You can establish one-on-one conversations through private messages and create personal relationships through instant communication.

Experiencing service recovery paradox

Where do people post their dissatisfaction for a product or service? On Facebook, of course. Negative posts from customers don't always have to be negative for you or your business. Showing your customers how well you can handle stressful situations can actually turn them into better and more loyal customers, a phenomenon known as service recovery paradox.

Don't ever delete a negative comment. Focus on that customer, fix the problem, and show how amazing your customer service is.

Advertising

Your business at Facebook is not just limited to a fan page or a group. Facebook also offers you a chance to gain followers and customers through paid advertising. You can build your advertisements and set your own budget. You can use hypertargeting to show your ad to the people who matter most to your business.

Using groups and events

You don't have to only use Facebook Business Pages to promote your business. You can create Facebook Events for your online and home parties, product launches, open houses, and vendor events (see the section "Setting up a Facebook Event" later in this chapter for more details). Facebook Groups are a great way to build an online community around a particular subject. You can use Facebook Groups for training your team, VIP hosts, and holiday specials. In these Groups, you share tips, sales, training, and more.

Increasing your search engine optimization (SEO)

SEO is a key aspect for anyone who wants to build a significant presence online. Having a Facebook page for your business can help you increase your chances of being found in search engines like Google. So be sure to post links and interesting content to your Facebook pages and remember to always use popular keywords in your industry! For example, *cooking, home recipes, slow cooker recipes, freezer meals,* and so on.

You can use an online tool like WordStream (www.wordstream.com) to help you find popular keywords in your industry.

Saving money

Facebook is free. And even if you do throw some money at it in terms of advertising, you are in complete control of your budget. Many direct sellers have very effective Business Pages without ever spending any money.

It's not about the number of likes. It's more important to genuinely connect with the people you engage with on Facebook. If you do, they'll help tell your story. Quality over quantity.

Setting up a Facebook Business Page

A Facebook Business Page is important when you have your own business. People utilize Facebook's search bar to find more information on businesses, companies, and products, just as they do on search engines like Google and Yahoo!. If someone is looking for your business, will they find you?

Setting up a Facebook Business Page is easy, and www.facebook.com/help will always give you the most correct, up-to-date information on how to create one. As of this writing, creating a Facebook page takes no more than a few simple steps.

At www.facebook.com/pages/create you can select a type of business. I suggest selecting either Local Business or Place, or Brand/Product. Local Business allows your customers to leave reviews, which is a plus. But keep in mind you must put in a physical address.

Once you've selected a business type, you can fill out information and details about your business.

When posting on your Business Page, think about what your customers and clients find interesting. Experiment with different types of posts. Follow a 90/10 rule. 90 percent of your posts should be lifestyle posts, and only 10 percent should be about your product and business opportunity. People dread the hard sell from direct sellers, so shock them with your compelling content. Always be authentic and personable and aim to start engaging conversations with your fans.

I suggest posting once a day. Play around with posting different times of day to see what times work best for you.

But what should I post, you may be asking? Here are some ideas:

✔ **Custom content:** You want your posts to be unique, personable, and true to your brand. Designing your own photos, blog posts, reviews, or tips will keep your business page fresh and your customers engaged.

✔ **Interesting facts:** People share things that they want their friends to know. Interesting articles, tips, tricks, and other content are an easy way to end up in more peoples' newsfeeds.

✔ **A or B questions:** Questions that require an easy answer help boost engagement. Use photos and ask your fans to vote on option A or option B. Always encourage them to share the post so their friends can vote too.

✔ **Videos:** Videos get a lot of attention on Facebook, and Facebook pushes them through into more newsfeeds and lets you play the video right there on the page, because the company doesn't want people to leave Facebook and go to YouTube. Your videos should last 15–45 seconds. Post videos on your Business Page about your products, how to use them, and so on.

Videos are also a great way to do your parties online (see the upcoming section "Hosting Facebook parties" for more). My daughter is a leader in the direct sales field, and for one of her Facebook parties in early 2014, she videotaped herself doing a home party. Not only did her guests love how interactive the online party was, it got a lot of attention from other potential customers and leads. Her bookings increased because of how fun she made a party look, and her recruiting increased because of how easy she made her job look. She still gets interest from the video, even to this day.

- ✔ **Links to your website:** Links to your website make for great calls-to-action. They give your fans somewhere to go after they've watched your videos and liked or commented on your posts. Posting links on Facebook also helps increase the SEO of those links on search engines like Google.

- ✔ **Personal testimonies:** Share what your customers think about you. Show off testimonials from past hosts and customers. When people know that other people love your product or service, they become more inclined to do business with you. You can also post statuses and photos where you ask fans to review your product by commenting on the status.

- ✔ **Scheduling posts:** Make your Facebook posts manageable. Pick an hour a week to decide what you are going to post to Facebook every day and schedule them on your Facebook page. This will allow you to keep a consistent flow of content on your business page.

Always ask for a *call to engagement.* You have to literally ask your fans to Like, Comment, or Share a post to get a post boosting action. For example, "Like this photo if you agree," "Comment below with your answer," or "Share with your friends and family!"

Likes, Comments, and Shares help get your content seen by your customers.

Using your personal Facebook account for personal branding

Using your personal account for professional networking is also a great way to grow your online presence and to spread the word about your business.

People used to talk about achieving a healthy work/life balance, but with the technology landscape changing, it makes it nearly impossible to leave work at work. We are in constant contact with those around us because of our mobile phones and on social media sites. So instead of trying to keep our personal and professional lives separate, more and more people are looking to integrate them.

When you are more candid and allow some of your personality to blend into your professional networking and conversations, you can gain likability, trust, and respect from your customers. People want to do business with people they want to be friends with, and you can use this style of attraction marketing to grow a loyal fan base.

When it comes to your personal brand, you want to show off the type of person your company makes you, not the products that you sell. Remember the 90/10 rule: 90 percent of your posts should be lifestyle-related, and only 10 percent about the product or opportunity.

People are often more drawn to the lifestyle and appeal of what your products give them. Women don't want to buy cosmetics. They want to buy confidence, attractiveness, and self-esteem. It's important that when you post on your personal page, you share the life your business has afforded you.

Don't duplicate content on your personal Wall and your Business Page. Remember, your friends and family will most likely be on both. Instead, focus your personal Wall on how the business affects you personally and contributes to your lifestyle, and keep your Business Page more about the product and industry.

But what is your personal brand? Personal branding is the commitment you make to define yourself. Ask yourself these questions:

What type of person am I?

What type of leader am I?

What type of friend, parent, or spouse am I?

What words define me?

What makes me great?

What makes me unique?

What makes me compelling?

By answering these questions, you make it easier to share your personal brand with others. In turn, when your customers understand who you are, it makes it easier for them to have a relationship with you.

Your personal brand is a great asset. It is how you represent yourself and how people identify you. But don't confuse it with acting. You want your brand to be who you naturally are.

Here are some other things you can do to enhance your personal Facebook page:

- ✔ **Update your occupation:** In the Work and Education section of your About tab, update your occupation to your business. You can also link this to your Facebook Business Page.

- ✔ **Protect your friends list:** Your Facebook friends list is like your email newsletter list. You have the option in Settings to hide your friends list. Hiding protects your clients and stops other representatives from reaching out to your prospects and database.

- ✔ **Celebrate moments:** Did you achieve a new rank in your company? Earn an incentive or award? Celebrate it! Show your friends, family, and customers how much your company appreciates you as a salesperson. And when people see how successful you are, they start to wonder if they can do it too.

- ✔ **Be Followed:** This allows people to Follow your posts without your having to friend them or see their updates in your newsfeed. This is especially important if you run out of space on your friends list (Facebook currently limits you to 5,000 friends).

- ✔ **Recognition:** Give recognition to other people! Create conversations with people. Comment on their photos. Like their status updates. Private message them asking how their kitchen renovation is going. People want to feel noticed. And the more you interact with them, the more they will interact with you.

- ✔ **Your "why" or "success" story:** Share bits and parts of why you started your business to your friends, family, and customers on Facebook. Show your friends how your business has changed your life.

- ✔ **Facebook lists:** On the left-hand side of your home page, you have the option to create Facebook lists. Lists give you the opportunity to filter your customers and clients. Now instead of seeing status updates from everyone on your list, you can choose to see updates from just that group of people. Lists make it easier to like, comment, and share posts with the people who are most relevant to your business.

Hosting Facebook parties

Virtual Facebook parties are *not* meant to replace your home parties, but they can be a great option for booking parties as well as hosting parties with your friends and family who live far away.

Don't overthink your Facebook and social media parties. Run your parties the exact way you would run a home party. It's just on a different platform.

Setting up a Facebook Event

I have seen direct sellers having parties in Facebook groups because guests are automatically added into groups, whereas Events require a response. But would you force a guest into attending a home party? No! So don't force them into a group either. Instead, set up all your parties as Facebook Events. (Note, you and your host must each have a Facebook account to run a Facebook party.)

Create your Event 7–10 days out. Follow these steps, but bear in mind that Facebook is constantly changing its interface and how it functions, so the exact method of setting up an Event is likely to change as well. Here is how it works as of this writing:

1. **Click Events in the left-hand menu on your home page.**

2. **Click +Create.**

3. **Fill in the details.**

   Include the event name, location, details, time, and so on in the Create Private Event box that pops up.

   The details section is very important! Make sure guests understand that they are being invited to an *online* event and *not* a home party. Many people use the events option on Facebook for live events, so make sure you state in the details section the party is being run completely online.

   You will also want to share with your guests what they should expect: the best tips in the industry, fun information, and so forth. Many direct sellers run a game to encourage participation. If you decide to do this, make sure it is mentioned here. Remember, the key to successful social media strategies, including parties, is engagement and participation from your audience.

4. **Click Create.**

   You're taken to your event where you can share posts, upload photos, invite more guests, and edit event details.

5. **Upload a cover photo.**

   This should be a photo of your products and your company name so everyone knows what type of party they are attending.

Pre-party posts and invitations

Once your page is set up, you'll write and post your first pre-party post. Do that before you invite the host to the page so that once she starts adding her friends, they will know exactly what to expect.

The first pre-party post should say something like:

   "Welcome! This online party will start June 15th at 9 p.m. EST!"

If you can, I suggest making this into a graphic so that it stands out to all those who check out the Event. For help on custom graphics, see the section "There's an App for That" later in this chapter.

Now it is time to invite your host . Once your hostess has joined the Event (make sure she knows to select Attending — this will be a part of your host coaching session as well), you can make her a host by clicking Edit at the top right-hand side and typing in her name under the Host section. This will enable her to add her friends and also let everyone know who the host of the party is.

Before the party, you need to do some more pre-party posts to help encourage attendance at the party. Train your host to comment on these posts.

Then you will post your point system. Your *point system* is a sort of game that you can use to help encourage engagement and participation. You offer "points" for things like joining the Event, placing an order beforehand, booking a party afterwards, placing an order or booking a party after the Event, inviting a friend and tagging them, for every item they purchase that you had featured during the Event — and so forth. At the end of the party, you will use these points as ballots for a giveaway.

Facebook party host checklist

Before we get to the night of the party, the next important step you need to take is coaching your host (for much more information on host coaching, see Chapter 10):

- ✔ **Book a date.** Always book a date when a client shows interest in hosting an online party. Even if it is only a tentative date.

- ✔ **Send the host a friend request and add her to the Event.** If you are not already Facebook friends with her, using the search bar at the top of your Facebook page, search for the name of your host. Always confirm with her the correct spelling of her name as well as what her profile picture is. Select your host and click Add as a Friend. Add her to the party through the Event page.

- ✔ **Share your enthusiasm with the host.** Every host deserves the best possible party. Make sure you share your excitement with her. If she knows you think it will be a great party, she will think it will be a great party too. Don't forget to remind her how easy a Facebook party is. Try to get her to book another date for a real party to be held in her home. Let her know how fun home parties are and remind her that her guests will be able to touch, feel, and interact with the product.

✔ **Register your party or set up an event online in your company's virtual/back office.** Set up your party online through your personal website for outside orders and pre-party orders. This is so important as it can increase party sales! (Reach out to your company or your leader for help on setting up an online event.)

✔ **Email or deliver her a host-coaching package.** This package should include things like any host specials or guest specials, catalogs for outside orders, samples, and other company literature. For more information on host packets, check out Chapter 10.

✔ **Encourage friends to bring a friend.** Let guests know that you will be giving away points (through the points system) for bringing a friend to the party online. People are more likely to engage in a party if a close friend of theirs is going. This will also help with engagement, attendance, and sales.

✔ **Encourage pre-party orders.** Let the guests know that they can place pre-party orders or set up orders on your personal website through the online party you created (if your system allows). Send them a link to your personal website and let them know they can easily add to the order the day of the party by saying, "Add that to my order!"

✔ **Send private messages.** Tell your host to send private messages to her friends to personally invite them to the Facebook party. Remind her *not* to send group messages, but to reach out to her friends individually. This will make her friends feel more important and more likely to engage.

✔ **Comment on all posts.** Tell her that her participation with the party is vital to its success. It will keep the party moving and energized and will encourage engagement on the event by all guests. Ask her to comment on every pre-party post that you make before the party and all posts you make during the party.

✔ **Remind her of your points game.** If you have decided to do a drawing for a free gift to encourage participation, make sure you remind your host to let her friends know that they can earn an amazing prize from you just for engaging.

Day of the party

Set up your party in five sections:

✔ **Welcome and intro posts:** At the beginning of the party, you want to find out who is there and engaged. You will see on your Event Page (usually located on the right-hand side) how many people have joined the event but that does not mean that all of those people are joining in on the party at that moment. Instead of just asking who is there, ask them a question that helps you find out a little more about their needs and wants. For example, "Would you rather be a better cook, a faster cook, or a more creative cook? Comment below!"

✔ **Industry trends:** Before you get into talking about the products, you want to create a want and a lifestyle. Why do people want your product? What need do they have for it? What need does society have for it? Is it useful, popular, trendy, seasonal?

✔ **Product posts.** Now is the time to show off what you got! You created a desire for your product, now give them the products to fulfill that desire. Remind them that by saying "Add that to my order" they will receive additional points towards the drawing.

✔ **Recruiting and booking seeds:** Now that the party is underway and you have showcased your company lifestyle and your products, it's time to plant some seeds for bookings and recruiting. (For more on booking seeds, see Chapter 7; for more on recruiting, see Chapter 14.)

✔ **The giveaway and closing:** Remind your guests about the points system and that you will be calculating the points and announcing the winner within the next few days. Give them the link to your personal website, ask if they need any help entering their order, and thank them for a wonderful time. Leave them with your contact information.

Follow-up

Now that the party is done, the next step is to follow up (Chapter 13 covers follow-up in detail). Here are some ideas for following up.

✔ Post images after the party that say "1 day left" or "only a few hours left" as a reminder for people to place their orders.

✔ Coach your host to personally contact those who attended to thank them for joining and to let them know when the party is closing.

✔ Go back to the event page and review the posts. What were people most interested in? Did they place an order for those items? Reach out to them. Don't forget to thank them for coming.

✔ Were there people who did not engage? Send them a message and let them know they still have time to order and look at the party posts.

✔ Post reminders on the Event about what they will receive when they order, such as chances to win a prize or any guest specials.

✔ Be sure ordering instructions are clear and simple. For example, share links that are easy to access from computer and mobile devices.

Staying out of Facebook jail

More and more direct sales consultants are landing in "Facebook jail" or "Facebook time-out." What this means is that many people, especially in the direct sales industry, are being blocked from actions like adding friends, sending private messages, joining Groups, liking Facebook pages, and commenting on posts. The most severe level of Facebook jail is having your page deleted altogether.

So why is Facebook putting you in jail? Because Facebook thinks you're a spammer or a computer-generated spam-bot. You want to avoid Facebook jail at all costs. Developing your personal brand is very important for your social media success, so it is important to always be authentic online and to avoid spamming users with sales pitches.

Here are four ways to stay out of jail and stop being labeled as a spammer:

✔ **Create custom content.** If Facebook notices one certain image or exact wording being used too many times across personal profiles, these images and posts get marked as spam. Post too many times, go to jail.

✔ **Don't add people you don't know.** If you start to add people you don't know, and people mark you as someone they don't actually know, Facebook will flag you. If it happens too many times — jail.

✔ **Don't add too many people at once to your page, profile, or Events.** If you go on an adding frenzy, Facebook assumes you're not a real person. Add too many people at once too often — jail.

✔ **Are you in too many Groups?** Facebook assumes you couldn't possibly be interested in that many things and decides your purpose is to spam. So, if you're in too many Groups — jail.

Bottom line, be authentic. Create real friendships and relationships with your customers and always follow the 90/10 rule of sharing: 90 percent lifestyle posts and only 10 percent product posts.

Instagram and Pinterest: The Power of Photos

Social media platforms like Instagram (www.instagram.com) and Pinterest (www.pinterest.com) are great ways to share your business, products, and brands through photos and short videos. Photos typically enjoy higher engagement (more Likes, Comments, and Shares) than text (a status post on Facebook, a tweet, or a blog post) and are more effective in terms of sharing your product.

Taking and sharing good quality photos is important. Be sure to take photos in good lighting. Focus by tapping on the subject on your phone as you're framing it and preparing to take the photo. You can also use filter apps and graphic design apps like Canva and Wordswag to make your photos more appealing.

When you post text statuses, they are usually contained to the platform that you posted it on. When you post photos, the chances are higher that people will save the photo and share it across numerous platforms by pinning it or posting it elsewhere, on Instagram, Twitter, or Facebook.

Thinking of promoting your business on photo-sharing social networks like Instagram and Pinterest? Check out the advantages of photo and video:

- **Getting your products noticed:** Photos and video give you the opportunity to showcase your product in a fun and appealing way, while supporting the type of lifestyle you are trying to sell to your customer. Your text can be very minimal in these cases because you are allowing the visual of the product to sell itself. Remember, users scroll through their feeds, often very quickly. You want to make sure you're always sharing the best, most eye-appealing photos.

- **Building your brand:** Your photos and videos show off who you are to your customers, which makes it easier for them to identify with you. Engagement on photos and video is typically higher than just status posts. I can't say it enough: People want to do business with people they like. So positioning yourself as an expert in your field is an easy way to grow your brand and increase sales and recruiting.

- **Before and after:** Are you in the beauty, health, or fitness industry? Show off before and after photos. Have you ever heard a picture is worth a thousand words? It's true. Showing how your product has worked for someone else through photo or video is much more powerful than written testimony.

- **Demonstrations:** Do you sell a product that requires demonstration? Showing a quick video or a photo to help explain how your product is used will help encourage sales because people will feel more comfortable and confident about using it.

- **Show off:** Show off your products, incentives you've earned, trips you've taken, friendships you've made — everything. Show off what your business has done for you and your family and what your products have done for you and your clientele.

Twitter: Community Presence

Twitter (www.twitter.com) is a powerful way to connect your business with your community. Even though the service restricts your posts to 140 characters, on Twitter you can jump in and out of conversations quickly and establish a strong presence online, especially with regard to your community.

Here are some reasons why you should be on Twitter:

- ✔ **Connection:** Establishing relationships is the main reason you should use any social media, including Twitter. Relationships create loyalty and likeability and increase sales.

- ✔ **Brand awareness:** You don't have to be a large brand to be noticed on Twitter. But be sure to have a photo of yourself and be personable. Large companies pay a lot of money to try to put a personality to their brand. *You* are the brand! Show off who you are. Don't have a profile photo of your products or your company logo.

- ✔ **Customer service:** Happy and unhappy customers post to Twitter. Respond to your customers in a timely manner and always help solve their problems. Other people will see how well you handle situations, good or bad, and will be more interested in following you.

- ✔ **Updates:** Share what you and your business are up to. Always post when you are at a party, event, or trade show. Show how you are involved in the community and what is new in your business. If you are at an event, always make it a point to find out its hashtag — you can usually find the hashtag in the events advertising or by contacting the coordinator. (See the upcoming section "Hashtags everywhere" for more.)

- ✔ **Contests:** A lot of people and businesses run contests on Twitter to help with their reach and drive traffic to their websites. According to Twitter, contests and sweepstakes may offer prizes for tweeting a particular update, for following a particular user, or for posting updates with a specific hashtag.

  For contests on any social media platform, always be sure to check their guidelines and regulations to see what you can and can't do.

- ✔ **Research:** Want to find out more about what your customers want? What about what your competitors are doing? Follow customers and competitors on Twitter, watch what they are posting, and check out hashtags that are relevant to your business. This will better help you provide the content your customers are craving and help you solve the problems they are having.

- ✔ **Staying current:** To be current, you have to be consistent. If a customer checks you out on Twitter and sees you haven't posted in months, they probably assume you're not engaged in any part of your business. This is why I always suggest starting with only 1–2 social media platforms.

  It is better not to be found than to be found and appear that you are no longer in business.

  Always make up a social media strategy that is manageable and stick to it. Making social media a part of your business routine is important. This will help you appear to be current and up-to-date in your industry and will help identify you as an expert/leader.

It's easy to incorporate a productive and successful social media routine into my proven system, the Power Hour. Check out how to run your business in 15-minute increments, four times a day, in Chapter 5.

✔ **Increase sales:** One of the reasons you went into business is to make money. Twitter is known for its heavy referral traffic. So, the more active you are on Twitter and the more you mention and share your personal website through posts, the more people will see your products.

✔ **Fundraising opportunities:** As mentioned earlier, Twitter is a great place for community-focused programs. Find out your community's hashtag. This is sometimes found on a city's website. You can also search influential people in your city and use the hashtags they use when mentioning the community. Get involved and show your community you are someone who wants to give back.

✔ **Finding local events:** Local trade shows and vendor events usually post updates to Twitter (again, a community-focused platform). This is a great way for you to stay updated on what events you can become a part of.

Building your audience on Twitter

If you don't have followers reading your content, then your posts have no value. It is important to have a strong audience. Here are some helpful hints on building your audience:

✔ **Have a plan.** What is your message? What is your brand identity? How often will you post? What is your ultimate goal? If you never set a goal, you will never know if you have reached it. Having a plan and a clear sense of who you are on Twitter helps grow your audience.

✔ **Be consistent.** You have to put in the work and walk the walk. The only way to grow a presence is work. It will not happen overnight, so you need to commit right now to posting everyday.

✔ **Be helpful.** Always give before you ask for something. Show people that you are looking out for them, not for you. When people think that you genuinely care about them, that builds trust and loyalty — for you and your business.

✔ **Find the people.** Identify your target audience and find them. Don't wait for them to come to you. Start conversations with potential customers and leads. Just make sure they're authentic conversations. Don't tweet them sales pitches.

✔ **Use existing networks.** Include your Twitter handle in your email signature and mention it in your other online marketing efforts (other social media platforms, email marketing, website, and so on).

✔ **Talk the talk.** Be relatable and use the lingo that your customers use. Positioning yourself as an expert shows them that they can trust what you offer.

✔ **Respond to everyone.** Respond to every reply and direct message you receive. Building solid relationships with people is important. And with our fast-paced culture, you need to move quickly and try to respond in real time.

✔ **Participate in hashtag chats.** *Hashtag chats* are scheduled chats on Twitter where you all connect using a hashtag. For example, say you sell food products and you want to do an online chat where people share their favorite pie recipes. You could start a hashtag, let's say #PieTalk. You would encourage people to join the conversation and share their favorite pies by using the hashtag. This helps connect like-minded people in one area and gets you noticed.

✔ **Promote others.** Always lift up others in the community first and give recognition to your fans and team members. People love to be noticed and recognized, especially on social media. This will again help with getting you noticed and getting you loyal followers.

✔ **Connect with stronger influencers.** Always be looking for ways to cross-promote and tap into other people's audiences. You want to look for the customers who will look up to you, but you also need to find who you are looking up to. Try to start conversations with them. If they reply or retweet you, that will get your Twitter handle in front of all of their followers. It's also important to watch what strong influencers are doing, especially in your industry, so that you can see what works best for them and adopt it.

Hashtags everywhere

Hashtags are a great way to categorize your posts, photos, and videos into categories that are easily accessible to users. Originally created by users on Twitter, hashtags now work across almost every social media platform and are being integrated into large-scale marketing campaigns across industries. The power of hashtags is huge.

There are two main reasons for adding hashtags to your photos and implementing them into your business:

✔ **Reaching more people.** Adding hashtags to your photos is a great way to attract new followers and share your content with more people. By using popular and relevant hashtags, you can get your posts in front of more customers.

✔ **Engaging more people.** Encourage your fan base to use your company's hashtags to categorize their own content. This will continue to build your brand awareness as well as find amazing customer reviews, testimonials, and photos for your business. For example, the hashtag #stelladot, for direct sales company Stella & Dot, has more than a million posts on Instagram alone!

Check out some of these other popular direct sales hashtags:

#itworks, for Network Marketing company It Works, has over 1.6 million posts on Instagram.

#jamberry, for direct sales company Jamberry, has over 340,000 posts on Instagram.

#directsales has over 90,000 posts on Instagram.

#MLM (multi-level marketing, also known as Network Marketing) has over 500,000 posts on Instagram.

#networkmarketing has over 350,000 posts on Instagram.

Clearly hashtags are an important way to spread your message online. The next sections contain tips on how to use hashtags to grow your business.

Be specific

Choosing specific tags will help you connect with other like-minded people. Your photo will then be added to a sort of virtual file folder where fans can easily search through content that is specific to what they are looking for.

For example, try adding #3dfiberlashes to your Instagram post instead of only using #makeup. Even though fewer posts use that hashtag (108,000 for #3dfiberlashes compared to 62 million for #makeup), your clients will get to what they are specifically looking for faster.

Being specific is much more beneficial than throwing your photo into a category that is filled with thousands, if not millions, of other photos.

Be relevant

Make sure your hashtags accurately describe your photos. Using general hashtags may get you some likes, but it isn't the best way to make your photos stand out on the platform or capture sales. Relevant hashtags will attract new followers who are genuinely interested in the content you are sharing. Remember, quality is always better than quantity when it comes to followers. Quality followers are interested in your content and are most likely to like and comment on your photos, especially over time. The biggest jackpot is when a customer Likes, Comments, Shares, retweets, and tags a friend in your post. This will help your reach grow exponentially.

Hashtag overkill?

But how many hashtags should you use? Is there a thing as too many hashtags? Not really. Studies on Twitter show that hashtagging is best done with 1–2 tags per post, as these have a higher chance of getting a retweet; Instagram engagement is highest on photos with *11+ tags.* Moral of the story? Don't be afraid to get tag crazy on Instagram.

Be topical

Watch what other people post and what they hashtag, especially photos that tend to get a lot of engagement. Others may be using hashtags you are unaware of or never would have thought to use. You should always be testing new tags on your photos to see what works best for you and your business. Are you in the fitness industry? Look up popular fitness gurus and check out the hashtags that bring them in a lot of followers and engagement.

Capturing the Social Sale

Here's the scoop: Even though you're on social media to sell to customers, you can't let *them* know that. People don't want the hard sell from you, and they don't want to feel tricked into purchasing something they don't need, just so you can make some extra money at the end of the month. You need to build trust and likability with your customers, and you do that through sharing your knowledge, positioning yourself as an expert and industry influencer — and, really, by sharing pretty photos.

Your biggest asset is you — not your product. People need *you* in their lives. Not your products or company. They need someone who solves problems for them, is current with trends, and is interesting. They need a *friend.* If you can get your customers to feel that way about you, and have an authentic relationship with you, then they will want to buy from you.

People go on social media networks to relax, not to get sold to. That's why you must be careful and get creative with what you post. Let your customers come to you. Do you sell food and beverage items? Share photos of what you are cooking up in the kitchen, your favorite recipes, and so on. Your fans will come to know you as a fantastic cook and will ask you for your advice. *That* is the perfect moment to share your products and opportunity.

Your content, whether a photo, video, or blog post, should always be interesting, engaging, and visually stimulating. You do not, I repeat do not, want to be seen as a spammer of products or as a "salesperson."

The market is crowded with other representatives, other companies, and other brands, so you need to stand out. Always offer content that your audience wants to engage with — and then be consistent. You can't start posting quality content to social media then disappear from it for months. Your customers will assume you are either not interested anymore in your business or, even worse, that you're not interested in them.

Once you show your customers that you share quality content, they will start sharing your content even more frequently, growing your brand presence and helping capture new customers.

So find out who your audience is, target them with what they actually want to see, and surprise them with your entertaining, inspiring, and compelling content in a variety of forms. If you do this, you will foster new relationships.

The Virtues of Blogging

The way we receive information is changing. The Internet and social media make it easier for us to get information from a variety of sources and from all over the world. And if the way we *receive* information is changing, it means the way we can *share* information is changing, too.

Many people have personal blogs that are not business related. Often they focus on hobbies. For example, food, fashion, parenting, gardening, cars, and so forth. People who have personal blogs don't normally get paid to do so — it is usually a hobby. However, if they generate enough web traffic, they often can bring in money through selling ad space.

Business blogging is different. Your blog is not a hobby, nor is it the primary way your business makes money. Instead, your blog serves as a way for you to market your business and as a social platform.

Blogging helps support your business growth and helps drive people to the place that matters most: your website and shopping carts. Your blog can provide fantastic opportunities for driving traffic to your website, capturing sales, customers, and leads, and establishing relationships with clients and readers.

Whether you are a small business or a multimillion dollar corporation, content marketing is key. Content is king in the online marketing world. Blogging is your way of sharing content.

There are many routes available to you for creating a blog. I don't have the space in this book to go through the process step by step. You might consider checking out www.blogger.com and www.wordpress.com as a couple of ways to get started for free. Once you've been blogging for a while, then you may consider upgrading to a more professional platform and getting your own customized URL, which then redirects to your blog. For much more on creating your own blog, check out *Blogging For Dummies* (Wiley, 2013) by Amy Lupold Bair and Susannah Gardner.

Increasing visitors to your website

Unlike you, your customers will care more about your blog and your other social media sites than they care about your website. Because representative websites are created by the company whose products you represent, you have little to no control over what the website looks like, what it says, or what you can share with your customers. Having a blog gives you the content control that you lack otherwise.

On your blog, you will always want to have a Shop My Products tab that leads directly to your corporate website (check with your policies and procedures to make sure this is okay). If you continue to update your blog and share posts, it will increase your visibility on search engines like Google, and will ultimately drive more traffic to your company website (where you actually sell products and offer the business opportunity).

Increasing search engine visibility

Updating your blog with fresh content means you will be found more easily on search engines like Google and Yahoo!. And this is important when trying to beat out your competition.

Always use popular keywords in your articles that your customers are likely to search for. Remember, you're not writing for yourself. The point is to serve interesting content to your clients. Using keywords, topics, and categories that your demographic is most interested in will help your blog be discovered.

Be consistent. Posting new content daily will help you find the customers you want.

Positioning yourself as an industry expert

When you share content that is interesting, engaging, and relevant to your demographic and customer base, you position yourself as someone who is knowledgeable and someone they can trust. The more you can show that you are knowledgeable in your industry, the more likely your consumers will trust you to supply what they need.

Don't make your products the topic of your blog posts. Doing so will turn almost everybody off. Say, for example, you sell for a make-up company. *Don't* write a blog post about your foundations. Instead, write a more general blog post about contouring and highlighting. Your customers are much more likely to search for make-up tips and tutorials rather than your particular product. If you supply them with information they want, they will continue to seek you out for advice. And of course, they will find your product tab on your website.

Creating customer relationships

Your blog will help you create deeper connections with your customers. It is important that your audience gets to know you as a person, because — and by now, I expect you can say it right along with me — *people do business with people they know, like, and trust.*

Large brands spend a lot of money trying to humanize their brand, whereas you come with that advantage built in. Show off who you are. Become a friend to your clients.

And just like on your other social media sites, your blog gives visitors the opportunity to comment. That allows you to respond and interact with your customers. One advantage blogs have over other social media is that your comments last longer than a tweet or a Facebook post and are more easily seen by everyone.

Selling through your blog

Whether you are selling online or in person, you need to forget the hard sell. The most important sales tactic you could ever master is authentically and actively engaging with your customers.

This industry really does enhance the lives of those involved, whether that be the income opportunity at the recruiting level, the social aspect at the host level, or the product benefits at the customer level. Sharing your personality and the benefits of your products is better and more profitable than directly selling to your customers.

Your primary goal should always be to build trust, likability, and credibility with your customers, as well as become a loyal and engaging community member. Once your customers come to know you as an expert and as someone they trust, you will never have to push your products on them, because they will be pushing themselves on your products.

Getting your blog noticed

The purpose of a blog is to get the word out there about your business and actually be seen by the people. And that means providing interesting content, not serving marketing material.

You want readers to "eat your content," so to speak. This means you want your readers to consume what you say, share it with friends, and keep coming back for more.

Your content should always be solving a problem for the reader, sharing a great story, and cultivating a captivated audience.

Here are some helpful tips to getting your blog noticed:

- ✔ **Be consistent with content.** Decide what your brand is. Who do you want to be? How do you want to define yourself? If you know who you are, your customers know who you are. Determine what kind of content is most useful for your customers and deliver that. Is it tutorial videos? Recipes? Design tips?

    Whatever the content is, make sure it is interesting and worth sharing — otherwise, it won't have any value for the reader. Then continue to deliver what you have committed to. It will make it easier for people to get to know you and to share who you are with friends.

- ✔ **Use your social media.** Include social media share buttons on your blog. This gives readers the opportunity to share your posts to Facebook, Twitter, and so on, as well as any photos used in your blog to Pinterest. Making your blog easy to share is very important.

    Also, any time you share a new blog post, be sure to share it on *all* your social media platforms as well.

- ✔ **Use quality photos.** People are drawn in by the way your blog looks at first glance. And again, you want your audience sharing your blog as much as possible, including pinning your images to Pinterest.

- ✔ **Be SEO-friendly.** What do your customers want to know? What are they searching for? Include those keywords in the title and body of your posts. The earlier into your post the keywords appear, the better your post will do on Google.

✔ **Be friendly in general.** Don't let your posts sound like a stuffy press release. Be casual, with a friendly tone. Use contractions as much as possible and talk in the present tense. Write like you speak. This is important because you always want to appear relatable to your audience — like a cool, knowledgeable older sister.

✔ **Be in the conversation.** Talk. Talk a lot. Talk to everyone. Always respond to your readers' comments, post comments on other blogs, and make relationships with other bloggers. The more you join the conversation and the community, the larger your presence will grow.

Don't delete negative comments. If you delete them, the person will go post them somewhere else. And then you wouldn't have the opportunity to change their mind. Be sure to always recover the situation and show your amazing customer service and personality. No one is perfect — not you and not our companies. But people will stay loyal to you, even through your mistakes, if you genuinely care about them and their experience.

There's an App for That

Technology was designed to make things easier, but at times it can be overwhelming and challenging. But even though it can be overwhelming, done properly, it can also be a very powerful tool to add to your belt. This section discusses some of my favorite apps and tips on how to use them.

Designing your own graphics and invites

✔ **Red Stamp Cards (www.redstamp.com):** Use Red Stamp to create invitations and announcements for everything from parties to special events. Click COLLECTIONS to see if your company offers pre-set templates. Red Stamp has limited font and text options, but with tons of templates, it's easy to create something that can be shared via text, email, or on social media. You can also choose to send a postcard of your creation or a card with envelope for a small fee.

✔ **Pic Collage (http://pic-collage.com):** Use Pic Collage to create invitations, announcements, special event notices, specials, and product collages. You can choose to add images from your camera roll/photo gallery or add them from the web. Lots of editing options. Also great for adding text to an image or combining multiple images into one. Your creation can be shared via text, email, or on social media. Apple users can also choose to send a postcard for a small price.

- ✔ **Canva (www.canva.com):** Use Canva to create all sorts of images, especially for sharing on social media. You can choose from pre-set image sizes such as a social media post or Facebook cover or click on Custom to create an image of any size. Canva has thousands of layout ideas and images, and you can customize the images to fit your needs. Use it to edit or create images. Canva is free to use, and many images/layouts are free as well. Paid images cost $1 each, or you can purchase a package (such as 22 images for $20). Canva also walks you through a quick tutorial when you sign up.

- ✔ **PicMonkey (www.picmonkey.com):** PicMonkey is great for editing all types of images. Add text, resize an image, touch up a photo, add a border, create a photo collage, and more. You can also use it to create images. There is a free version of PicMonkey that includes tons of options, but some options are only available with a subscription. This subscription is currently $4.99 a month or $33 a year.

- ✔ **Word Swag (http://wordswag.co):** This $2.99 app lets you turn quotes or messages into amazing images that you can share on social media. Simply choose a background, add text, and then choose from tons of font styles that make your words come to life.

Organizing your material

- ✔ **Evernote (https://evernote.com):** The ultimate organizing tool for everything you want to save, share, and find. It syncs across all your devices and is perfect for staying organized on the go.

Keeping an eye on time management

- ✔ **Wunderlist (www.wunderlist.com):** The ultimate "to-do" list tool. Set tasks and reminders from your computer, phone, or tablet. You can create multiple lists, set priorities, get push notifications, and even share task lists with others.

- ✔ **EasilyDo (www.easilydo.com):** Easily Do is like a snapshot of upcoming events and random "things to know." This intuitive app finds information from your email and other apps and uses it to help you keep important information in one place. It notifies you of upcoming flights and shipped packages, for example, and even allows you to schedule Facebook birthday posts without leaving the app.

Incorporating business services

- ✔ **Flint (www.flint.com) and Square (http://squareup.com):** Both of these apps are for credit card processing. If your company offers this to you for free, then you may not need apps like these. However, there may be a time when you want/need to collect payment with a debit or credit card, and these are two inexpensive options. Sign up for free online and then download the app so you're prepared if needed.

- ✔ **Quickbooks Online (http://quickbooks.intuit.com):** Been hesitant to use Quickbooks because the software is expensive? Quickbooks Online is another option that allows you access to all the great Quickbooks features for a small monthly fee. Track business expenses and then give your accountant access to "view" your account so they can complete your taxes.

- ✔ **Expensify (www.expensify.com):** Helps you track business expenses, including mileage. Run reports and get your taxes done in a flash.

- ✔ **MileIQ (https://www.mileiq.com):** Automatically tracks your travel and allows you to designate trips as personal or business with one swipe. It's the easiest way to track travel for business reimbursements and mileage deductions.

Chapter 12

The Power of One-on-One Selling

In This Chapter

▶ Getting the importance of one-on-one selling

▶ Securing appointments

▶ Finding the right service for your customers

▶ Selling one-on-one while out and about

The power of one-on-one selling is ideal for anyone in direct sales — Party Plan, Network Marketing, and Hybrid representatives. One-on-one selling is about the customer experience and customer service. One-on-one appointments are commonly used in the Network Marketing industry as a primary means for product sales and recruiting. However, many Party Plan companies are finding that one-on-one appointments are a great option for people who may never consider hosting a party.

Home parties (discussed in Chapter 9) are an ideal way to reach a group of people at one time, especially in the Party Plan model, but one-on-one appointments are another kind of asset in your arsenal. They create a personal shopping experience for your clients.

Just because someone isn't interested in a hosting a party doesn't mean they're not interested in your product or your service. For example, I once overheard a conversation between a customer and a representative. The woman mentioned she was interested in purchasing a product that the other woman sold. The representative offered the woman the option of hosting a party so she could earn free and discounted items. The woman replied that she wasn't interested in having a party, as she only wanted to purchase a particular item. Instead of listening to her customer, the representative continued to offer the benefits of hosting a home party. Eventually, the other woman just walked away.

The representative missed the opportunity for a sale. She didn't understand that even though the woman didn't want to hold a party, she still wanted to make a purchase — just in a different fashion.

Your one-on-one clients or prospects can become very profitable and sometimes lead to referrals of other people who may have turned down the idea of a party, too.

When my son was in college he sold a high-end product line that focused on bedroom linens and decor. Because of the price point of the products and the type of person the product attracted, he found it difficult to find people who wanted to have a home party.

He found his niche in people who wanted to completely redo their bedrooms. With these potential customers, he would share the benefits of a one-on-one consultation, rather than the benefits of a home party. He would bring samples, swatches, and other decorating ideas to show his client. Most of the time he would enjoy a healthy sale equal to that of a home party. However, by entering the order as a home party, he was able to offer his client an amazing deal with free credits and half-priced items. He would show them what it would have been at retail, and how much they saved.

Instead of pushing a party or the idea of host credit, he reworked it so that his clients felt like they were getting a personal shopping experience with an amazing deal. His clients were always happy with their experience and often referred someone else who wanted to redo their bedroom or asked him to come design another bedroom or bathroom in their house.

One-on-one selling is an excellent way to gain new clients, party hosts, and recruits. It gives you the opportunity to discover your prospects' needs and cater your presentation to offer them a specific solution. Again, this is very commonly done in Network Marketing and Hybrid (as Hybrid is a combination of both models).

As a direct seller, it is important to offer value to your customers. One way to do that is to personalize their experience with you, meeting a need or solving a problem they have, so that they appreciate your effort. This creates loyalty, excitement, and ultimately, profitability.

Selling with One-on-One Appointments

Selling through one-on-one appointments is a great way to achieve sales. *One-on-one* is where you offer a personalized service to an individual client. Say, for example, you sell beauty products. At a one-on-one appointment, you would sit down with a client to present your make-up line. You could give your client a makeover, give tutorials, and/or update her current make-up selection.

Although one-on-one appointments aren't as efficient as selling to a group of people, they nevertheless can be an important profit center for your business. And although it's true that one-on-one appointments don't yield the same total sales as a home party, you can get a higher per-person sale because the presentation is completely catered to the individual. You can reach a different clientele than you might otherwise service, as well as building your business network.

At a home party, you present your products to a group of people, so you don't have much opportunity to only discuss the products that each guest is most interested in, although you can give a brief personalized service as you total the personal orders and offer further services during that final phase of the party.

During your one-on-one appointments, you explore the precise needs of your client (for example, perhaps they're most interested in your skincare line) and focus on the products that will solve their challenges. You still up-sell and show other products that you think may benefit them from the line, but the customized presentation begins with addressing an expressed need or desire (see Chapter 9 for more on upselling).

This personal experience is the perfect situation for relationship-building, so it also helps set you up for re-servicing. When you call to offer other products or refill the existing order, you're already familiar with her priorities (because you'll have made several notes on her immediately following the appointment, so that you can remember what she talked about).

Always ask for referrals! Ask your one-on-one clients if they have any friends who would enjoy the same service. You can also ask if they have any friends who would enjoy hosting a party. You can even suggest she host one herself to share the products with her family and friends.

In Network Marketing, one-on-one appointments focus more on the opportunity than the product. The main goal of one-on-ones in Network Marketing is to sign representatives who are interested in the income potential of building a business. Key to success is not only signing up a new representative but also helping them choose the right amount of product for personal consumption on an automatic shipping program (auto-ship).

The Party Plan model focuses on continually gaining and servicing new customers. For the Network Marketing model, the typical goal is to have approximately six customers on auto-ship and to focus on continually gaining and serving new representatives to help them build their businesses. Of course, Hybrid models encompass both of these.

Getting One-on-One Appointments

Being ready for business wherever you go is important, and that's especially true when it comes to securing one-on-one appointments. You should be equipped with business cards or promo cards and catalogs at all times, of course. But more importantly, you should be upbeat and ready to engage in conversations that can lead to business opportunities.

Engaging in conversations with potential clients is fundamental to your success. During these conversations, the most important thing you will do is *find out the priorities of the potential client.* The best way to do that is to make a friendly observation, followed by a question. For example:

"That's a great necklace. Where did you get it?"

The second most important thing is to be ready to offer a way to help them meet that priority with your service or business, because that's how you'll get the appointment:

"I help women expand their wardrobes by creating new looks with accessories. I think there are several pieces that are just your style in this season's line."

This particular example incorporates a 30-second commercial into the conversation. Your *30-second commercial* is the answer you give when someone asks what you do or where you're working. It should always tell people what you do, not who you are. For example, instead of saying, "I'm a jewelry representative," you might say, "I help women create personalized looks with great accessories." Your 30-second commercial should paint a picture of your product or service, create an interest/wow factor, and meet a need. (Chapter 6 talks more about 30-second commercials.)

Then, before the conversation turns, simply ask for the appointment:

"I'd love to get together with you and show you those pieces that are just your style! I would love to come by and bring my jewelry and help you accessorize your wardrobe with our newest selections."

You want to make sure you get clients excited about the appointment and the product. Pique their interest and get them looking forward to meeting with you.

The one-on-one appointment is the time where you secure the potential client as a customer or even as a representative. So be sure to build a desire for the product during this conversation.

When securing an appointment, always be sure to build credibility for yourself by sharing how the product and business has worked for you, often called a *testimonial* or *success story.* Your testimonial may mention either how the product has improved your life or how the opportunity has impacted your family and your financial situation:

"I see how much you love our products, and you know that's what really attracted me to the business in the beginning. I can't begin to tell you how many awesome things this business has done for my family financially, when I really joined just to get my product at a discount."

Perfecting the Details: What to Do and Say

For a Party Plan representative, your one-on-one appointments may focus on one of two things (a Network Marketing representative typically focuses more on just the second one, and of course, Hybrid can focus on both):

✔ **Sharing the product:** This is where the main purpose of your appointment is to sell product. In this situation, you do a mini-presentation of the products that your client/customer is most interested in. You cater the selling experience to solve a problem for them. You will have learned what their challenge or priority is during your initial conversation. And you'll take time during this appointment to learn more.

✔ **Sharing the business:** This is where the main focus is to gain a new recruit or representative. You still want to build a desire for the product because that is one of the factors that drive people to join a direct sales company — they need to believe that the product is something that is marketable, easy to sell, and in demand. But the focus of this appointment will be to share the benefits of the business opportunity.

To help you with your one-on-one appointments, follow this format:

1. **Introduce you and your product or opportunity.** At the beginning of your appointment, thank your client for meeting you. Briefly remind them of what got them excited about the product or business in the first place.

2. **Find out more about their needs and wants.** Focus on them. Ask again what their needs and wants are. If it is product and sales based, ask specific questions that deal with your product type. For example, if you sell cleaning products, ask things like this:

   "What type of cleaning solutions do you currently use? What are your biggest issues or concerns with your current household cleaners? Do you have any problem areas in your home that you need a solution for?"

   If you're focused on the opportunity, you would ask things like the following:

   "What do you want from a job? What is your favorite part of your current position? If you could change anything about your career, what would it be?"

3. **Share your story and offer a solution.** It is important to let your client share her story first — that way, you have the opportunity to make your story relatable to theirs. For example, maybe she wishes her job was

more flexible because she has small children at home. If you also have children, you could say something like this:

"Carol, I completely understand. When I was working at the bank, it was difficult for me to juggle the kids and the demands of a job with different shifts. When I started my own business, it gave me the opportunity to stay home with my kids and work around my existing priorities."

Such a statement not only shows off the benefits of your business, it also helps you appear more relatable. That, in turn, can boost their confidence that this opportunity is right for them.

The key to successful one-on-ones is relationship-building. Take time to find out about your client's life, challenges, and hopes. Your role during one-on-one appointments is to listen and learn how you can best serve the client.

Even if the two of you seem to be very similar, don't assume you have the same priorities. For example, you may love the product because of the overall luxury experience of textures and scents, but she may be drawn to it because it is environmentally friendly and not tested on animals. Or perhaps you love that you can work the business full-time on a schedule you love, but she may be initially interested in just an extra $400 a month.

By listening, you can focus on her interests and priorities and learn more about them. You can share things about yourself as appropriate, but keep the focus on them. Just by doing that, you will create an experience that is unique and enjoyable.

Additionally, as mentioned earlier, because of the time you spend learning about your clients, you'll be able to continue meeting her needs and priorities in the future. For example, if she tells you that her son is graduating high school next month, when you call to re-service, mention that in the conversation. If you sell cosmetics, ask whether she would be interested in a fresh look for the event, using the new spring colors.

Selling While Out and About

Meeting new people — or *networking* — is important because you never know where you will find business. So always be prepared to talk to the people around you.

Being prepared means being ready mentally and physically. You want to look professional, have your 30-second commercial prepared and rehearsed, and be sure your marketing items are on hand. If someone asks you what you do, you want to be able to follow up with marketing materials such as promo cards, catalogs, and business cards.

Of course, if you carry a very popular item that's priced reasonably, you can always have that available on hand as well.

Selling while out and about is a great way to boost your sales every month as well as take of advantage of the day-to-day situations you find yourself in. For example, many nail and cosmetics representatives carry additional product with them while out and about because of the interest their products create. For example, when nail reps are complimented on their unique nail wraps, having product on hand gives them the opportunity to sell a set right on the spot, without any real effort. So even if you don't run your business full-time, it's important to always be ready to take advantage of opportunities that present themselves.

Executing a show-on-the-go

Your mini show-on-the-go is an excellent opportunity to sell your product one-on-one while you're out running errands. An afternoon out at the mall can quickly turn into a sale, a booking, or a new recruit for your team.

Chapter 6 talks in detail about your show-on-the-go, but in a nutshell, I'm talking about a mini-kit that you carry with you in a tote bag that contains some items that you can throw a mini-party with. Carrying around your large kit that you take to your parties is unrealistic, but having some items in a small bag is an easy way to show off *some* of your products while you're out.

You can quickly create a show-on-the-go kit by putting three catalogs (or mini-catalogs or product brochures) into a tote bag with five to eight product samples, a host packet, and an opportunity packet (see Chapter 6). If you sell jewelry or items that you usually display on a black tablecloth, then you may want to put a small piece of black fabric in the tote bag, also. Choose something that won't wrinkle easily when rolled up.

Keep your show-on-the-go tote bag in your car so that it's always ready. When you're prepared for business, you'll discover that opportunities arise more frequently. For example, you may be sitting at the pool watching your kids when you and several of the moms begin chatting about what they do. When you mention what you do, if they express interest, offer to show them a few samples. Suddenly, an outing at the pool turns into potential sales and bookings.

Starting conversations

Starting a conversation can help you meet new prospective customers, hosts, or recruits.

It's important to learn how to network and to engage yourself in conversations. The easiest way to start a conversation with people is by complimenting them, perhaps on something that they are wearing. This is especially important if they're wearing something that you sell — like jewelry, make-up, clothing, and so on.

Shared experience and interests are also great conversation starters. Perhaps the person next to you in line has in their shopping cart a product you like or are interested in trying. It is perfectly appropriate and friendly to say, "I've been wanting to try that. Is this the first time you've bought it?"

 Be sure to choose a conversation starter that is positive. It can be tempting to mention long lines or a terrible call by an umpire at a little league game, but it's important to start a relationship the way you want to continue it. Be someone who is enjoyable to interact with.

Distributing promo cards

A promo card is a combination of a postcard and a business card. Promo cards are often made available through the direct sales company as selling tools. A promo card should have your contact information on it as well as key information about the product.

Promo cards work best for direct sales companies that have a major line of products or a very popular product. They often feature a photo of the product, before and after results, and so on.

Promo cards are given out to people in place of a business card and catalog (though you can still give these to potential clients who are interested in more of the product line). They typically have an offer, such as a special price on a product when hosting a party, but they may also direct prospects toward your website where they can purchase the product line or choose to join your company.

Using wear-to-share and other promotables

If you sell a product you can wear, this is something you should be doing every time you go out, or as often as you can. Wearing your products or using them for personal use is a great way to market yourself and your business.

For example, if you sell beauty products like make-up or nail art, you should use these items as a part of your own daily routine. That also goes for clothing companies and ones that carry accessories like bags, purses, and jewelry.

One of the best ways to get a conversation started while on the go is *wear-to-share* apparel. Effective wear-to-share is more than just a polo with a logo. In fact, unless your company's logo is particularly intriguing, the polo won't help you share your products at all. Great wear-to-share apparel fits well and is flattering — but most of all, it has a "conversation-starting" factor. Many representatives have shirts, hats, and sweaters made that feature catchy phrases, cute sayings, or even jokes.

Wear-to-share conversation starters also include things like logo stickers to apply to the back of your tablet or the top of your laptop, a reusable water bottle, phone cases, or car magnets. Many direct selling companies offer wear-to-share apparel along with marketing materials and other business tools.

There are also other ways you can share your products even if you can't wear them:

- ✔ **Cleaning products:** Always have samples of your cleaning product in your purse. If you're picking up your son from daycare, at a restaurant, or even at work, and you notice a spill — that could be the perfect opportunity to show how quickly and easy your company's cloth or favorite cleaning spray works.

- ✔ **Food and beverage:** Use products from your line when making your lunch or your spouse's lunch for work. And always bring extra for people to sample in the lunchroom.

- ✔ **Spa products:** Bring a few samples of your soaps or lotions to work, your daughter's dance studio, your hairdresser's salon, and so on. Ask the owner if you can leave the products in the bathroom with copies of your business card or promo card.

- ✔ **Decor items:** Have a desk or an office at work? Decorate your space with the products you sell. When people compliment you, let them know you offer those products as part of a line you represent.

Think outside the box. Grab a notebook and pen and brainstorm all the different ways and places where you could share your product line.

Having product handy

In some cases, it's a good idea to have product on hand. If the direct selling company you work with has a single product that is in high demand, and it is affordably priced, then investing in a small stock of product may be beneficial, even if it isn't necessary. It enhances your opportunity to sell while out and about, especially if you're meeting people who are only interested in that product, and hence are one-on-one prospects rather than potential party hosts.

When you first start out, it's next to impossible to predict what your future customers will want, so it's often wiser to simply let customers order from you and let them know when to expect their products to arrive. Amazon.com has used this e-commerce model with incredible success, so don't feel as if you need to purchase inventory up front to be successful.

Although your sponsor and upline leaders may encourage you to purchase a certain amount of inventory, keep in mind that other than your company's "business starter kit," there is no inventory requirement. That's one of the benefits of working with a direct sales company.

When you have product on hand, you may want to take some with you when you're out driving around, especially when you're handing out promo cards. You can also take a photo of the stock you have on hand and post a photo on your business page on Facebook, to let friends know that you have inventory you'd like to move quickly.

It's also a good idea to keep product on hand during seasons where your products are extremely popular. For example, for several years I sold a line of crystal products and I rarely carried any inventory at all, except during the summer at wedding season. I always kept crystal vases, picture frames, and toasted flutes on hand, because neighbors and friends would often call on me to see if I had a wedding gift for them.

Be sure to check your company's policies and procedures with concerns to ordering product to keep as inventory for re-sale.

Enhancing the Personal Shopping Experience

You don't only offer home parties. You offer a magnitude of ways that clients and customers can purchase from you. Recall my anecdote from Chapter 7 about the woman who complimented the necklace I was wearing? She loved it but didn't want to host a party. Instead of accepting defeat, I let her know that I also offered one-on-one appointments. I would bring my jewelry to her house and help her match the selections to her outfits.

When you're booking one-on-one appointments to sell product, you want your client to feel as if it is personal to her. Find out her interests and needs and create an experience for her that really is unique.

Identifying the target audience

Your job is to find people who are interested in your industry and your products. For example, if you sell health products, you may get many people who buy once from you because they are looking for a quick weight loss. These are great to top off your sales every month. But to get consistent monthly customers, your primary goal will be to find the people who are interested in their health on an ongoing basis and already spend money on their health every month (such as on gym memberships, nutritional programs, vitamins, supplements, and so on). These people can be your best profit centers and most loyal customers because they're already interested in your type of products.

One of the best ways to identify people who may be interested is by listening to them. In fact, listening is one of the most helpful skills you will utilize in your business. You have to know and understand your customer in order to sell to her effectively, and the only way you can do that is to listen to her. Listening is especially important in one-on-one appointments. So ask the relevant questions, and then listen.

Don't write off the people who initially were looking for a quick fix. Instead, use the opportunity as a way to teach them about the benefits and continue to re-service them every month using my 2+2+2 follow-up method, discussed in Chapter 13.

Finding the right service to introduce your product

Earlier, I mentioned the benefits of offering personal shopping experiences as part of your one-on-one selling. For some products, it's easy to imagine a service you can offer, but others may take a little bit of creativity.

Another way to effectively sell in a one-on-one situation is to charge for your service or consultation. You could offer to come in for a fee and help update someone's kitchen, pantry, closet, make-up bag, and so on.

Spend a bit of time brainstorming about the ways people use your products and the challenges they may have associated with similar types of products. Here are some examples or ways you can introduce your produce:

- ✔ **Cosmetics:** Offer makeovers, or even "makeunders," where you share how she can look her best in five minutes. This could be a consultation where you come over to teach her new make-up tricks or even assess her current make-up bag and recommend products that would be best for her.

✔ **Jewelry:** Offer a service of visiting clients in their homes and accessorizing several outfits. If your client wasn't interested in a home party, but still had an occasion where she and friends would be attending (like a wedding, gala, and so on), you could plan to go to her house and pair jewelry to each of their dresses for that specific occasion.

✔ **Kitchenware:** Think about your average customers. They probably have at least two jumbled drawers full of kitchen tools, most of which don't get used. Offer a kitchen tool review, going through drawers and cabinets to pare down and offering tools that fill in the gaps or replace worn ones.

✔ **Organizational products:** Speaking of overflowing drawers and cabinets, those who sell storage products could offer an organization service for the kitchen, bedroom, laundry room, office, and so on.

✔ **Clothing:** Clients may prefer a private fitting. Bring over sample sizes for them to try and order the specific styles or patterns they want.

✔ **Food and beverage:** You could offer one-on-one cooking lessons, fridge or freezer overhauls, as well as freezer meals.

Bottom line, *be creative.* Figure out what service you could offer that will meet a need or priority your prospective clients have. It may be something no one ever thought of before. Remember, you can charge a flat fee for your service, and let the fee apply towards any purchases they make.

Get referrals. Always close your one-on-one selling appointment by asking *who do you know who . . .* that is, who your client knows who would appreciate your service. And of course, when you get to service one of the referred clients, be sure to send a thank-you note to your original client. You could also offer a *referral gift:* Offer a certain amount for a referral that ends in a sale, another amount for a referral that ends in a booking, and another amount for a referral that ends in a new team member joining.

When it comes to your business, it is up to you to be creative and to listen to your customers to determine exactly what service they are most interested in. Never forget, there are many ways for you to work your business other than a home party.

Chapter 13

Sustaining Growth: The Fortune Is in the Follow-Up

. . . .

In This Chapter

▶ Understanding the importance of customer follow-up and re-servicing

▶ Using the 2+2+2 method for follow-up

▶ Following up with booking leads, hosts, customers, and recruit leads

. . . .

I have found that consistent follow-up can increase a direct sales representative's income by as much as 50 percent. The more you connect with people and show interest in them, the more likely they will do business with you time and time again.

In direct sales, your consistent business activities put you in contact with *leads* — people who show interest in your offerings. You have to cultivate and develop your leads in order for your business to grow. This chapter discusses how to provide good customer service for your customers and leads:

✔ **Hosts or preferred customers** have already hosted a party for you or, in the Network Marketing model, are subscribed to your monthly product auto-ship program.

✔ **Booking leads** are those who express an interest in hosting a party.

✔ **Customer leads** may be interested in purchasing your product.

✔ **Recruit leads** say they'd like to learn more about starting a business just like yours. Recruit leads are important in all three models, but are the main focus of the Network Marketing model.

Here is a common life cycle, or progression, of contacts:

Party guest > Customer > Host or preferred customer > Recruit

To be sure, not all contacts ultimately progress through that pattern, but it is a common evolution. Implementing a solid system of following up leads to more success in maintaining your customers in the long term, generating higher sales, and having more contacts progress further into that life cycle. Some people leapfrog right over customer and host and become recruit leads. But it is far more common for people to warm up to you and your business over time.

Follow-up is the most important part of your business, but it's the part most neglected by representatives. Take advantage: When you follow up, provide great customer care, and build stronger ties to your contacts, they become your leads, and you set yourself apart from many other representatives.

Warm and Cold Markets

When you begin your direct sales business, your family and friends are naturally your first customers and/or hosts. They are considered your *warm market,* because they already know, trust, and like you. People do business with people they know, like, and trust, so it makes sense to begin marketing your products and building your business with your friendly and open warm market.

Everybody else is your *cold market.* It's easier to connect with your warm market, but occasionally people don't have much of a warm market to begin with or, as they grow their business, they find themselves needing to rely on making new "cold" contacts to expand their network. The beauty of cold contacts is that they warm up as you do more follow-up and get to know them. Once someone becomes your customer, they are part of your warm market. Excellent customer service can make them a "customer for life," and that's the way to go, because it is much easier to keep your customers than it is to continually search for new business.

Being likable and trusted

What does it take for people to like you? Well, first they need to be exposed to you and feel like you are someone they *want to know.* Take the time to get to know them, find out what their interests are, what their children's interests are, and what they enjoy most from your product line. When the items they like are on sale, call them. When items you think they might like are featured or there is a good deal, call them again. Take good notes after your conversations, so you can reference those details during future calls. As you really get to know people, they will begin to think of you as their friend — as someone they really know.

To be *likable* to the people who know you, you must show your good personality and authentically come from a place of service, not sales. When you serve, the sales will come. Specifically, you want to be known as friendly and someone who offers solutions for people's challenges. Reinforce your friendly image with little extras, such as throwing in free samples when someone places an order or sending thank-you notes for their order.

For someone to *trust* you, be someone who is reliable, who is known for doing the right thing, and who is trustworthy. You can reinforce your trustworthiness by providing superior customer service. Make sure customers receive their products in a timely fashion and answer any questions they may have. Being trustworthy in business means *following up:* calling when you said you would call, being on time, and gracefully handling product returns. When customers are unhappy with any aspect of your products or business, acknowledge them and support them by doing whatever you can to correct the situation. You'll find that when people feel you are really listening to them and hearing their concerns, they will trust you even more.

Getting referrals

When people like and trust you, have good commerce experiences with you, and feel like you're consistent, they're more open to referring their friends to you. The bar is higher with referrals than with sales: People need "more" to go that next step and recommend you to others. When people make referrals, it is their own reputation on the line. When they feel they can trust you to take care of their friends as well as you take care of them, they will be more likely to refer their friends to you.

Being someone people will want to recommend to their friends is an ongoing goal and requires consistent behavior. Referrals can be a big part of your business, so you may want to offer gifts for referrals. A gift can never replace the know-like-trust part of the equation, but it can be a nice way to thank and incentivize your best customers to continue to send others your way.

Being systematic about customer service

Later on in this chapter, you'll find my 2+2+2 system for placing follow-up calls with your customers and knowing whom to contact when. You'll read about how to schedule those calls, how to balance all your follow-up calls, so that you build a balanced business, and create other good follow-up habits (using my concept of the Power Hour, also discussed in Chapter 5).

The first step to making sure you're conducting effective, consistent, and profitable follow-up is to capture the leads as they come in. You must capture relevant contact information for calls to your previous hosts and your customer care calls through the paperwork related to your parties and your order tracking. (The Power Hour discussed in Chapter 5 is also essential for this.) With follow-up calls to your booking leads and recruit leads in particular, you need to create a habit for capturing the contact information for these leads. Many of those leads will also come from your parties, but you'll find that as you grow your business, network, and get referrals, booking and recruit leads will come to you in other ways.

For example, imagine you've just come home from your party with a booking lead — or even from grocery shopping where you met someone you now consider a booking lead. What does it mean to capture that lead? It means you immediately get that person's contact information, along with some details about the person while they're still fresh in your mind. This collection of leads is what you reference when you are making follow-up calls. Once you get home, you will want to record in a designated area.

Keep four specific file folders or notebooks to record information that you'll use for later follow-up — one for booking leads, one for recruit leads, one for current hosts, and one for customers. I used to come home from a party or my errands, go straight to my workspace, take my little slips of paper out, and right then add the details: name, where I met them, any information on what they were most interested in, anything they told me about their family, and so on. All the information I needed was right there, at my fingertips. For people who had asked me to call them later, for some reason, I'd include the details so that I'd be able to reference them when I called. Details like: "Daughter getting married in July. Call first week of August to book a party."

Chapter 5 describes a good tracking system for your calls, but one method that I've found to be successful for people, even in this high-tech age, is to just have an old-fashioned paper system, where you just have a small index card for each customer that lists what they ordered. Store that card in a card file with tabs for the months of the year. When you call the customer in February for that third check-in call, move the card to April. When April comes and you call again, move it to June, and so on. Low-tech, but reliable and simple, so you're more likely to do it. Even better, if all the details of what they've ordered are easily accessible on your computer, each data card will just have that customer's name and phone number on it. Then you can pull up the order details on the computer when you pull out the card to make the call.

Following Up with Booking Leads

Booking parties or future appointments is critical to your successful ongoing business. I call bookings *the heartbeat of your business* because without them, your business will die. And because, by monitoring them, you can track the health of your business.

You meet great potential hosts all the time, but often they don't want to commit to a date. Perhaps they don't have their calendar with them or they have another quite legitimate reason why they prefer that you contact them at a later date to schedule. People are busy these days. But if you don't make a practice of effectively capturing leads and following up as promised, you will be leaving a lot of money on the table.

To protect yourself from forgetting, to develop a reputation of being dependable, and to maximize your earning power, you must have a reliable plan for follow-up that does not rely on your memory. And you need to make regular follow-up calls, including calls to booking leads, even when you're not feeling "desperate" for bookings.

Making booking calls when your calendar feels empty or after you panic about potentially being out of bookings is a big mistake. Trying to get business when you have no business is, quite honestly, the worst time to do it. You're thinking: "I've got to get on the phone. I *need* to make some calls. I don't have anything! I'm not even going to make my numbers this month! What am I going to do?" Get on the phone like that, and the result is desperation, insecurity, nervousness, fast talking, and begging. Don't do it!

The best time to work on getting new business is when you have a lot of business, because you're fired up and confident and you're feeling good. That energy comes through the phone, and people want to work with fun, successful, exciting people. Even when you have a full calendar, you should make booking calls at least twice per week, touching base with people and making the effort to fit them into your calendar — or at least making sure you stay fresh in their minds.

Your voice will be brimming with confidence, certainty, and enthusiasm. Be sure to call with your booking lead information in front of you so that you can reference the last conversation you had and their reasons for waiting to book a party. For example, she was remodeling her kitchen, or she was moving, or her daughter was getting married. Then invite her to book the party she wanted to host when you met and you two started to get to know each other.

> You: "Hey, Brenda, I just wanted to touch base to see how your kitchen remodel was coming along?"
>
> Susan: "Its great! It's almost done!"

(Here is where you will also ask a few more questions, like how she's liking it, what colors did she do and so on, to show interest.)

> You: "The reason I'm calling is that you asked me to give you a call once the kitchen remodel was complete so we could go ahead and set a date for your party. Your friends are going to love the specials we have

going on. I have a couple of dates left for the latter half of the month. So Susan — were you thinking a weekday? Or a weekend? What would work best for you?"

Susan: "Weekend."

You: "Awesome. Let me give you the choices I have for weekends."

When you meet an interested person and they tell you that now is not a good time to book a party, but they *are* interested, pay attention and gather information about them so that when the time is right, you can call, have a personalized conversation, and help them get a party booked on your calendar.

You may hear things like, "I'd love to, I just can't right now because during hockey season, I'm at the rink early every morning with my boys for practice. There is just no way I could host a party."

That's your cue to get more information so you can plan your follow-up and fit her into your calendar later.

You: "So when is that over?"

Hockey Mom: "The last week of March and I can't wait."

You: "Well, why don't I give you a call in early April to get your party booked?"

Then find out her sons' names, write down the details about the hockey season, and when you call, reference your previous conversation, and ask how things went.

Why is such detail important? Because it shows you care and that establishes a connection. It's endearing, and they are more likely to do business with you, including booking their party when they said they would.

Following Up with Hosts

There is no greater asset in your business than these golden customers who host a party for you. If you treat them right, they will host parties again and again and will lead you to a never-ending stream of referrals. Happy hosts will recommend you to their friends and will sing your praises. There is no better ambassador for you in the marketplace than your previous hosts.

Due to their special nature, you want to provide incredible service for your hosts. Many representatives have a motto: "Hosts *Never* Pay Full Price." In addition to representing the perks a host receives from a party, this motto translates into offering special discounts, gifts with purchase, and even exclusive sales just for your previous hosts. Representatives often have special customer-appreciation events they host around the holidays and to make their previous hosts feel special, they sometimes hold a separate event just for them.

Be creative. Think of ways you can surprise and delight your previous hosts so that the message is unmistakable: *I truly value you.* Incorporate special touches that represent a level of above-and-beyond service, and you will keep these golden customers for life.

Following Up with Customers

You want to create lifelong, repeat, satisfied customers, and the best way to do that is to provide excellent customer care. What would be a one-time customer can become a repeat customer, who later becomes a host, and possibly even becomes your recruit someday. Happy customers will refer other customers to you and help you grow a more successful business.

When you master a system of providing consistent and excellent customer care that's focused on effective and well-timed customer-care calls following their orders, you will be able to get everything else you need from your business: bookings, re-orders, more sales, and recruit leads.

According to my years of focus groups and studies, shockingly few independent representatives make follow-up calls to their customers after taking their initial order. This is a shame, because it's quite likely that your customers don't order everything they want from your product offerings. If you call them periodically, these customers will invariably order additional products, in addition to re-ordering consumable products they've run out of.

So why don't more representatives make those calls? In my experience, they are afraid they will be seen as pushy. They fear that the customer will resent the call, because she's already placed a large order. That's an understandable fear, but it's unwarranted. In fact, the flip side might shock you. I've heard things like the following statements:

> "I'm put off because I go to the party and connect with the rep and never hear from her again."

> "I haven't used my product. I didn't order the right thing and needed something else, but never heard from the rep."

> "I didn't even know whether the rep was still in business."

> "I lost her number and ended up going with a lady I know from Facebook for my re-orders."

Imagine how much you could distinguish yourself and how much more business you could generate if you behaved with a level of professionalism that included showing your gratitude for each customer's business and providing excellent, ongoing customer service?

Representatives who make customer-care calls have bigger businesses, are happier and are taken more seriously.

Following Up with Recruit Leads

It's especially important to follow up with recruit leads more than once because timing is everything. Circumstances change, and you want to be checking in with people who, at one time, have expressed an interest in the business. They may not be ready today, but they may feel differently in the weeks and months to come.

Recruiting is a numbers game. On average, whether you meet them at a party or in some other way, about one in ten recruit leads will join your business at some point. To ensure that you don't miss out on great potential team members in the future, your follow-up system needs to factor in this potentially long lifecycle from recruit lead to recruit.

Hot and warm recruit leads

To maintain an accurate picture of which recruit leads are most likely to join your team in the next 30 days, you want to assign them as *hot* leads — labeled H — or *warm* leads — or W.

People who request information on the business or take a business-information packet at a party are definitely H's. Write an H next to their contact information and contact the hot lead within 24 to 48 hours. If you do not follow up with them in that timeframe, they become a lot less hot. Schedule the call so you don't forget and make sure you call them during that period, no matter what.

Here's an example of the type of thing that happens a lot and why your hot lead can appear to have had a complete change of heart. You meet a lady who seems excited about joining, and she goes home to tell her husband:

Hot Lead: "Honey, guess what? I'm going to join this company."

Husband: "Do you really have to do that right now? I thought you were taking the summer off and we'd be doing a lot of camping."

Hot Lead: "Oh, you're right. Maybe I'll wait until the kids are back in school."

You call her up 24 hours after meeting her:

You: "Hi! How are you doing? Did you get a chance to look over that packet of information?"

Hot Lead: "You know what? I did, but I was talking it over with my husband, and right now, I just think the timing is bad and that I'm going to pass."

In that instant, she has gone from H to W. It's important to engage her, acknowledge the validity of her situation, and make an agreement to follow up with her in the future so the door stays open.

You: "I completely understand. That makes sense, and I want you to start at a time when you'll really be able to give it the attention that it deserves. How would you like it if I just keep you updated on any relevant specials that come up? I'll just touch base periodically and definitely reach out in the fall. How does that sound?"

You'll find that most people you recruit will be warm leads. It's uncommon for people to just decide to join your team after one meeting with you. The vast majority of your new recruits will come as a result of your consistent and repeated follow-up.

You want to touch base with your W recruit leads about every three months. These contacts are really just temperature reads and opportunities to reconnect, deepen the relationship, and remind the lead that you're still around.

Have a simple conversation around questions like the following:

"How are you doing?"

"Just checking to see how you're doing with the products."

"Is there anything I can do for you or any additional products you may need?"

"What products might you need at the moment?"

Not every check-in like this needs to be phone call. It can even be a postcard, Facebook message, email, text, or note that lets them know you're thinking of them, want to keep in touch, or have a great special going on. If you do get her voicemail, it is completely acceptable to leave a message with the same sentiments. You may want to alternate methods of contacting them, just make sure you are making some kind of contact every three months.

Timing is crucial when following up with recruit leads because people's lives change all the time: job changes, moves, marriages, separations, new children, health changes — any number of things. You want to be ahead of that curve, because when they're ready to try something different or their needs change, you want to have recently been in contact with them so that they feel comfortable calling you. You want to be in their minds when they consider earning extra income or changing their routine by starting businesses.

Exception to the quarterly call schedule: Any time your company offers a special promotion related to getting started, you want to call all your Ws to let them know. It's a courtesy, and even if they don't join in the moment, it plants the seed for the future and reminds them that you're watching out for them.

In this call regarding the special promotion, acknowledge that you don't know whether the timing is even right for them, but you didn't want them to miss the special. Sometimes the timing of these calls will be ideal and on some of those calls the W will say something like, "I can't believe you're calling me today because, actually. . . ." Your timing is sometimes coincidentally so good, the lead feels like it was "meant to be."

About half the guests leave a party considering your job for themselves. That doesn't mean that half the people you meet will ultimately join your team. But it does mean that half wonder whether they can do it, whether you make decent money doing it, and whether they'd be good at it and make decent money themselves. That's why you stay in contact with them, because there is potential there, when the time is right.

Most people are looking for ways to make more money and for solutions to their current challenges. Your business could be a great fit for a lot of the people you meet and who see the potential, as long as you stay in touch with them.

Brrr! Cold recruit leads

Let's go back to the example of the lady whose husband wanted her to wait until summer was over before she started a business and explore a different scenario. You call her up 48 hours after you've met:

You: "Hi! Did you get a chance to look over that packet of information?"

Hot Lead: "Right now, I just think the timing is bad, and I'm just going to pass."

You: "I understand. How would you like it if I just keep you updated on any relevant specials that come up? I'll just touch base periodically. How does that sound?"

Hot Lead: "No, that's okay. If things change, I'll call you."

Now, unfortunately, this lead has moved from an H to a C — she is now a *cold* lead. You don't need to keep calling cold leads to bug them about signing up. You do keep their information among your recruit leads, but you follow up more generally about other aspects related to them being your customer. Call your C recruit leads when you have a new catalog, a great customer promotion, or even to see whether they want to host a party. But not to recruit.

Often your old recruit leads can still be a good source of business. Keep in touch with them about things other than the business opportunity. Often, once you're in front of them again, it can renew their original interest.

Removing the Guesswork: Using the 2+2+2 Method of Follow-Up

Some reps neglect to call not just because they fear being pushy, but because they're also overwhelmed with when to call, how to call, and what to say when they do call. My 2+2+2 Method solves this issue by providing a systemic approach that takes the guesswork out of when to call and what to say. When combined with the Power Hour (see Chapter 5 for more), the 2+2+2 Method will catapult your business.

2+2+2 helps increase your sales, bookings, and recruiting by ensuring that you contact your customers at predetermined intervals that are proven to be optimal times to connect with them. Some estimates attribute the 2+2+2 Method with increasing a rep's income by 50 percent!

2+2+2 stands for two days, two weeks, and two months.

2-day follow-up

The first call you make to each customer is two days after they place their order or make their purchase from you, whether that was at a party, online, in person, or by calling you.

The *only* purpose of this call is to thank the customer. That's it! You're not asking for anything. You make this call to demonstrate your gratitude. Simply, thank you:

> "Hi, Mary! This is Belinda, I just wanted to say what a pleasure it was meeting you at Sandy's house, and I wanted to thank you again for your order."

Tell her when she can expect to receive her order and make sure she knows she can call you with questions. That's all. The call takes less than a minute, and being brief is important, because you'll complete more of your calls, and she'll remember that you are respectful of her time.

The reason you want to call in two days is because through the focus groups I have conducted, I have found that things stay exciting or top of mind for about three days. After that, the interest fades. This is true of a great restaurant you ate at, a concert you attended, or a cute pair of shoes you passed on while shopping. It is also the case with the party or presentation your customer attended.

Sometimes you'll call a customer for your thank-you call two days after their purchase at a party and things will go differently. Your customer may have already been talking up your party and your products with her coworkers or friends. Maybe they asked her for a catalog. Imagine what your thank-you call sounds like in those situations?

> "I was talking to my friends and a few ladies from work asked whether I could bring in a catalog. Could you send me one?"

This is your opportunity to suggest hosting a party with you:

> "Sure, Allison, I can send you a catalog. But to be perfectly honest, your best bet would be to host a party. You already have friends who want to order, and I would much rather give you the credit for those orders instead of me just taking the orders."

You will be amazed at how often someone like this will book a party. Suddenly your two-day customer-care call has secured another booking.

Or perhaps your customer got home and realized she wished she'd ordered other items. Maybe she gushed to her husband about an item she loved but didn't get. And he said, "If you loved it, you should just have gotten it!" Imagine your thank-you call in those situations:

> "Is it too late to add onto my order? Because I wanted to go ahead and get _____."

Or they say something like this:

> "I was talking about it to my husband, and I do want to get that cookware. I thought it was too much to spend, but he said go ahead."

This is *also* your opportunity to suggest hosting a party with you:

> "Well, Mary, would you like to go ahead and book a party so that you can get that cookware half off?"

You will be amazed at how often someone who had second thoughts and wanted to add to the original order decides to accept your offer to host a party during your thank-you call two days later. Suddenly your two-day customer-care call has secured another booking for you.

Now, what I have found is only about 10 percent of your two-day calls will result in add-on orders, but about 20 percent of these types of calls will turn into parties on your calendar. It's also important to understand that it's rare for someone who has realized that they'd like to add to their order to pick up the phone and call you. They presume it's too late. Plus, people are busy and they forget. Your two-day thank-you call provides an easy opportunity for them to update their order — and you're already providing superior service to them.

People often ask me, "Do I have to make a phone call for every one of these 2+2+2 or can I text or use email?" I always answer that I prefer calling but other communication is fine. For the biggest impact, I recommend always using the phone for this first two-day call.

2-weeks later

The second call you make to each customer is two weeks after they have received their order. This call is to provide service. You still aren't going to ask for an order or a booking. You are showing up to be of service to them as one of your existing customers:

> You: "I just wanted to make sure you received your products and see if you had any questions."

> Recent Customer: "I did. Thank you!"

> You: "Are you enjoying your product?" or "How is your product working?" or "What have you noticed with your new product?" — or some other question tailored to the product she ordered.

The positive feedback you get during these calls is valuable, because you can use those stories during your presentations or when you're sharing the benefits of your products with others. Any feedback that is not so positive gives you an opportunity to shine and address any issues. This is your chance to help her correct the way she's using the product if it's not optimal, or suggest a different additional product, or help her get her money back if appropriate.

Regardless of how glowing the feedback is, ask how you can help her today and reiterate that you are available and that she should feel free to contact you with any questions going forward.

Here's the last thing you say:

> "Is there anything else I can help you with today, Carolyn?" And then: "I value you as a customer, and customer service is very important to me. From time to time, I would like to touch base with you to see if there's anything else I can do to take care of your needs. Would that be okay with you?"

That last part is crucial, because you're making a commitment to keep in touch, which will make it more likely that you will actually call. And you're getting her agreement, so you can feel good about calling to provide excellent service.

Exception: In the rare case that your customer responds to your offer to touch base periodically with something like, "Don't bother!" or "I'll call you if I need anything," consider it a great time saver for you. Just be gracious, agree, thank them, and move on. You may feel a little rejected, but that will pass, and you have just saved yourself a ton of time spent calling someone who isn't interested in hearing from you (or likely any representative).

2-months later

The third call you make to each customer doesn't have to be precisely two months after your second call, but you will want to schedule these for yourself so that you don't have anyone fall through the cracks. In Chapter 5, where I talk about the Power Hour, you learn a system that can help you stay on track for all the 2+2+2 Methods of customer care, as well as your other follow-up calls to booking and recruit leads.

You're checking in with a customer who now feels like she knows you better. This call is more of a free-form, touching-base kind of call. The topics are going to depend on what you learned when you originally met along with any details that came up in previous calls.

Again, this is why it's so important to record good notes after each time you encounter them.

The more you can engage with your customers and make them feel important the more connected to you they'll feel and the more likely they'll be to do further business with you and refer people to you. So, in this third call, you make pleasant conversation about what's going on in her life:

> You: "Well, I was calling to see if there's anything I can help you out with right now, any gift-giving items or special things I can do for you?"

You can also connect it to an upcoming celebration or event:

> "Wedding season is coming up. Is there any way I can help you with that?"

> "Mother's Day is right around the corner. Can I help you out with any of the special ladies in your life, including yourself?"

That's it. These calls don't take much more than about two minutes. The power is in having a systematic approach so that the calls are not random. You're contacting people on a regular basis and are positioned to have a stronger business and a more professional reputation.

After this third call, especially if your product line is something consumable like food, nutrition products, or skincare, you will want to stick to a check-in call just like this one every two months. If your product is something more like jewelry, clothing, or home decor, you can probably stick to a quarterly call to each customer after you've completed the initial 2+2+2 calls.

Re-Servicing: Customer Care Is Key

It's easier to get new orders, referrals, and new business from happy existing customers than constantly needing to look for new customers. It's also more gratifying and more fun.

In fact, when you have a large, satisfied customer base, including previous hosts, you also have a ready marketplace at your fingertips for when you want to increase sales for any reason. Let's say you want to increase your production in the spring, because you have a fun vacation planned in the summer and want to pay all cash for it. Or maybe your company is running a promotion, and the sales thresholds for that trip or reward are just a tad higher than what you normally average.

In both cases, if you've used the 2+2+2 Method and kept in touch with your customers, you'll be able to increase your sales by going to your current customers to re-service them. To *re-service* is to go back and take replenishment orders (in the case of nutrition, food, skincare, and so on) or to secure additional orders from an existing customer.

For best results, call the customers who are scheduled for their third call from you in the 2+2+2 Method or those who you now have on a two-month or quarterly check-in schedule. Why? Because these are your established customers, they're accustomed to hearing from you, and they're more likely to "need" something.

When you make these calls, lead with a featured product or special. Even if your company doesn't currently have a special or a featured item, you can highlight a particularly appealing item when you make these calls:

> "I wanted to call you and share our featured item this month. (Go on and talk about how exciting the product is.) I'm placing a special order for my good customers this Friday. Is there anything you need right now, or is this featured item something you would be interested in?"

This works well because you're presenting something specific, which makes it an easy yes for your valued customer. The other reason this works well is that you're reminding your customer that she can order from you at any time — not just when she attends a party or runs out of product. This awareness helps you provide even better support for your customer.

My findings show that even though you provide a website for re-ordering, 70 percent of people feel they need to attend a party or be in touch with a representative to order. Some representatives feel that when people are on auto-ship, they don't have to make these calls. But the more your customer feels valued and connected to you, the longer they are likely to stay on auto-ship.

Part IV
Building an Organization

Six Ways to Help Your Recruit with a Party

- ✔ Use your recruit's starter kit.
- ✔ Do the opening talk.
- ✔ Have the rep do the product presentation.
- ✔ Do the closing talk.
- ✔ Allow the rep to complete order checkout.
- ✔ Know the rep's schedule.

Read a free online article on promoting leaders and training your team at www.dummies.com/extras/directsales.

In this part . . .

- ✔ Recruiting new representatives to become team members
- ✔ Interviewing potential recruits
- ✔ Getting started on leading your new team
- ✔ Holding events to promote the business opportunity

Chapter 14

Attracting New Team Members: Recruiting and Sponsoring

In This Chapter

▶ Exploring the rewards of recruiting and what the opportunity could mean for others

▶ Finding recruit leads and getting people interested in the opportunity

▶ Understanding people's behavior and what that could mean for your recruiting efforts

▶ Providing excellent follow-up and customer care to leads

▶ Using social media in your recruiting

*I*f, as I have said in previous chapters, bookings are the heartbeat of your business, recruiting is its lifeline. As long as you have bookings, you can generate an income. But to generate a large income, you need recruiting. Recruiting means you are paid for the efforts of others, and from that you can create an amazing income that builds on itself month after month.

In addition to the financial rewards, there are very personal rewards that come from recruiting; the opportunity to help people achieve their goals and dreams and have a better lifestyle, and to know that you have helped contribute to someone else's success is extremely rewarding. Bringing new people into your group brings a level of excitement to your business as well; each new person is on a new journey with the hope of making his or her life better.

Of all of the areas of your business, recruiting is the one that truly requires the right attitude. It's also the area where I see many people struggle the hardest. I hear people all the time say, "I'm just not a recruiter. It's really not for me. I'll just focus on my personal business." When you change your attitude to one that is confident, passionate, and positive, it's like a switch has been turned on. Many people actually refer to it as a light bulb going off. Then suddenly recruiting becomes easy and exciting.

As I see it, there are basically three parts of recruiting:

- ✔ The basic rules
- ✔ The why
- ✔ The how

This chapter covers all three.

The Rewards of Recruiting

Many people have issues with recruiting because the focus is on them. This is understandable because you are told that you need to recruit in order to advance in the company's career plan, or to earn a travel incentive trip, or to qualify for additional cash bonuses. It is usually a part of your company's Fast Start program. In fact, I hear a lot of things like, "You only need to get one more and you'll be promoted" or, "If you recruit someone this month you can earn this rolling tote bag with the company logo on it."

We are always talking about what *you, the rep,* need to get. But those who are good at recruiting aren't thinking about what they want to get; it's all about what they can give. It's in our nature to want to nurture others, help others, and do something nice for someone. And that's what recruiting *really* is all about — what you have to give to others. You have the amazing privilege — not just opportunity, but privilege — to change the course of someone else's life. You may think that's an exaggeration, but it's true. Whether it is on a small scale or a large scale, people's lives can truly be impacted by this business, and you get to play a part in that.

That's when the light bulb goes on for most people. For many families, an extra $600 a month could make an impact on a household budget. Anyone who comes into this business and puts forth an effort can earn an extra income every month. People have challenges. Sometimes it comes on suddenly, like a car breaks down. Or maybe it is a special camp or sport that your children want to participate in. It could be home repairs that need immediate attention, or medical bills that need to be taken care of.

That's how I like to think of recruiting — as solutions for people's challenges. When you start to really think of it this way, you will suddenly have an attitude change and you will be excited about sharing this amazing opportunity with others.

I once spoke at a scrapbooking conference. A lot of people do this business as a hobby because they enjoy it and it allows them to get their products at a discount. It also allows them to share this fun hobby with a group of like-minded individuals. But of course, I gave my normal recruiting speech that I always do at conferences to help them see a different side of the business.

About seven weeks later I was doing a seminar in another city, when a woman came up to me and said the following:

> "I saw you speak at our conference a few weeks ago, and I wanted to share this with you: I had never really wanted to recruit anyone — in fact, I told my leader I'm not interested in doing this as a business. This is just my fun hobby. It's my therapy and I'm not interested in anything else. I don't plan on recruiting.

> "I have been in the business for nearly four years and have recruited two people, and that was by accident. They just asked me if they could join. I never talked about recruiting at any of my workshops. But when I heard you talk at our conference, I realized how incredibly selfish I had been. What if another woman needed an awesome hobby, or therapy? I just changed up a bit of what I said at my workshops, and I have sponsored nine people since I saw you seven weeks ago!"

That's what can happen when you suddenly change your attitude. She was now coming at it from her heart instead of her head. The funny thing was, she said to me, "Now I think I may want to do this as a business."

I think we are afraid to admit that we want something for ourselves, but when we are doing something for others we generally end up benefitting in the end. That is coming from a place of giving.

Sometimes new people come into this business and recruit straight out of the gate. They are very happy with what they have found and can't wait to tell everyone. Others are hesitant and felt like they need to know everything before they start. Often a simple approach, honesty combined with enthusiasm, will attract someone.

I would like to share my story with you because it has several learning points. I started playing the drums at the age of 10 and worked very hard throughout my school years to be the best drummer I could be. I was quite accomplished with all the school programs and lessons I'd participated in and began playing in clubs at a fairly young age.

All I really wanted to be in life was a rock star, and I was very serious. I *was going* to be a rock star. That's all there was to it, and I didn't need to do anything else. So, at the age of 18, after graduating from high school, I was in a band and I was sure I was going to make it to the top.

Meanwhile, I worked at a doctor's office as a receptionist in order to appease my mother, which meant I had to get up at 7 a.m., which is not my favorite time of the day. One day at work, a patient approached me and said, "I'm just getting started in my new crystal business, and I need six parties. You seem like you're fun and bubbly! You would make a good hostess. Would you host a party for me?" And I said, "Okay, sure." She didn't make a big, long pitch asking me to have a party. It was very simple: *I need help, and I think you're my gal.*

Then I thought, *I'm an 18-year-old rock-and-roll drummer. What do I need crystal for?* But I did the party to help her. Remember, she was a brand-spanking new representative. She said, "If you want your party to be really good, you need to have five orders before I get there." So I said, "Okay." I went out and showed the catalog to anybody who wasn't coming and then I invited all my mother's friends as well. This was in 1979 when the party average was about $200. I had a $600 party! She said, "Wow, you're way better at this than I am. You should just do it." That was her entire recruiting campaign.

I said, "Okay," because I was thinking in my 18-year-old brain, *If I do two parties a week, and I'm playing in the band three nights a week, I will never have to wake up early.* Avoiding mornings was the whole reason I joined.

I tell that story because one of the things I hear from people is that they don't know enough information to recruit.

The simple, easy approach works just as well as trying to explain every aspect of the business to a potential recruit.

Initially, I worked the business for about 18 months. I did my shows, and I made money. I made more money than I could have made anywhere else. Back then, the minimum wage was $2.35, and it went up to a whopping $2.65 right after I started. Needless to say, making $75–$100 for a couple hours worth of work was extremely exciting.

In the meantime, the band I was playing in started taking off, and we were playing five to six nights a week. I began travelling, and it was a very exciting time. It seemed that there was less time for my sales business, so I all but quit having parties. Over the next several years I also got married and had a baby girl. Life had suddenly changed.

Here I am with this precious little baby, and suddenly it didn't feel so glamorous to be at the bar until 4 in the morning and wake up at 6 to feed her. At that point I thought, *I don't think this is the life I need, so what can I do? What am I good at? I was pretty good at that direct sales thing. I'm going to go back. I'm going to call my leader and get re-started.*

At this point I became fully engaged in the business and got very serious about it. We needed that income as part of our household budget. We were new homeowners and our new house suddenly needed a new roof and a new well. I was doing about four parties a week on average to make enough money to pay for all of that. I started recruiting consistently, but more importantly, I showed my *recruits* how to recruit and helped them bring *others* into the business. This is what helped me start to grow a large organization. By the age of 29, I was making a consistent six-figure income and was at the highest leadership level of my company's career plan. My husband and I were now able to use that income on the extras outside of our household budget.

After many years of growing my direct sales business, I was being asked by others to teach them my methods. I decided to start my own training business, sharing my knowledge with others in the direct sales world. I've now been training and speaking on direct sales for 20 years and I'm one of the most sought-after speakers in this industry. And it all started because I wanted to sleep in.

The Rules of Recruiting

This section talks about the four basic strategies, or as I like to call them, the rules of recruiting:

- ✔ Always invite.
- ✔ Never prejudge.
- ✔ Always do the recruiting talk no matter what.
- ✔ Look for leads instead of recruits.

Always invite

With bookings, you *ask*. With recruiting, you *invite*. When you ask someone something, they generally feel like they have to give an answer. With hosting a party or buying a product, it's not a difficult decision. But choosing to try a new job or invest money requires some consideration, and many people just won't be ready to give you an answer. That's why you invite. You invite people to take a look. With this approach, you're not asking for a commitment or decision but rather seeing whether they are interested.

I like to think of this as creating a safe zone for people to be interested without making a decision. I find that about half the people at parties leave with a level of interest. Half won't usually join, but they leave thinking,

I wonder if I could do this. Would my friends support me? Would I be good at it? Could I really make good money? Your objective is to identify the leads so you can give them information and follow up with them. That also helps you get over that fear of rejection.

You want to use soft word choices, not hard word choices. Soft words would be ones like the following:

> "So if you would like to take a look, please let me know."

> "If you would just like some information to take home with you, I'll be happy to send it with you."

> "If you would like to find out more of what we are all about, let me know."

> "If you would like take a closer look at what the company has to offer, I can explain it to you."

Hard word choices would go more like this:

> "If you would like to join my company, let me know."

> "If you would like to get started with this ground floor opportunity . . ."

> "If you would like to be a part of my team . . ."

> "If you would like to take advantage of this great kit sale, let me know."

This approach sounds too final, and most won't in that moment decide to join, and therefore will never even let you know they are the least bit interested.

Never prejudge

As much as I will say this, everyone does it. It's human nature. But try as much as you can to avoid falling into this trap. The best way to do this is by inviting everyone.

You can't stand in front of a room or meet someone for the first time and determine how much they have in their bank account or know whether they need a more flexible schedule or whether they're never recognized or appreciated for what they do. You just can't. You can't look at someone and determine whether they would be a good fit or would do a good job.

So often people say to themselves, "Oh, they don't need the money," or, "They just don't have the time," or, "They wouldn't want to do something like this."

A lady once said the following to me:

> "You know, I'm a doctor's wife, and I've worked in my husband's office for 22 years as a receptionist. We live in a very nice area. It's a rural area, but our house is likely considered one of the nicer homes in the whole little town. Everyone knows me as the doctor's wife.

> "I went to a ton of parties, and no one ever asked me if I would be interested in this business. No one ever talked to me about the business. They never invited me to join the business. So I just always went along until, finally, somebody shared the business opportunity with me. I joined up, and now, I'm the jewelry lady in town."

It's not about money, it's about identity.

I have another colleague who does direct sales part-time and has a PhD in chemical engineering. She works for a large pharmaceutical company. She gets paid very well and has a very prestigious job. Yet she still does direct sales. She says:

> "I generally do about three parties a month. I get so much grief about it, especially from the people in my family, mostly from my father. He can't understand. He says why do you waste your time with this? I say, because one night a week, I get to be a girl. I get to go and have fun. I don't have to think about protocols. I just get to go help people dress up, and it's fun."

I have another colleague who said for years she would go to parties and was always intrigued by direct sales. She truly wanted to make a better life for herself and her two boys. But she said no one ever asked her. They would always walk up to the person sitting next to her and say, "Oh, you would be perfect at this." It always made her feel like no one thought she would be any good. She did eventually join a company on her own and went on to become one of the top leaders there. She says she invites everyone because she wouldn't want anyone to feel the way she did.

People have all kinds of different needs. You can't afford to prejudge.

Always do the recruiting talk no matter what

When I first joined this business, I had a kind of hard-edged leader. These were her words to me, in training:

> "You do the recruiting talk no matter what! You don't ever leave it out! You keep it short, sweet, and simple, but do not ever leave it out! You never know who needs what you have to give!"

I was scared to death. But every single time I would be at a party and I would think, "No one here looks like they're interested," I would hear her in my head, "Do the recruiting talk, no matter what!" Then I would do it.

A recruiting talk takes all of 90 seconds. Ninety seconds to invite people to join you, to take a look at what your business has to offer, and to say, "What could an extra $600 to $800 do for you and your family at the end of the month?"

Yet you look out into the audience, and maybe somebody's sitting there, and she looks bored. Maybe she's looked at her watch three times. Maybe she's got her arms crossed and she has kind of like a scowl on her face, and you think, "Oh, I'm wasting time. She isn't going to want to hear about this, so I'm just going to skip it."

For the people who aren't interested, it is going to go in one ear and out the other. By the time they pull out of the driveway, they won't even remember your name. Why put so much concern in these people? What about the young mom sitting there whose little boy just came home from school saying, "Mommy, all the kids at school are going to baseball camp! I want to go!" When you say, "What could an extra $600 to $800 do for you and your family at the end of the month, working one night a week?" she thinks, *That's how I could afford the baseball camp.*

In 90 seconds, you changed the dynamic of that family, even if it's for one summer. Who are you more concerned with? The person who won't remember your name or the lives you're going to change?

My friend Carol has a big circle of friends, so she's invited to a lot of different parties. She has said to me, when they don't do the recruiting talk, "I wonder, wow, she must not think any of us would be any good." Have you ever stopped and looked at recruiting that way?

Look for leads instead of recruits

Mastering this concept is an art. It means changing your mindset, and when you do, you open your eyes to countless opportunities for recruiting. Looking for leads will help you get past the fear of rejection as well as recruit multiple people. Recruiting is a numbers game, and as much as I'm not a fan of the saying *some will, some won't, so what, who's next* — there is some truth in it. I suggest just taking a slightly different attitude.

You're only looking for leads. Your primary job in the area of recruiting is creating the interest. The more interest you create, the more leads you will get. The more leads that you get, the more people who will sign.

You're not looking for "the one" and definitely not "perfect one." I hear so often, "I wish I could find someone just like me" or, "I'm trying to find my next go-getter." You probably won't. If you do, it will take a long time. In the meantime, you miss out on a lot of people with great potential who are simply interested.

Your goal is to give out two to three information packets at each party or event. (More if you are at a trade show.) Now, will you be able to do this every time? Probably not. But if you set the expectation and go prepared, you will have a greater chance.

Let's look at the numbers. If you did two parties a week and gave out two to three information packets at each one, that's 16–24 packets. Statistically, one out of about seven will join, so you're looking at two, even three recruits a month as you become more experienced. Even if you only did one party a week, that is 8–12 packets, meaning you're still likely to sign one person a month. Anyone can have a healthy growing business recruiting one person a month — especially if you teach each one of your new people to do the same.

First, make the packets and then take them with you. I can't tell you how many parties I've been to where the rep has nothing with her and says, "Oh, I'll send it to you." In today's busy technology world, the customer will move on to someone else. You should also have a *digital packet* with online versions of your recruiting information ready on your computer if anyone inquires online or if you don't have physical packets.

 People always ask what should be in a packet. Keep it simple. Here's what people want to know: a little about the company, what comes in the kit, what is the cost, and what kind of money can you make. Don't overwhelm people with the whole compensation plan — unless they ask, which may indicate that they have previous direct sales experience.

Always take six packets with you to a party and always have one to two in your car. I have found that the more you give out, the more you're likely to give out. This sounds funny, but a lot of people want the information but are too afraid to ask for it. When they see you giving out the packets without harassment, they are likely to ask for one also.

The "Why" of Recruiting: What's in It for Them

There are five key benefits to this business, or five things that attract people to this business. I like to think of them as gifts. Thinking about it this way makes it easier to talk about. It's fun to give a gift away. Every single person who comes to your show or party, or even those you come into contact with, is in need of at least one if not all five benefits:

- ✔ Financial freedom or income
- ✔ Flexibility of time
- ✔ Friendships
- ✔ Recognition
- ✔ Personal growth and self-esteem

Even when you are in conversations or planting seeds, keep these five benefits in mind. If you put a cover letter in your packets, these are the things you should be mentioning.

Remember that even with friends, or people you have talked to in the past, lives can change and suddenly they have a need or challenge. For the most part, everyone's life shifts or changes about every six months. Always refer to the five benefits in conversations. This section goes through them one by one in detail.

Financial freedom or income

Eighty percent of people join for the extra income or money. Don't be afraid to talk about the income. Financial freedom is different for every single person. It may be getting out of credit card debt, extracurricular activities for your children, or private schooling. It may be living in a dream home or fixing up an old beloved home. It may mean being able to go on a special vacation with your family, paying into a college fund that you're desperately behind on, or building a retirement fund.

For every single person, financial freedom means something different. This is why you can't prejudge.

Flexibility of time

If people don't need money, they need time. Most people would love to be able to spend more time with the people they love. As a matter of fact, if you ask people what they consider a better quality of life, most say something like, "To make good money and be able to spend it with the people I care about." You can offer that by letting them choose the hours they want to work, by allowing them to work a minimal amount of hours, and by enabling them to be able to make the income they desire.

Flexibility of time affects many different types of people. The rest of this section describes some of these people.

The full-time worker

This is the largest group. Often we think they don't need the money or have enough time. Right now, about 90 percent of people who work in direct sales also work another job. People in this category are drawn to it because they may be on a set salary with no opportunity for raises or bonuses. Their income may take care of their household bills, but they don't have enough money for the extras. Direct sales allows them to generate the income for whatever goal or project they have.

Many people work on a sales, or commission, basis, and their bonus structures have been taken away. They think, *I'm working here, but I need to make extra money.* Are they going to go work in a department store making $8 an hour, so they spend four more hours away from their family for $32? They know that's not worth it. With direct sales, they can go out and spend a couple hours working and make a couple hundred dollars.

For some full-time workers, direct sales is just an outlet, to do something different. A long-time accountant might say, "I've got a pension coming. I've got retirement coming. I've got my health benefits. I'm not leaving, but I'm tired of doing the same thing."

Direct sales allows them to try something different, have a little bit of fun, and meet a different group of people. This represents huge flexibility of time, to make the maximum amount of money spending the minimum amount of time.

The stay-at-home mom

This business has always worked for the stay-at-home mom. It allows them to be with their children, save on daycare, and still help contribute to household income. They want to be able to do things like volunteer at their children's school, or be there when their children are sick.

Many women aren't ready to return to work right after they've had a baby. But they're getting up at 5:30 in the morning to get themselves ready for work. Then they get their kids up and take them to daycare. They drive to work, spend eight or nine hours there, pick their children up from daycare, drive home in rush hour traffic to get home by 6 or 7, make dinner, and spend all of 45 minutes with their precious babies before crashing into bed, so they can get up at 5:30 the next morning and repeat the same miserable thing all over again. All while they're giving 75 percent of their income to daycare. They think, *There has to be a better way than this.* You have the answer for them.

The college student

Not all college students are going to be great at this, but every once in a while you get a little gem. They make direct sales work for them because even doing two parties a month, they can make more money than most of their friends can working at a cafeteria or in a bar, staying up until midnight. I know plenty of college students who have helped support themselves in college doing this. It's not the biggest group of people, but it's a group you shouldn't forget about.

The retiree

Retirees are looking for a way to add that extra stream of income as well. Maybe they worked at the post office, maybe they were a teacher for 35 years, and they're not ready to just sit at home doing nothing. Direct sales allows them to meet new people and create a stream of income, choosing the times when they want to work.

Once, when I was in my late 20s, I was conducting a party. A 68-year-old retired lady approached me and said, "I think I could do this. This would be perfect for me." I said, "Great!" So she came on board and she ended up averaging two parties a week.

When it was time to go to conference, I said, "I want you to come to convention with us." She said, "I'm not going to go to that convention. You girls go. You all have fun, go dancing and all of your crazy things. I'm just going to stay home."

I said, "Oh, no. It will be so much fun." I knew that she had earned a diamond ring and that she was going to be receiving it at the conference. I said, "I really want you to go." So she went.

I always had a post-convention meeting the Monday after each convention weekend. At the meeting, I would cover some of the highlights of conference and talk about where the next travel incentive trip would be. I would also ask what they enjoyed, what they received, and what they learned. This made for a really great set of testimonials for the guests I invited. These testimonials allowed us to do additional recruiting at the meeting.

It was my retired friend's turn to do a testimonial of what the convention meant to her. She stood up and said, "Four years ago, I lost my very best friend, my husband. He was always so wonderful to me, buying me flowers and jewelry. When he died, I never thought I would ever get a diamond ring again. When I walked across that stage and received this diamond ring, I couldn't believe it."

That would have never been anything I would have ever suspected about why she would want to be in this business, or the effect it would have on her. We don't always know the effect of what this business has on people's lives. And of course, there wasn't a dry eye in the house.

Friendships

One of the great benefits of this industry is the wonderful friendships and relationships you will develop. It's fun to do this business with people you have a lot in common with. Some people will join simply to have a new group of friends to be around.

If you work a full-time job, you're lucky if you really have one true friend at that workplace. In direct sales, you're surrounded by like-minded, positive people who want you to succeed. They want to offer ideas, support, and encouragement. You may even find that the people on your team and within the company are more supportive than your own friends and family. And unlike many other industries, where coworkers may be hesitant to help you because you may get the promotion they want, in direct sales, everyone can move ahead at whatever pace they choose.

The friendships in direct sales are amazing, and you'll create some that last a lifetime. I know I have.

Recognition

When people are asked what they value most in a job, the number one answer I get is, "I just want to be recognized and appreciated for a job well done." Yet so often people aren't appreciated and aren't given any recognition.

The corporate world's idea of recognition is, "Gee, Tammy, you've done such an awesome job that we're going to give you more work. We can't pay you more, but keep it up." In direct sales, recognition is everywhere. You have people congratulating you on your Facebook group page. You earn additional products through your Fast Start program. You can earn jewelry rewards or iPads based on your efforts, and you can earn an all-expense paid vacation to destinations all over the world — simply for doing your job. You can potentially earn all of this, in addition to the income. Plus it feels really good. So many people tell me they didn't come in for the recognition but they love it.

Personal growth and self-esteem

This isn't the gift that people are necessarily always looking for, but I can promise you it is the one benefit that every single person in direct sales walks away with.

I've watched people who couldn't speak in front of a group suddenly be able to and also feel like they are able to take on other added responsibilities. People's lives change when their confidence grows. I've seen relationships change. I've seen people transform in how they carry themselves and feel about themselves. I've had people tell me they were promoted at their day job simply because of the new confidence they have gained.

One evening at one of my crystal parties, a young girl walked up to my table. She had holes in her jeans and a sweatshirt hanging off her shoulders. She said, "I just got my own apartment and I'm living on my own for the first time. I have a full-time job with UPS, but I don't know if I'm really making enough money to support myself. Do you honestly think I can earn an extra $400 a month?"

I said, "Absolutely. If you did one party a week, you would be able to make $400 a month without any problem at all." So she came onboard and she was what I call a great steady eddy. She did her one party a week and started to make money. Then she started coming to the monthly meetings and began to make friends. She ended up renting a house with one of the other women in our organization.

Four years later, she came to me and said, "I am moving. I'm getting married and I'm moving out west and I just wanted to let you know that I'm quitting." I said, "Oh, gosh, you don't have to quit. That's the awesome thing about this. You can take it with you."

She said, "I know, but I just want to dedicate this time to my new husband. Once I get out there and get to know some people, maybe I'll restart." I said, "Well, the door is always open and I'll be happy to help you in any way that I can." She said, "I don't think you understand what you've already done for me. When I met you, I had been in foster care for my entire life, and basically at 18 years old, they throw you out the door with $250. You have given me the one thing that I never really had, and that's family. You have also given me more self-confidence than any foster family that I ever lived with had." The reward for me, knowing that I had made such an impact, was worth more than any money I would earn from working with her.

That is what you can't see when you prejudge someone. Is your heart wide open? The why of recruiting comes from your heart.

Getting People Interested

Science tells us that people need to hear something roughly five times before it really sinks in. When it comes to recruiting, people tend to do the all-or-nothing approach — nothing meaning looking around the room and determining that no one is interested, and all meaning telling their entire life story at one time, usually at the beginning of the party.

Make sure you mention or plant seeds for recruiting at least five different times throughout each party.

I really like to get to know what people think about this business — customers, hosts, and people who attend parties. I've done many surveys that consist of two questions: "When you go to a party, do you mind if the representative does a recruiting talk?" Fifty to sixty percent say they don't mind. For the other 40–50 percent of the population, I ask, "What don't you like about the recruiting talk?"

This is the number one answer: "I don't like it when representatives tell you their whole life story."

Too many reps stand up and say something like this:

> "Hi, I'd like to tell you a little bit about myself and how I got involved with my company. I have been doing this now for five years. I was a teacher for eight years and after my third child I just really wanted to be able to stay home with my kids.

> At first, I was just doing the business part time, making a little bit of extra money and trying to supplement that income. After a year and a half, I was able to make the same money I was making as a teacher. Now I've been doing this five years and have doubled my income.

> I've been on five fabulous trips. My husband and I have been to Hawaii. We've been to Cancun. We've been on a cruise, and this past year at our national conference, I was the queen!"

That is how a lot of consultants sound. Now there are some good points in there, but too much at once is overwhelming, and people tend to tune you out. At first you may have grabbed their attention, but by the end they've stopped listening. You want people to relate to you, to think, *Oh, that's my situation* or *We have a lot in common, this could possibly work for me.*

So many companies teach you to do your "I" story, where you talk about what the business has done for you. I totally agree that you need to share your "I," but I don't believe you should start with it. You should start with a "you" story, meaning what could this business do for *you,* the people at the party. This grabs their attention and will likely result in them paying more attention throughout the party.

Planting your first seed of interest would go something this:

> "Ladies, I would like you to watch me do the party this evening. You'll see that my job is fun and it's really quite simple; and I would like to invite you to take a look at what we offer. Maybe you're looking for a way to add an extreme stream of income to your household budget. If you would like to take home some information with you this evening, I would be more than happy to send you home with a packet. On an average, we make between $150 and $200 in a night."

That's a simple way to do it. If you don't even want to talk about the money, you can simply say this:

> "Ladies, I'd like you to watch me do the party this evening. You'll find that I really enjoy my job. I find it fun, simple, and extremely rewarding. Maybe you're looking for a little extra money for the extras with your family. If any of you would like to take a look at what our business has to offer, I would be happy to send you home with an information packet this evening."

If you want to get a little more detailed, it could sound more like the following:

> "Ladies, I would like to invite you to take a look at what our business has to offer. On an average, we make between $150 and $200 in an evening, and I would like you to think about for a moment what an extra $600–$800 could do for you and your family. That could easily be a car payment or even part of a house payment. It could be an easy way to get out of credit card debt or pay for your kids' extracurricular activities. Or even a special vacation."

You don't want to say something like this:

> "If you would like to join, we give you everything you need. You just pay a small amount for your kit. We give you all the training, and a personal website. We can assist you with your very first party."

That's like *decide, decide, decide,* and *commit, commit, commit.* They don't want to decide right now. They don't want to commit right now. They don't even tell you that they're the least bit interested. Instead say, "If you would like some information, I will gladly send it home with you."

The next points of interest (numbers 2, 3, and 4) you should hit are part of your "I" story and should be sprinkled throughout the presentation. These will cover why you joined, how the business has benefitted you financially, and finally, how your business has benefitted you personally. You don't want to cover these all at once.

Again, the first should be what drew you to the business, why you joined:

> "One of the things I love about this business is . . ."

> "One of the reasons I was drawn to this . . ."

> "One reason I decided to sell this was because . . ."

> "I fell in love with the product . . ."

Then you should mention something the business has done for you financially. Something along these lines:

> "I was recently able to take my family on a trip to Disney World with the income I've earned."

> "I was able to pay off my student loans."

> "My extra income pays for my son's hockey and my daughter's dance classes."

And finally, talk about something personal the business has done for you:

> "My confidence in myself has grown tremendously."

> "I love the great friends I've made."

> "In addition to a really great income, the company also offers fabulous travel trips. My husband and I just returned from Hawaii."

Sprinkle these. Don't tell a big story about all your trips.

Toward the end, the fifth point of interest is your actual recruiting talk. It could sound something like the following:

> "Ladies, you've watched me do the party this evening. You've seen that my job is quite simple and that it's a lot of fun. Now maybe many of you are thinking, *Wow, an extra $800 a month really would be nice* or *But I've never been in sales. I've never done anything like this before. What if I don't like it once I've started?* That's what's really awesome about our company. They literally give you a chance to give it a try.

> It's a pretty minimal investment, and if you give us a month to a month and a half, do a handful of parties, you will typically have your investment paid off and start to earn an income. If any one of you would like an information packet to take home with you this evening, please let me know, and I will be more than happy to send it home with you.

> If you find that it's not for you, you can simply walk away with nothing lost. But you may find that you like it. It's a great way to make friends, earn income, and have a more flexible schedule."

If you have properly sprinkled these five points of interest, you are going to get people wanting more information.

How to Lose a Recruit Lead

Now let's talk about how you are likely to blow it. Here is a perfect example. Two ladies, Rachel and Brittany, are both interested. Brittany wants a packet, but she's not checking it off. Rachel checked *Yes, I'll take a packet.* Brittany is thinking, *Oh, I'm just going to watch and see how this goes down. I'm not going to say anything.*

You read the sheet. Rachel has checked yes and you're excited. What do you do? You run right over there and blurt out the following:

> "Oh, Rachel, I see here you wanted an information packet. You're going to love this. This company is so wonderful. I've been in this company now for three years . . . *me, me, me, I, I, I* . . . In fact, we have a special kit sale that ends soon. If you sign up now, you can take advantage of that!"

And Brittany is thinking *I'm so glad I didn't check yes.*

What should you do instead? If it were me, I'd walk over and say something like this:

> "Well, Rachel, I see here that you wanted an information packet, and I have one for you. You know, why don't you take this home and look it over, and I would love to give you a call tomorrow or the next day to see if you have any questions. How does that sound? Okay. Wonderful. Does tomorrow work for you? Awesome. I'll look forward to chatting with you then."

Walk away. As much as it kills you, walk away — and as you're walking away, what do you think might happen? Brittany now says, "Excuse me, do you have an extra packet I can take?"

This is where you planned ahead. You pull out another packet. Stay calm. Take it to Brittany and say this:

> "Brittany, just like I told Rachel, take this home and look it over, and I'd love to give you a call tomorrow or the next day. Does tomorrow work well for you, too? Okay. Wonderful. I look forward to chatting with you then."

And walk away.

Recruiting is like fishing. You've got a line. You've got bait on it. You throw it out. You get a bite. What do you do? The first thing is set the hook. It's just a little click. Then reel it in slowly. If it's a big fish, pull back, give it a little room then reel it in. If you scream, "Wow, I got a fish! I got a fish!" You start reeling it in quickly. What's going to happen to your fish? It's going to break the line. With recruiting, give them a little room and then follow up.

Let's talk about the three types of people who are at your party. As I said earlier, the statistics show that you have grabbed about 50 percent of your guests' attention. Only 10 percent of those people are likely to check *Yes, I want a packet.* The rest are going to sit back and watch. They don't want anybody bugging them. Interestingly enough, the people who check *Yes, I'll take a packet* are not the most likely candidates to join.

Seventy percent of that other 50 percent are ones I call *the fish.* When do the fish come out to swim? At the end, when you're packing up. This group wants a packet, but they may lack the confidence to ask for it. They want you to ask them if they would like a packet.

They even look like fish. They come over and ask you a series of questions. This group starts asking questions:

> "How long have you been doing this?"
>
> "How many nights a week do you work?"

The most common question, though, is: "Would you like some help packing up?" And what do reps say? "No, thank you. I've got a system. I've got a special way."

Wrong! What is happening here is that she is trying to get you alone and you're indicating *Go away.* Instead say, "Oh, that would be wonderful. Thank you so much. That's very kind of you to offer."

She starts helping you and asking questions:

> "How long have you been doing this?"
>
> "How many nights a week do you work?"
>
> "Can you really make good money?"
>
> "Does your husband mind you doing this?"
>
> "What did your friends think when you first got into this?"

Try to answer for her, not for yourself. You're going to say something like this:

> "Well, I try to average two a week, but you know what I love is I can do as much or as little as I want, depending on the amount of money I want to make."

After a few more questions, say to her, like it just occurred to you:

> "How would you like to take home an information packet?"

She'll say, "Oh, do you mind?" And Carol, sitting next to her, will say, "If you have an extra one, I wouldn't mind one also." You'll usually give away two more like that if people are standing around.

These are the 70 percent, and they are the most likely to sign. They're interested. They're a little bit nervous. They just need some coaching from you.

The last are the ones who have no confidence. They want you to read their minds. You'll recognize them because they'll come up to your table and will touch everything. They'll pick up absolutely everything and stare at it, and they'll stare through it, like they're not really looking at it. It's almost like they're thinking, *Could I do this? Would anybody buy this?* This is the body language you need to pay attention to.

Say someone does this. You say, "That's a pretty piece, isn't it?" And she answers, "It's all nice." When you get that answer, you know you've got to go easy with her and not bombard her right away with recruiting information. Instead, make small talk with her to make her more comfortable. You ask where she lives. You say, "Oh, my goodness, I haven't done a party in that area in a long time. I would love to get back to that area." "Really?" "Absolutely." Then continue to pack and say, "Tell me, where do you work?" "Right now I'm between jobs and I haven't really found anything I really want to do." You ask, "Is this something you have ever considered?" "Oh, I don't know."

She doesn't say yes and doesn't say no.

Then you say, "How would you like to just take a packet home? I'll put some information in there on hosting as well as our business opportunity and I'll talk to you in a couple of days, and if nothing else we could do a party. I would love to get back in that area." She says, "That sounds great."

If you pay attention to these three types of people, you are going to give out your three packets, and the more interest you create, the more leads you'll get. The more leads you get, the more people will join, and your recruiting will completely explode.

To summarize, recruiting uses three of your five senses:

✔ Speak with your mouth to create interest

✔ Listen with your ears for clues that people are interested

✔ Watch with your eyes for body language that people are trying to get your attention

If you work on these, you will begin to master recruiting.

Using Follow-up and Good Customer Care

When it comes to recruiting, there is probably nothing as important as follow-up. Chapter 13 talks a whole lot about follow-up and customer care, but it is important to mention when recruiting. It is vital to your business. Without good follow-up, it is quite possible to lose the leads that you worked so hard to get.

So many times I see people skip over this part of the recruiting process, when really it is easier than capturing the lead in the first place. If you have a lead from a party who is ready to sign, literally all you have to do is follow up and get her signed up. Whether that means helping her sign up over the phone or sending her the link to your website, it shouldn't take more than five minutes.

If you have a lead from a party who is on the fence, and you told her you would be in touch within a couple of days, don't wait a week. By then, she has already talked to someone else and signed up with a different company. Pick up the phone and call her.

If you're new to recruiting and are unsure of some of the questions she may ask, it is a good idea to call up your upline leader for some coaching. Ask if your leader wants to be on the phone as well. In fact, I encourage this with your first recruit. That way, you'll know what to say with your future leads.

Recruiting on Social Media

As you might imagine, social media is a great place to find leads. Many direct sellers run their entire businesses online, with their hosts becoming the perfect new recruits. (Don't miss Chapter 11, which has detailed coverage on using social media in direct sales.)

Facebook

Facebook (www.facebook.com) Groups for direct sales are the perfect place to meet new people, trade business secrets, plan events, and purchase products.

I am a member of several direct sales Groups on Facebook. I'm always seeing people posting questions about new direct sales companies, many of which are asking because they themselves want to join. They say, "I'm looking to start a new business. Why should I join with you?" That is the perfect opportunity for a new recruit and you didn't even do any work.

Other Groups have different theme days, such as Opportunity Wednesdays, where you are able to post about your business and how great your company is. It is a good idea to join many Groups. Each has different unique attributes and reaches many different demographics. There may even be Groups in your area where you can set up local events to help generate leads as well.

LinkedIn

LinkedIn (www.linkedin.com) is another great place for generating leads for your business. LinkedIn is a little bit of a more professional platform, where you can find people in your area and connect with business associates. What's great about LinkedIn is that you can build onto your business with just your profile. You can set up your profile with as many keywords as you'd like in order for people to find you. It is one of the best places for recruiting on the web.

YouTube

I love YouTube (www.youtube.com) for generating leads, because when I put a video out there, it's me. People can see who I am, how I present myself, and what I have to say. It's the perfect place to show your true self. Besides that, people love videos. They would much rather watch a two-minute video about you talking about your products and company than read about it.

In talking to representatives, they tell me that they generate more leads from their YouTube videos than anywhere else. Making and uploading videos is so easy, too. Most computers have webcams built in. All you have to do is turn it on, start talking, and upload. Use your tablet or smartphone as well. Use popular keywords in your YouTube video descriptions and be sure to keep your videos under three minutes.

Chapter 15

Conducting Interviews

In This Chapter

▶ Drumming up interest in the opportunity

▶ Interviewing potential recruits

As wonderful as it would be if people would come to you and ask to join your businesses, that's usually not how it happens. In fact, it hardly ever happens that way. I've done close to 3,000 parties, and this scenario has only happened to me a handful of times.

In this chapter, you'll find out how to stir interest in your prospects about joining your team, help them learn about the opportunity without intimidating them, and interview them to determine whether they would be a good fit.

When you get right down to it, there's a simple formula for adding people to your team: You create interest by creating desire for your job. You then generate leads by handing out information packets and then follow up with an interview.

To be absolutely clear, I don't mean *interview* in the sense of a traditional job interview. I mean interview in the truest sense of the word, where you discover information about your prospect, and the two of you together determine whether the opportunity is a good match.

Setting the Stage: Creating Interest

In Chapter 9 you learned how to sprinkle opportunity seeds throughout the party. *Opportunity seeds* are references to the benefits of being a representative of the direct selling company.

Always offer an opportunity packet to guests three times. First at the opening, then in your recruiting talk, and finally when you are closing the customer.

Here's an example of a recruiting talk I've done hundreds of times:

> "Ladies, you've watched me do the party this evening. You've seen that my job is quite simple and it is a lot of fun. Now, maybe many of you are thinking *Wow, an extra $800 a month really would be nice, but I've never been in sales. I've never done anything like this before. What if I get in? What if I don't like it?* What's really awesome about our company is they literally give you a chance to give it a try.
>
> "There is a small investment when you purchase the kit. And if you just come in and do a handful of parties with some friends of your own, you will likely have that investment paid and have cash in your pocket. So if any one of you would like an information packet to take home with you this evening, please let me know and I will be more than happy to send one home with you."

When you've helped guests have a great time and quickly shared the benefits of the opportunity, people will *want* an opportunity packet because it's a low-risk way to learn more.

You can also create interest online, on your social media sites (see Chapter 11 for more). Videos are a popular way to create interest because they are easy and quick to watch and share — plus they give people a really good idea of what your company is all about. People like to do product videos and "unboxing" videos (where you open your kit and show the products), upload them to YouTube, and post links to them on social media and through email.

When you offer the opportunity to a room full of guests, give very minimal information because too much information can be overwhelming. Don't share facts about the compensation plan, don't share details on incentive trips, don't talk about the various ranks of leadership the company offers, and so on. When leads hear too much information, self-doubt can creep in — doubt about whether they can hit a qualification on a compensation plan, earn a large amount of points for an incentive trip, or recruit a large number of people. Simply let guests know that this opportunity could meet a need they have right now and offer them the packet.

Asking for an Interview

Remember, this is just follow-up. Although you may be nervous about asking for the opportunity to interview her, you won't be using the word *interview*, and she likely won't even realize that she is being interviewed. She'll just think you're getting to know her. And that's exactly what you'll be doing: getting to know her so you can give her the information she needs to make an informed decision.

How to ask

As you hand the opportunity packet to a guest, even though you're very excited, you'll simply say something like this:

> "Why don't you take that home and look it over, and I would love to give you a call tomorrow or the next day to see if you have any questions. How does that sound? Okay. Wonderful. Tuesday or Thursday, which one works better for you? Thursday? Awesome. I'll look forward to chatting with you then."

When you find prospects online, you need to send them a packet as well, via email or mail. It is a good idea to follow up with these leads as soon as possible — within 12 hours.

And now your first interview is scheduled. It's really that simple!

Although it may go against every instinct you have, after confirming the interview time, *stop talking and walk away.* The reason it's important to calmly walk away is because the person sitting quietly near her has been carefully watching, wanting to know whether *she* should risk asking for the packet or whether she'll be overwhelmed with questions or a hard sell on the opportunity. By making that process low-pressure, you just proved that asking for a packet of information on the opportunity is a low-risk question.

Another common way to ask for an interview comes at the close of the party, when you are sitting with each guest individually to take orders. Part of a full-service checkout is asking, "Are you interested in learning more about the company?" If she says yes, simply use the same kind of verbiage to get her interview scheduled.

Who to ask

There's a simple answer to who to ask, and no matter how often it's said, it can't be said too often. The answer is: anyone who shows interest enough to take an opportunity packet.

It can't be said too often because it's human nature to minimize the risk of rejection. As soon as you consider sharing the opportunity with someone, your brain will immediately tell you all the reasons why they wouldn't want to enjoy the benefits of being an independent representative:

- ✔ Doesn't need the money
- ✔ Too busy as a mom/career woman/PTA president
- ✔ Doesn't really know anyone
- ✔ Would never do this business

But the truth is that it's impossible to know what is going on in someone's mind and heart. There's no way to predict what will motivate someone to consider going into this business. So it's important not to prejudge anyone.

Interviewing a Potential Recruit: Phase 1

There are two phases of the interview. The first phase is the follow-up, and in fact, your potential recruit usually won't even recognize that you're interviewing her. Which means, if all goes as planned, she will have her guard down and won't be nervous.

What to say

The first interview phase is done when you follow up with a person who accepted an information packet on becoming a consultant. This interview is conducted by phone and is really very casual.

There are just three steps to this short interview:

1. Ask whether there are any unanswered questions after reading the packet.

2. Answer those questions.

3. Ask how ready she is, on a scale from 1–10, to get started. One means *I am not ready to get started,* and 10 means *I'm ready to sign up right now.*

   For in-between numbers: For a response ranging from 2–4, ask, "What are some of your concerns?" If she replied with a 5–8, I would say, "Okay, what is holding you back and how can we get you to a ten?"

What to do about indecision

A potential recruit may be on the fence and have difficulty making a decision about the business. When that's the case, offer her the win/win option of having a "decider party." A *decider party* is simply a party she hosts, and at the end of the party, she decides whether she wants the paycheck and the host credit, or just the host credit. If she decides she wants the paycheck, then that evening she signs up as a consultant online, and you help her enter the evening's orders as her first party. If she decides not to join, she will walk away with free credit and half-priced items. A win/win for sure.

Really, this first interview phase is all about getting someone to closure, to making a decision to give the business a try.

What no really means

As a direct seller, you will hear no. And you will most likely hear it often. Get used to it. But here's something important to understand: *No* doesn't mean *I don't like you* or *You're stupid for asking me. No* means *Not right now.*

Lives change. Right now, your recruit isn't interested. The timing isn't right. Stay friendly and stay in touch, because one day circumstances may be different, and the timing may be perfect.

In my experience, you will hear yes just once for every ten times you offer the opportunity. This rate will improve to two or three in ten as you gain more experience. I tell you these numbers for two reasons. First, so you're not surprised when you don't hear yes more frequently. But also so that when you set a goal of bringing three team members aboard, you are mentally prepared that, statistically, you'll offer the opportunity about 30 times.

That's also why this first phase of the interview is just a simple phone call. It's easy to make 30 phone calls, and it doesn't require an inordinate investment of your time. If the number 30 seems overwhelming to you, remember that you won't be making these calls all at once. More like in bunches of three to six, using the Power Hour system (See Chapter 5). Unless you happen to hand out 30 opportunity packs in one week, which is absolutely *amazing* — and you'd be well on your way to quicker success than most people have ever dreamed.

Interviewing a Potential Recruit: Phase 2

Once your new recruit has signed, you should immediately schedule the second phase of the interview. Say something like this:

> "Lisa, I'm so excited that we'll be on the same team! There are a few things you'll need to know, so let's plan to get together for about 30 minutes as soon as possible. Can you meet me for coffee on Thursday evening or Saturday morning?"

Ideally, the second phase should be a place that's conveniently located and that will allow you to have a conversation with few interruptions. Being able to meet and have an interview face to face allows you to bond and cultivate a friendship. Showing her that this business is flexible will allow her to see how simple it really can be.

Ask her to please bring a calendar and a notebook to the meeting.

If she doesn't live in your area or can't meet you, doing a phone interview works as well. If the second part of the interview has to take place over the phone, email her a couple of things to prepare for it. Include a *goal sheet* (where she writes down her goals, how many days she wants to work, how much income she wants to make, and so on). And include any questions that you will ask her, including possible dates for her launch party as well as a sheet outlining her contact list.

What to say

When you arrive, smile warmly and let her know how happy you are to have her on the team.

Start by getting to know her. Ask about her and her family, where she's lived and worked, and what she enjoys. This will relax her, because everyone is comfortable telling their own stories. They know all the "right" answers to those! While she's becoming at ease, you're learning what you have in common, which creates a good feeling and engenders trust. ("My uncle is also from Syracuse!" "Reading is my favorite hobby, too!")

Next, steer the conversation to find out what her "why" is without actually asking that (possibly intimidating) question. Alternate asking questions and giving up answers. Say things like, "What drew you to this company? For me it was . . ." and, "What do you hope to gain from this experience?" These are a couple of really good questions that get you talking about the company and why she joined.

Next, you want to find out how much she wants to work, how much she wants to make, and whether the two of those things are in line. I often use a goal sheet to do this. This is a sheet that helps organize your team member's goals and consists of questions like "How many parties are you willing and able to hold each week?" and "How much money do you want to make each week?" You may find this shocking, but what often happens is that people want to make $1,000 a month, but they only want to work one day a week. Using a goal sheet can really help her key into what is reasonable for her by clearly laying out her goals and making a plan to achieve them. When you find out how much money she wants to earn, find out what she wants to do with her income — go on a trip, pay off a car loan, get rid of credit card debt? This will help you discover what her *why* really is and will help you later coach her to success.

One of the biggest reasons that people leave direct sales is because their expectations and goals don't match. You need to tell her to adjust how much she wants to earn or how much she wants to work. People leave because they never earned the $1,000 but the truth is, they never worked enough to make that income.

The beginning of training

The last part of this interview is actually the beginning of training. During this part, you'll give your new recruit simple tasks she can accomplish immediately:

- **Schedule a launch party:** Have her set a date for her very first party. Depending on the company you're with, this may be called a launch party, grand opening, or starter party, or some such. You also want to explain to them what a back-up launch is and why it's important. See Chapter 8 for a lot more on launch parties.

- **Booking lead notebook:** You'll help her begin creating her contact list, which she'll use for inviting people to her initial party. Make sure you explain why she needs to invite people from all aspects of her life and not only her friends. See Chapter 7 for more on this.

- **Business hours:** Next, have her get her calendar out. Ask whether there are any regularly scheduled family or career commitments, such as little league practice on Tuesdays. Have her make sure those days are on her calendar for the next few months. Then ask your new recruit which days she would like to have parties on and emphasize the benefits of circling those days in her calendar, explaining that by having a regular schedule, this business is much easier and more fun.

- **Company programs:** You'll also go over your company's 90-day Fast Start program, or whatever yours is called. This will usually reward three levels of accomplishment. Help her set a few goals for achieving the first level — but don't overwhelm her by planning out the entire first 90 days of her business.

- **Bringing a friend:** Finally — and this is one of the most important things you need to do — talk to her about a friend who she thinks would enjoy the business too. Explain to her that convincing a friend to join not only helps with earning the rewards of the 90-day starter program, it also makes the business fun. Having a friend join gives her someone she can bounce ideas off of, go to parties and share experiences with, and celebrate achievements together.

That's it! That's the entire second phase of the interview.

The best part about this meeting is that you've begun building a relationship that includes personal trust and professional respect. The second best thing is that using this system makes the interview and the new relationship easy.

Going to your recruit's launch party

One way to help get your new recruit off to a great start is by attending her launch party. By doing this, you can help her through the presentation and with the opening and the closing. She can focus on the products and gaining confidence for her upcoming parties, while you focus on helping her get future parties booked and recruiting interviews scheduled.

If it is logistically not possible, you can video-conference (using Skype or FaceTime, for example) or offer to be on call to answer any questions that arise during the party. Be sure to call your new recruit before to offer encouragement and afterwards to congratulate her.

For detailed coverage on working with a new team member, see Chapter 16.

Chapter 16

Sponsoring New Recruits and Leading Teams

....

In This Chapter

▶ Helping new team members create healthy business habits

▶ Assisting your new recruit with a launch party

▶ Understanding what it means to be a leader

....

Sponsoring a new recruit and becoming a leader shouldn't be scary or overwhelming. It's an exciting time; you've got your first recruit! That's awesome!

Do you remember, when you joined the business, how were you trained? What types of things did your upline leader do to help you get started in your business?

A good way to ease into leadership and training is to think about how you were trained and start there. I will help you fine-tune the rest.

Often I see representatives wait to start really leading their teams because, they say, "My team isn't big enough" or " I don't know how to lead."

Wrong. You begin leading the minute you sign your first recruit. Your purpose as a leader is to help build confidence in your new team member, support them with their first parties, and be a friend and encourager. When your new team member gets off to a strong start, they are setting the pace for their business.

Ideally, like you, they should begin by starting their business with two launch events (parties or mixers), scheduling five additional appointments or parties on their calendar, and recruiting one new team member. Obviously, not every person who joins your team wants to be in the business full-time. Many just want to be a hobbyist. However, by having these things accomplished within the first 30 to 45 days, they are more likely to continue with a successful business.

It is important to interview new team members when they join so you can get to know them personally and find out what their goals are for themselves and for their business. See Chapter 15 for information on interviewing.

Being an encourager and establishing a relationship is an important part of building self-confidence and excitement for their new business. Instead of hours of training, it's more important to have quick, consistent contact with your new recruit.

Nowadays people want information in bite-sized chunks — they don't want numerous guides and documents to follow. In fact, when I ask individuals why they joined a direct sales company and then never did anything with it, the top answer is: "I signed and then never heard from the person who sponsored me." They feel abandoned. That's why consistent, quick communication helps people feel connected.

The next most-common answer goes like this: "There was so much information, it was overwhelming. I work full-time and have three kids and there is no way I will have time to learn everything."

This is where giving your new reps small bits of information is best. Let them know that it will take them months to get through the training in their virtual office, so it is important and completely okay to take their time, and that you (the leader) will help them with the most important things they need to know. Focus on your company's Fast Start program (or whatever your company's is called). These are designed to help new people achieve success and earn product rewards in their first three months of business.

If you help team members with these accomplishments, they'll most likely recoup the money they invested in their business starter kit and earn additional profit. They'll also achieve Fast Start program bonuses offered by most direct sales companies. Accomplishing these goals will get them established and often help catapult them to a new level in the compensation plan.

Helping new team members get off to a great start is important because a large percentage of people who purchase a business starter kit from a direct sales company never make a single sale or recruit a team member — often because they don't have anyone to guide them to success. By helping your new team member, you become the mentor who guides them.

This chapter focuses on the areas that you, the sponsor, can focus on while working with new recruits to help them create habits that will bring them success from the very beginning of their business.

First steps first: Establish a relationship, set a date for their launch, and get them familiar with the Fast Start program. Help them find a friend to join also.

Getting a New Team Member Off to a Great Start

Whether you work with a Network Marketing model, Party Plan model, or Hybrid model (see Chapter 3 for more on models), you definitely want your new recruits to take advantage of having a business grand opening, usually called a launch party (see Chapter 8 for more on launch parties).

Imagine how excited you would be if most of your new recruits had a launch party that resulted in above average sales, four to five bookings, and their very own, first team member? I've found that with a little time investment, that can often be reality. It's how I built several million-dollar teams myself, and it's how I've trained thousands of leaders to build them, too. Some of the most successful leaders I've trained produce millions of dollars a year in team sales.

I believe the very best way to get your new team members off to a great start is to help them with their first launch party. By allowing your recruits to learn from you in a party setting, they will discover how to conduct a successful party, get bookings, and secure strong recruit leads.

Obviously, if you live far apart, or if you are recruiting several people a month and you are trying to maintain your own business, helping with every launch party may be impossible. But if you're adding one to three new team members a month, helping them with their launch parties is a great use of your time and will generally result in higher sales, more bookings, and a recruit, all in their first party.

Your success at holding parties, securing bookings, and recruiting team members took practice for you to develop. Even though your new recruit has likely seen you do a presentation (if you recruited them from a previous party), she was viewing the party with a different set of eyes — either as a host or as a guest. She probably didn't have the mindset of "I'd better remember what she says — I might be doing this in a few weeks, too!"

By assisting her with the party — by doing her opening, closing, booking, and recruiting talks — you are giving your recruit the help she needs to get her business off to a great start. All you will leave for her to do will likely be the product demonstration.

Here are some tips you can use to help assist your new recruit at her launch party:

✔ **Use her starter kit:** You've probably had the opportunity to build up your kit with products from your Fast Start program, held your launch party, and so on. However, while you're training your new recruit, you want to show them that their kit is all they need to be successful.

You can, however, bring a few additional items that your new recruit would like to earn from their launch party or if there is an item in particular that her guests are interested in. But your new recruit's investment in their new starter kit should be all they need to run effective parties.

✔ **Do the opening talk.** Helping your new recruit with her party opening is very beneficial not only to her, but to her guests as well. Welcome all the guests and let them know their friend has started a new business with some really great products. Talk to the guests about how they can be helpful by booking their own parties to help their friend get off to a great start. Don't forget to mention the wonderful benefits of starting their own business. See Chapter 9 for more on opening talks.

✔ **Allow your new recruit to do the presentation.** As the new representative, she should do the "guts" of the party — the product presentation. She will want to share with her friends and family why *she* loves the products. Of course, you will be there to assist if anyone has any questions she can't answer. You will want your new recruit's passion for her business to shine through during the presentation.

✔ **Do the closing talk.** This is another part of the party that you will want to do for your new recruit. Thank the guests and let them know that everything they purchase tonight helps their friend get started with her new business. You will always want to give effective booking and recruiting talks for your new recruit — especially if she has forgotten to.

Tell the guests that if they want to join, they can grow their business together with their friend. Let them know that statistics show that people who join the business with a friend have greater chances of being successful, so if they were interested in joining, now would be the perfect time. See Chapter 9 for more on booking and recruiting talks.

✔ **Have the new representative complete the order checkout.** It's important to make sure that your new recruit goes through the checkout process with her guests. This reminds her friends that their purchases are helping their friend and not you. Of course, you will still be available to answer questions, encourage bookings, and create the desire for starting a business.

✔ **Know your recruit's schedule.** Before the launch party, discuss with your new recruit what her schedule is and what days she plans to work her business. Be sure to have a copy of her calendar with you with highlighted dates so that you can go ahead and actually get bookings dated for her.

The goal of assisting your new recruit with her launch party is:

- Help her achieve above average sales.
- Secure four to five bookings within 30 to 45 days of her new business.
- Get at least one recruit.

If you don't live in the same area or it is against your company policy, or if you find you are just too busy with your own calendar, then coach your recruit appropriately on how to do an effective launch party.

REMEMBER

Even though the launch party may not be directly income producing for you, it produces income in the long run because you are setting them up for success.

See Chapter 8 for much more on launch parties.

Incorporating Fast Start programs

Most companies have a Fast Start (or similarly named) program to assist new representatives in achieving profit and rewards quickly. Such programs are designed to help representatives build a strong foundation for their business during their first three months. As a leader, it is your job to both direct and inspire your new recruits as they work toward achieving sales and recruiting goals. As your new representatives follow simple and proven benchmarks, they'll find themselves on the road to business success.

One of your main objectives is to get all of your new recruits through their programs. It not only acts as their first achievable goal, but it also helps them earn additional product and rewards, earn commission, and build a team.

Most Fast Start programs are laid out with mini-goals to help new representatives achieve bookings, sales, and new team members quickly. Usually, the end result of completing the program is a promotion to a higher rank, sometimes with an increase in pay. It also helps establish healthy habit patterns in their new business.

Revisit the program regularly. When people are new, sometimes they miss deadline dates. Some don't even know where they are in sales because they don't know how to read their sales volume, and it is up to you, as their leader, to explain your company's compensation plan to them. Don't assume everyone will understand everything. It's a shame for people to miss out because they are just a few dollars short.

What It Means to Be a Leader

Some will join your team because they want to earn extra income or be recognized for their accomplishments. Some will join because they want to be a part of something bigger than they are. Regardless of why someone joined your team, though, they'll engage and participate more when they know that you appreciate and value them.

I've said it again and again, people usually join because of the product but they stay because of the people.

When things get tough, as they often do in sales, it's *relationships* that will power them through the challenging times. Making people feel important and showing that you care will often contribute more to their success than extensive training can.

During the first month of your direct selling business, your sponsor will most likely help lead and train those you recruit to be your team members because you'll still be mastering the skills of booking, coaching, and recruiting new team members, as well as learning how to do a product presentation.

After you master these skills, you'll begin learning qualities and characteristics of a good leader. A leader does four key things:

✔ Builds vision in others

✔ Coaches team members

✔ Mentors team members

✔ Trains team members

Setting goals and building vision in others

Building vision in others is one of the most important things you'll do as a leader. Many people don't have a vision for their lives, and even among the ones that do, very few of them set *goals,* which are the steps for achieving a life vision.

A *vision* is a big picture of what a person wants in life. Building vision in others is important because it helps them remember *why* the challenges they face are worth going through. As someone who has become a leader, you know that whether it's hearing *no,* adhering to a busy personal schedule, working with an unorganized calendar, or dealing with personal situations, there will be challenges to building a business.

When those challenges come, your new representatives need to be able to focus on the vision they're working toward, so the challenges are put in perspective. Without your help, the majority of your team members may not have a clear vision of how they want their new business to impact their lives; so when the challenges come, the challenges are what they focus on. By helping them build vision, you give them *staying power!*

Once you've helped a team member clarify her vision with plenty of details, next you'll have to help her identify the goals she'll need to reach her vision. Initially, these could be things like achieving the company's Fast Start program, booking four parties a month, or bringing in two new team members.

Have your recruit share her vision with three people who will be supportive — perhaps another upline leader, a family member, a friend, or member of her team. These people will help her keep her eye on the prize (her vision) as well as hold her accountable for doing what it takes to achieve it. I've found that having team members create a Vision Board, with pictures that represent what they are working toward, is helpful.

Remember, regardless of how big the vision is, it is achieved the same way; you break it down into small steps (goals) and meet each goal until the vision is accomplished.

Becoming a trainer

I think this part is the scariest for most people. It's one of the biggest things that hold people back from recruiting: the fear of training. Many people avoid leadership within a company because of this fear.

Being a trainer to a new representative is not difficult. Some people have natural abilities in this area (this has always been my strength). But it can be taught, and you can learn how to be a good trainer. The good news is, with all the technology and multiple resources available to you, you don't have to figure out what to train — you just have to execute a good system.

Usually a company can provide nearly endless resources. You don't have to reinvent the wheel. You may have to pull the most important pieces of information and feed it to your new recruits in bite-size chunks. You may need to email them a cheat sheet, so to speak, telling them where to find the necessary information. But the *what* of training is probably already done for you.

Put together a checklist of things your recruits need to learn and where to find them. Then follow up with them. Post some of these trainings in your social media.

Here are the main things your recruits need to learn right away:

- ✔ How to get bookings
- ✔ How to bring in their first recruit
- ✔ How to host coach
- ✔ How to place an order
- ✔ Where and how to order additional business supplies

Knowing when to coach

Plenty of programs out there will let you spend thousands of dollars on becoming a "certified coach." You probably don't need those programs. This section outlines basic skills you need to coach a team member to success.

First, let's talk about what a coach does not do: *instruct and teach*. Instruction and teaching are done when you're wearing your *trainer* hat. Coaches also do not work alongside people, allowing them to gain from observing a more seasoned professional — that's *mentoring*.

In business, coaches help people determine a game plan based on the team-mate's individual desires. They then encourage, direct, and redirect toward those goals.

As a leader in direct sales, you'll wear your coach's hat most frequently during individual coaching calls to team members. Coaching calls should not be more than 30 minutes but can take as little as 10.

While coaching, one of the most important steps is to find out what the individual's personal goals are. When I first began coaching, I made the mistake of assuming that all my team members wanted what I wanted — to create a full-time income with their business — so I was encouraging them to meet goals of eight parties and two recruits a month. You can imagine how overwhelming that was for representatives who only wanted to earn a part-time income.

Ask questions and be a great listener. During an initial call with a new team member, ask what she wants to achieve with her business within five years, three years, and one year. (Asking about her long-term goals first will help her begin to think realistically about what she'll need to do to reach short-term goals.) Then ask her what that would look like for each quarter, and then for each month.

For example, she wants an income of $60,000 a year. That's $15,000 a quarter — $5,000 a month. Based on her average party, you can help her determine how many parties she needs to hold each month and how many team members she'll need to achieve that.

Once you know their goals, you'll begin coaching recruits based on what they want — representatives who want to earn $400 a month won't want a weekly or even bi-weekly call from you; touching base once a month will be sufficient.

After the goals are determined, you won't need to discuss them in depth during each call. Instead, you'll ask them how they're doing regarding their business. When they respond, ask them if they are happy with that. Your conversation might go something like this:

> "So, Katie, how are you doing with your business?"
>
> "Well, I've had three parties this month, and sales were good."
>
> "Are you happy with that?"
>
> "I'd really like to get more bookings."

Although her initial response sounded positive ". . . sales were good," by asking whether she was happy with that, you allow her to tell you exactly what she wants to be coached on, rather than assuming she's satisfied because she gave you an upbeat answer.

Once you know what they want coaching on, ask more questions:

> "Tell me, what do you say during your booking talks?" or "What booking seeds do you sprinkle throughout your parties?"

The more you ask about, the more you can pinpoint where they may need to do some tweaking.

Your coaching allows your team members the benefit of being accountable to someone — some people will actually work harder because they know they will have to "account for their ability" to you. For some people, being self-employed is difficult; knowing they will be accountable to you makes them achieve more.

Great coaches are also cheerleaders. They recognize and congratulate those who are doing well. One of the mistakes I think people make is that they tend to only coach people who need help. I hear this all the time: "I am typically one of the top sellers on our team, so I rarely hear from my leader." I also hear: "I never hear from my leader because I'm not a top achiever." You need to make each person feel they are an important part of the team so they will stay in your organization and be productive.

A coach doesn't always need to have a solution or fix problems. Sometimes people just need to be heard. If you're offering advice, always start with a compliment first — mention something they do well. Then offer advice on what they may need to improve on.

As a coach, you're a listener and an encourager. What you learn during your calls will help you direct each representative to the training they need. You'll also discover opportunities to mentor those who are interested in a closer business relationship.

Mentoring Team Members

I'm glad *mentoring* is becoming a more commonly used term, and more of a familiar relationship. That's because I've discovered that mentoring is an incredibly powerful tool and creates an incredibly effective relationship. In fact, I personally believe that no matter where you are in life, you should have a mentor and also be a mentor.

Mentoring doesn't mean "teaching" someone the ropes, nor is it simply being encouraging while redirecting efforts. Mentoring means working alongside someone, allowing them to gain from observing a more seasoned professional.

Being a good mentor requires you to be accessible and vulnerable, willing to share the mistakes you've made as well as what's worked. The goal isn't to seem like the *all-wise expert,* but rather to let them know that you have been where they are, and then show them how to get to where you are now.

One thing those I've mentored really identify with is when I share how I felt when I completely ran out of bookings. (Because who hasn't been there?) Usually, once they learn that I know exactly how they feel because I experienced that or something similar, they are pretty eager to find out what I did to change the situation. They also feel a stronger connection to me, and it makes me, as a leader, seem more relatable.

Mentoring does require an investment of time. Often, I would allow a representative I was mentoring to listen while I made calls and watch my parties. And I would watch their parties. They would drive to my home to ride with me to one of my parties, or pick me up for me to watch one of theirs. This meant we had great discussions during travel time — often discussing what to watch for, or analyzing what was said and done.

When a representative I was mentoring needed help with phone calls, I would allow her to come to my house to make them so I could overhear. After just a few calls, I could provide a tweak that would help them get better results.

You can mentor team members who don't live nearby, too, even for phone calls. Simply utilize three-way calling or video conferencing. Simple introductions so that the third party understands what is happening will make everyone more comfortable. Skype is a common video-conferencing program. It's easy to use, and most computers and tablets have the capability to run it.

Some other ways to mentor include having team members work alongside you at trade shows or sit in to observe you doing an interview.

As your relationship with those you mentor grows, you'll discover more and more joy in helping others achieve their goals. Some you mentor will grow quickly and may reach the same level in the business as you in no time. Others will take much longer. And yes, there will be some who simply decide that now isn't the right time for them to pursue the business or mentoring relationship with you.

Each of those situations has happened with those I've mentored. And because we developed our relationship through vulnerability and personal investment, we became more than team members. I'm still in touch with many of those I've mentored over the years.

You should get a mentor, too, if you don't have one. Your mentor should be someone who is where you want to be professionally. Often, it's a good idea to choose someone who is at least two levels above you.

I think you'll find that mentor relationships are some of the most rewarding you'll experience. I believe they're absolutely essential to success, and I treasure them for the richness they add to life.

Sometimes your personality may not click with others on your team. Selecting accountability partners on your team can be a great way for them to find similarities and work with a personality more like their own.

Working with Different Personalities

I've discovered that the key to succeeding in this business is not by having the most outgoing personality, but having the right attitude as well as a willingness to work to achieve your dreams. Quieter personalities can have successful direct selling businesses when they are properly trained, coached, and mentored.

There are many programs and books available that discuss working with different personalities. Some of my favorite programs are Briggs Meyers, True Colors Personality Test, and StrengthsFinder.

You don't have to be everyone's best friend — just treat everyone with respect.

Communication is an important priority of an effective leader. There are four main types of communication methods, and each can be an important part of your business. The secret is knowing when to use which method.

Electronic/Digital communication

Email and *texting* are quick and efficient, and they can be incredibly effective for use as reminders or giving quick information. Send texts and emails to your team so that they have a record of information, such as when and where a meeting is and so on.

What electronic communication simply can't do is build relationships well. The reason is obvious: It's so easy for the receiver to mistake your tone.

One thing you may want to keep in mind is that age matters when it comes to digital communication. Those in their 30s through 50s are generally more comfortable with both texting and emails. Those under 30 prefer texts, whereas those over 50 tend to prefer email or a phone call.

Facebook Groups are an excellent way to share information, recognition, and encouragement with your team. You can have one Group where you share all your information, or multiple Groups for your team for different purposes — for example, photo and marketing images, new representative training, incentives, elites, downline, and so on. You don't want to share time-sensitive information with your team on Facebook. Not everyone checks their Facebook daily or keeps up with all of their notifications. See the upcoming section "Using Team Facebook Groups" for more on this.

You should also encourage each new team member to set up a Facebook page for their business — separate from their personal page. Point them to Chapter 11.

Phone calls and video-conference calls

Phone calls and video-conference calls are great for coaching team members. Video-conferences are a wonderful way to supplement your monthly meetings, especially for those on your team who don't live nearby.

They're both effective because they allow you to share your tone of voice and allow the listener to really hear and understand what you're saying. Even if you aren't using a webcam, it's easy to know when you're smiling, because it comes through in your voice.

When using the phone or video-conferencing to coach a team member, keep the difference between coaching and training in mind: Coaches encourage and ask questions so that the team member discovers good answers. Trainers give instructions on how to do a task or activity well.

You can use weekly conference calls (whether they're on webcam or not) for sharing up-to-date information and statistics, as well as encouragement. It's fine to do some recognition during these calls, but be sure that you also do the same recognition at live meetings, too.

For your conference calls, I recommend emailing outlines for the calls ahead of time so the team can follow along. You can even have a few "fill in the blank" spots for really important ideas. This helps your team members engage in the calls, rather than be distracted by other tasks.

You can also hold opportunity calls throughout the month where your leads and your downline's leads can learn more about the business.

Snail mail

Is there anything you love more than being surprised by a card in the mail? Okay, perhaps a check in the mail is better, but we all love to get a card or handwritten note from someone special. Snail mail is a wonderful way to brighten someone's day, congratulate them on a promotion or earning an incentive, encourage them, or let them know you're thinking about them.

People tend to hang onto cards and thus be reminded of their special accomplishment. Facebook posts get buried quickly, and emails get deleted. But a card is a special extension of yourself, showing you care, that has lasting meaning. To make this easy for you, keep a little basket of cards handy so they're within reach after a conference or coaching call.

Face-to-face meetings

Whether it's one on one or as a group, there's no substitute for the energy and enthusiasm generated by a face-to-face (or F2F, as the kids say) meeting. This is absolutely the best way to build relationships and create a team spirit or culture. During these meetings you should recognize team members, share information, explain opportunities, and train people. You already know this is true: Don't you generally earn more money at a home party than a catalog or online party? People are designed to interact in a live community — even the crankiest among us are likely to share laughter and fun.

Make your meetings enjoyable. Play energetic music before starting and after finishing. Make announcements fun, and allow as many people as possible to actively participate, because communication is always best when it's interactive. I know it can be disheartening when few are attending your meetings. If you make your meetings more engaging and fun, attendance should rise. When people quit coming to meetings, in a way, they quit their business. So add some energy and fun into your meetings.

Doing meetings at a fun place such as a restaurant often creates more engagement. Also, plan some fun activities as a group that aren't necessarily business related, such as an outing to a play or musical, or shopping at a local boutique.

By building camaraderie, it helps people have a more positive feeling about their business. Often people learn more from fun side conversations than from official business meetings.

Using Team Facebook Groups

Having a team Facebook Group is a great way to build a community, share information, give recognition, and really motivate your team. Creating a Group connects your representatives from other areas and gives them the opportunity to learn from each other and share tips, tricks, and ideas.

As a leader, you will be the administrator (or Admin) of this group. If you have a very large downline, you can also assign other leaders on your team Admin status to help you manage the page.

Encourage your team members to visit the Group page rather than to simply wait to see if posts appear in their feeds. This helps ensure that they are getting the information you and the other page Admins post. Not everything ends up in a Facebook feed, and what does is ultimately up to Facebook.

Here are some easy but effective tips for running team pages:

✔ **Have multiple team pages.** If you have a large downline and a lot of information to share, sometimes it's easier to create multiple team pages. You can have a photo-sharing Group, recipe Group, one for your entire downline, elites and directors, new representatives, and so on. But don't feel overwhelmed by having more than one — you can enlist the help of some of your leaders to help manage the Groups as well.

✔ **Use your cover photo.** Be sure to monitor and frequently update your cover photo in your Groups — especially your downline page. You can post the special of the month, current incentives, reminders about conference/convention, and so on. This is a great way to showcase any important reminders for that month.

✔ **Pin posts.** In Groups, you can pin posts to the top so that people don't miss something important. These can be reminders about order deadlines for shipping and incentives, information about new programs, product spotlights, and so on.

✔ **Use the Files tab.** Create an archive for your team. Post useful files in the Files tab section of your Group for your downline to access. You can allow others to post to the Files tab as well, or you can have it only available for admins to update.

✔ **Create albums.** People love photos. Create and share albums from conference, incentive trips, meetings, parties, and so on.

✔ **Promote Events.** Create Facebook Events for your team meetings, conference, and so on. Post these in your Groups so your team members don't miss out.

Challenging Your New Recruits

The digital age we live in has created new ways to do business in direct sales. Before social media, sponsoring and recruiting happened mainly in the local area you lived in; you welcomed new team members through your parties/shows, one-on-one appointments, and events.

Social media allows us to reach more people than ever before — and in places we may have never been! Direct sellers have the opportunity to grow their organizations across their city, region, country — and yes, even world!

But with vast physical distance between us, how do you communicate with your team and help them grow to an amazing level of success? Monthly, physical meetings with your local team are still important. But for those who live farther away, you can use social media to train, motivate, and communicate with your teams. This section talks about setting up some specific goals/challenges for new recruits.

Create a Facebook Group just for your new recruits. As soon as someone joins your organization (even before they receive their kit), add her into the Group for new representative challenges.

The new representative challenges are divided up into tasks for new team members to do. You create a post for each task. Once the recruit has completed a task, encourage them to comment DONE! on the original post. This keeps your new starts engaged and accountable for their success.

Complete training guides are still important for companies to have, but quick challenges are easy to implement with your busy representatives.

Challenge: Announce your business to the world

This challenge is the first to growing your recruit's business online. The day you join, you post on your Facebook wall announcing to your friends and family that you just joined [your company]. You do not want to wait to do this because it keeps your momentum going and your level of excitement up.

Here is a great example to use, or you can create your own:

> FAMILY & FRIENDS! I am so excited to announce that I have started my very own business.
>
> When I heard about [company], I knew it was an opportunity that I could not pass up! [company] is famous for their _____. I went to a party, had an amazing time with my friends, and learned that I could make some extra money doing the same thing.
>
> You know that I would never promote anything I didn't back 100%. I LOVE the product! You're going to be seeing a lot of posts from me. If you take the time to read them, I know you will be intrigued! I am so excited to start my very own business and I would love your support. PM me to be one of my first hosts or one of my first new team members. I appreciate all of you!

Comment below with DONE!

Challenge: Explore your virtual office

Today's challenge is to get to know your office.

Learn how to place an order.

Learn how to enroll your first team member.

Familiarize yourself with the layout.

Watch any training videos or calls that are located in the virtual office.

Learn where to order business supplies.

Learn how to keep track of your monthly sales and commissions.

Having trouble? Contact your leader!

Comment below with DONE!

Challenge: Get organized

We hope you have been enjoying your business so far!

Part of doing your business, outside of parties, is to work in your "office" and set a schedule. It's absolutely vital to your business that you treat it like a business! Being organized will help you become confident and savvy. When you are confident, you are creating a great business image. This is key to additional bookings as well as sponsoring more representatives.

Be sure to set aside a space to make your office. This could be an actual office, a desk, or even the kitchen or dining room table. Whatever you choose for your workspace, make sure it is filled with the essentials. You will need a filing system, a telephone, and a board (bulletin board or dry erase/magnetic) for goal tracking. *A goal is a dream until you put it in writing!*

A calendar/date book is your intent to be successful. Make sure to keep your calendar/date book visible and filled with events. Plan your parties, office time, family time, and so on to keep you on target to your goals.

This is a FUN business. When you work a FUN business, it is very easy to spend hours on Facebook, texting and talking about your business without a lot of productivity — meaning, without making any money. Therefore, it is critical to be intentional with your time and your schedule. You can get a lot accomplished in 15-minute or 30-minute increments if you block them out and assign specific tasks to the time! Remember, always make sure your tasks are income-producing activities. Don't waste time on the things that won't grow your business!

Comment below with DONE!

Challenge: Make a graphic

Graphics and images are not only visually appealing, they work! Experts say that people are more likely to interact with your post on social media if it has a photo attached to it.

Play around with some graphic apps and start to create your very own! You can take photos, upload them, and put text and other images on top of them. Or you can create graphics right from scratch.

Play with these websites: picmonkey.com, canva.com, madewithover. com, pinwords.com. And check out these applications: WordSwag, Typic+, and Rhonna.

Note: These applications are made for beginners and non-graphic designers! They are extremely easy AND effective.

Remember to make your graphics using photos that are not copyrighted. This means that although you want to be creative, you don't want to use celebrity images or even logos from your company's business. Using copyrighted images to promote your business could result in you landing in "Facebook jail," where you aren't allowed to post any images. It's always a good idea to check your company's policies and procedures on this as well.

Comment below DONE! when you have explored a few of these.

Challenge: Your "why" story

Your why story is the most important story you will ever tell. Your why story tells people why you joined the company and what the business has done for you and your family.

For example, maybe the business has helped you pay off school debt or pay for your daughter's dance lessons or your son's hockey. Maybe it has allowed you and your family to take that much-needed vacation, save for a new car, or stay home with your kids.

If you're very new in the business, you still have a why story! Share what your goals are or what you plan to do. Something as small as the fact that the commission paid for your gas this week is worth sharing! You can also use your leader's why stories and share with your friends the amazing success they are having in the company.

Why stories help create sponsoring leads. People will become interested in your story and start to wonder if this is something they could do too. So share your why story with everyone!

Comment below with DONE! And feel free to share.

Challenge: Invite some friends

So many people believe that you need to wait to be in the business for a while to start sponsoring. That is completely untrue! There is no better time to sponsor than right at the beginning of your journey.

Studies show that people who sign up with a friend are more likely to work the business and be successful at it. Not to mention how fun it is to share the excitement of this opportunity with someone else, share ideas, and have someone to brainstorm with.

Your challenge this week is to reach out to ten friends and say, "I would love for you to do this with me!"

Here are some tips and scripting you can use:

> "Hey Mary, I just started this new business and I think it would be really fun for us to do it together!"

> or

> "I'm so excited about my new business! In fact, I've been so impressed with what the company has to offer as a business, I wondered if you've ever thought about doing something like this? I would love to share more about it. When can we get together?"

> or

> "I've started my own business and I would really value your opinion. I need the practice. Would you mind if I did a trial run with you? That way, you will also get a better understanding of what I'm up to. Actually, it is something you may want to consider."

Sponsoring is merely having a positive attitude and expectancy. You've got so much to offer — make a difference in someone's life today! Take the focus off yourself and share with others to help them with their needs. You will also benefit through personal growth, additional income, and building a team.

Comment below with DONE!

Challenge: Fortune is in the follow-up

By now, you're becoming comfortable with parties and are learning the ins and outs of your new business. You have probably also met some AMAZING people along the way! When you build relationships with your customers and team members, your success will go to a whole new level!

This week's challenge is to FOLLOW UP!

Don't forget you're in the *relationship business!* Keep a steady, positive relationship with all your customers, so that when they are out of product, they think of you!

Let's get started on the 2+2+2 Service Plan!

As soon as your party is over, set up a customer care card or file sheet with the customer's information and what they ordered.

Follow up using 2+2+2. That stands for 2 days (to thank them), 2 weeks (to see how they are enjoying their product), and 2 months (to see if they need to replenish their stock or add to their collection)!

Don't be afraid to pick up the phone. Customers will not often call you — it's up to you to build the relationship. Following up is a great investment in long-term success!

Comment below with DONE!

It's Always a Learning Process

Remember, above all else, this is a learning process, and I promise that you will make mistakes along the way. It's okay! No one expects you to know everything overnight. You will learn and grow as you go. There are a lot of people behind you willing to help, offer advice, and share what they have learned along the way. You have multiple resources, both within your company and outside it. There's an app for almost everything — check out Chapter 22 for more. Stay positive, be honest, and sincere. Be an encourager. You will gain respect from your team members and together you will navigate through this amazing industry.

Chapter 17

Group Recruiting: Holding Opportunity Events

In This Chapter

▶ Knowing best practices for different types of opportunity events

▶ Recruiting in a group

▶ Staging and planning events

Group recruiting requires a different approach than one-on-one recruiting does, but the great news is that it can be exponentially more effective. *Group recruiting* is when you share your company's products, profits, and programs with a group of people. Here's the exciting part: The group of people don't have to be, and actually would rarely be, all your own prospects.

You can do group recruiting at any number of different events, for your entire team to bring guests to. This means that your newest team members — those who are the most excited, the most scared, and the least knowledgeable — can bring their prospects to the event and leave with a new team member (see Chapter 16 for much more on working with new team members).

As a direct selling leader, you'll hold various kinds of events: team meetings, product launches, host-appreciation events, and take-a-looks (just to name a few). The next section talks more about these.

Encourage team members to bring a guest with them to every opportunity event, and you'll start to see your downline team growing exponentially.

One thing I discovered when I ran my team was that if I planned an "opportunity night," then team members who didn't have anyone to bring simply didn't show up. But when I included the opportunity in our regularly scheduled meetings and encouraged team members to bring a guest, we had a more exciting evening. Representatives felt confident enough to bring their leads to a meeting, and people who didn't have any leads still felt comfortable coming and participating. This meant more bodies in the room and a lot more energy. As a leader, you want your team to come to your events feeling confident about recruiting because they know that you are there to help.

Independent representatives often have a fear of recruiting when they start their businesses. They say things like, "I don't know enough yet," and, "I haven't read through the entire compensation plan, nor do I understand it enough to answer questions," and, "I'm still so new, I can't be a leader."

It's your job as a leader to make sure your new reps understand that you're there to help them every step of the way. Your new team members will feel more secure in attending opportunity events if they know that for the most part you will be doing the recruiting for them. That is, you will be doing the recruiting talk, discussing the company, and answering any questions. Remind your reps that you will continue to be with them and their new recruits every step of the way until they feel more confident in their abilities.

Creating this kind of encouraging space for your reps helps create momentum for your entire team.

Looking at the Best Types of Opportunity Events

The best types of events are where enthusiasm and excitement are built through recognizing achievements, sharing tips on how to succeed in direct sales, reinforcing individual goals and vision, and talking about the amazing benefits of this opportunity.

There are several types of opportunity events that you can hold:

- ✔ **Take-a-look:** These types of events can be done weekly, bi-weekly, or monthly in your home. *Take-a-looks* are evenings when representatives on your team can come with their potential leads to learn more about the opportunity. Take-a-looks are casual events, often held right after work. You will have a kit set up and serve light food such as pizza or vegetables and dip, cheese and crackers, salad, and so on.

  The first part of the take-a-look is the meet and greet, where people mingle and get to know each other. After they have eaten and networked, you go over the kit, talk about what direct selling means, and share the benefits of your company's business opportunity.

If you have a team spread across the country, you can also do this on the phone using a conference line. The main objective is to create a casual atmosphere where your team can bring their leads to learn more about starting a business of their own.

✔ **Team meeting:** Depending on your company culture, this may be a weekly or monthly gathering. I always encouraged everyone to bring along potential recruits. The reps would get to stand and introduce their guests, which served as recognition. Having guests at team meetings is a great way for them to see a variety of different representatives that they can relate to, see a meeting in action, and envision what it would be like to be a part of your organization.

✔ **Host-appreciation events:** These are most exciting when you make them team-wide events, inviting anyone who hosted a party for any member of your team. On the invitation and promotions, be sure to mention that there will be prizes for the top sales, best-attended party, and any other category appropriate to your company. Hosts are always your best recruiting candidates, and a room full of them is super exciting. You can use the time to honor the hosts by saying something like this:

"Thank you all so much for supporting our representatives. We certainly do value and appreciate you. Many of us started out as hosts just like you." Then go on with your regular opportunity talk.

✔ **Service seminars:** These are great to invite the general public to. They can be more than just events for team members who didn't attend the annual conference. These events can be set up as seminars where you discuss things like the latest fashion trends, how to perfect your spring cleaning, eat healthier, become a label detective, and so on. Have team members invite guests, because the value added by the information creates an exciting atmosphere for ending the presentation with a recruiting talk. This causes people to become interested in learning more about the business, and you can continue with a recruiting talk.

✔ **Product launches:** These events show off your new products. Depending on the company, there may be a couple opportunities for these, such as when your company launches a new catalog or additional seasonal products. These can be a lot of fun. Invite your past hosts and guests to preview the new products. Product launches are perfect opportunities to get new bookings, as well as turn those hosts and guests into new recruits.

Recruiting at Events

Once you establish that you will be giving recruiting talks at all your events, you'll discover that team members are likely to bring recruiting leads. Your talks boost their confidence. And because you're recruiting to help your team members succeed, you'll find that *you* become more confident when delivering your recruiting talk as well.

This dynamic lends itself to great recruiting results. I remember how I felt when I heard team members telling each other, "If you bring them, she'll get them to join!" It really was one of the highlights of my week.

Don't be concerned that these recruits won't be your "personal" or "front-line" recruits. They will help your team members, and ultimately you, build a very solid and successful business.

Explaining the business model

No matter what type of opportunity event you choose to hold, I always like to start the recruiting portion of my meeting with a brief description of the direct selling business model. Although most people would say they know what direct selling is, most don't understand how it actually works. I remember once, when I had been a representative of a company for many years and had built a very large and profitable sales organization, a friend asked my mother, "Hasn't she collected all the product she wants yet?" She didn't realize that I was making a substantial income on every sale I made — she thought I was being compensated with product alone.

So, take time to briefly explain what direct sales is. You can say something like this:

> "No matter what stage of life you're in, being in direct sales can offer you many opportunities. Whether you need some extra spending money, want to stay at home with young children, or are looking to take a well-deserved vacation, a business in direct sales can give you the income every month to help you achieve the things you want most.

> "Whatever your *why* is, this business can fit in many different areas of your life. It has provided me a wonderful journey and source of income throughout the different stages of mine."

This is a great time to ask, "How many of you have ever dreamed of owning your own business?" According to studies I have conducted over the years, approximately 80 percent of people dream of owning their own business. But fewer than one out of ten ever takes that chance.

You can then explain to the group that the reason people don't take this chance is usually two-fold: The first reason is the risk factor — risk of money and risk of time. Starting a business such as a restaurant, bakery, florist, or a gift boutique could require as much as a few hundred thousand dollars in startup costs, and you may expect very little income for the first few years. It also requires a substantial investment of time — you can go weeks without spending time with your family.

The second reason is that even though you may be passionate or good at baking or designing floral arrangements, that doesn't mean you know how to run a business, or that you necessarily want the responsibilities involved. You may not want to deal with bookkeeping, hiring and firing, inventory, shipping, operations, and so on.

You then contrast that kind of thing with direct sales. You can say something like this:

> "Direct sales is a wonderful way to try your hand at owning your own business with very low start-up costs. There is no risk involved. To join this company, for example, you just need \$___ to purchase your business starter kit, and you'll get about \$___ worth of products and business aids to start your business immediately.

> "The average party with us results in about \$___ to \$___ in sales, which will earn you on average \$___ to \$___. You'll easily pay back the cost of your kit within your first two parties. However, if you decide the business isn't for you, you haven't really lost anything. You'll have earned some income and if nothing else, you can continue to enjoy your own purchases at a discounted price. But you may discover that you love it, and this could be the beginning of a whole new, exciting journey.

> "Now the other thing that holds people back from starting their own business is having to wear all the hats. With direct selling, you get to focus on sharing your love for these great products. You don't have to worry about selections, warehouses, inventory, bookkeeping, merchant accounts, and so on. The company handles all that for you, and even provides you with your own personal website. So, you get to enjoy all the benefits of being an independent business owner, without all the risk and all of the responsibility that usually comes with it. You just get to do the fun part of the business: sharing the love of the product."

Emphasizing the five needs direct sales fulfills

Next you should address the five needs and desires that direct selling meets:

- ✔ **Financial freedom or income:** You can make *extra* income or you can make a very nice *full-time* income. You can create and choose what you want depending on how many hours you have to put into it. A lot of people do direct sales as a fun hobby, sharing the products with friends and family for some extra spending money. Others do one or two parties a week for a part-time income. And then some work on average at least two parties per week and start to build a team to make a very nice full-time income.

The amazing thing about direct sales is that you generate the income you deserve. You are in charge of your own business and get from it exactly what you put into it. You determine when you're open for business and how much money you want to make.

✔ **Flexibility of time:** Your direct sales business can work around your existing priorities and responsibilities. You can work your business at 2 p.m. or 2 a.m. — it's completely up to you. College students can schedule parties around major exams and classes. Moms can remain at home with their children and choose to work when they want to. Those with a full-time job can schedule their business around family and work commitments.

✔ **Friendships:** Another major benefit you get from starting a direct sales business are the friendships you create with other reps. With your business, you'll network and make connections with like-minded people who all share the same passion as you. Your team members will become some of your best friends as well as your biggest motivators and cheerleaders. Annual conference/convention is an amazing time to get to meet more people within your company and establish those connections.

✔ **Recognition:** Representatives are constantly rewarded by their companies with great gifts, ranging from small rewards to incentive trips that amount to fully paid vacations. Many 9–5 jobs rarely provide the recognition people deserve for their hard work, or the appreciation. Direct sales not only gives you an income you deserve and a schedule you want, it celebrates all of your achievements. And the friendships you make along the way also join in on these celebrations.

✔ **Self-esteem and personal growth:** Although very few people actually join for this reason, I rarely see anyone who doesn't experience an increase in their confidence and self-esteem through the new skill sets they learn, the recognition they receive, and the meaningful connections that they make.

Sharing the three Ps: Products, programs, and profits

There are three main things to talk about when doing group recruiting: products, programs, and profits.

Products

Who is the product marketable to and how marketable is it? Talk about whether there are any age barriers to your product or gender barriers. When representing a consumable product, you should emphasize that a representative can build her client base and continue to serve it. Personally, I love the compound effect of continuing to get new customers while servicing existing ones.

Programs

Tell the group what types of programs the company has to support you in your direct selling business. These include the Fast Start program your company probably offers, the training programs, the host program, and any regular incentive programs that occur. Other programs your company may offer include merchant accounts provided on your website that take credit cards, newsletters for you and your customers, and professional fundraising programs that allow you to simply facilitate the program and earn the commission.

Profits

Finally, you talk about money. I suggest being forthright. You can also inject a little bit of humor into a subject many people find uncomfortable. I would usually say something like this:

"So, now you're saying to yourself, 'Okay, it sounds like you've got a great product and you've got great programs, but how much money can I really make?'"

"The answer is that you can make a lot of money or you can make a little bit of money, depending on how much time and effort you're willing to give. You can make the amount of money you want!

"Our reps start out making __ percent on sales, which will typically earn you about $___ to $___ for an average party. Many of our representatives have $800 parties or $1,000 parties and end up walking away with $___ for themselves. Our best party last month generated about $____ in sales. Just imagine what you can make for just a few hours of fun with a group of friends. So, just on the basis of selling, you certainly can make a very good income.

"Then you can start to share this amazing business with your friends and I highly recommend that you do so, because it is so much more fun to have a friend along. As those people join, you make additional income. We have new leaders that are making an extra $___ in a month, just from sharing the business opportunity. And that can be you in no time.

"So, that is just a little bit about the product, the programs, and the profits. I know this was a lot of information presented very quickly. Now I want you to ask yourself, 'What do I have to lose?'

"And you know what, the answer is: *really not much.* The business starter kit costs $___, and you should earn that back within a couple of parties. You literally get to give something a try, and if it's not for you, you can simply walk away without a lot of loss. The real question is what do you have to gain? The answer is everything — a world of possibilities. The opportunity to make great friends, to present a product you already like, to call something your own, and to make an income that you never dreamed was really possible. So, the possibilities are actually limitless."

Encouraging them to make a decision

At this point, it's effective to have them make a decision. I offer three choices on a small card that I placed on their seats before the event started:

1. I'm interested in purchasing products.

2. I'd like to host a party and receive the products free.

3. I'd like to represent the products and start earning an income.

The card also has a space for their contact information, as well as the name of the person who invited them. Once they fill them out, I ask them to put them in one of three baskets that correlate to the number they circled on the card.

The basket method was very effective for me. I recommend it because it heightens excitement when you do a drawing for gifts for the three baskets. Make the gift for basket 2 worth more than basket 1, and basket 3's worth more than basket 2's. Do a drawing from baskets 1 and 2. Then, using the cards from basket 3 (starting a business), welcome each new team member up to the front of the room. You will welcome each one of the people to your company. From those, you can do a drawing from the third basket. This is great recognition for them and affirms that they are going to be starting their new business.

Planning and Staging Events

Events are part of creating excitement and motivation for a direct selling team. They don't have to be expensive, but they do need to be well thought out. Follow this checklist to execute the perfect opportunity event:

✔ Pick a location and facility to host the event in a central location for you, your team, and your attendees. It could be a banquet hall, hotel, restaurant, coffee shop, or even your home, depending on your budget and size of attendees.

✔ You and your team should invite all past leads with an invitation, an email, and a phone call. Send invitations at least two weeks before the event and invite more guests as you meet them and get closer to the date.

✔ Always ask for an RSVP and reconfirm the day before the event with a reminder call, email, or text.

✔ Promote your opportunity event at all your other events, including home parties, online parties, and one-on-one appointments.

✔ Keep a master RSVP list so you know how many guests to plan for.

✔ Have each recruiter confirm their leads' attendance with you one to two days prior to the event.

✔ Have a check-in table with a master list of attendees. You can assign someone on your team to help with this.

✔ Have a sign-in sheet that asks for name, contact information, and name of person who invited them. Use this as a follow-up sheet.

✔ Have them fill out a customer information slip in exchange for a chance at a door prize. The survey should include space for their name, contact information, and what their interests are (purchasing product, hosting a party, or starting a business).

✔ Have recruiting packets, host packets, catalogs, and any other promotional material ready to pass on to interested attendees.

✔ Have a business starter kit on display. You should also have an additional kit of all the products or if you are doing a product launch, have a section featuring the newest products.

✔ Offer light refreshments like cookies, water, coffee, fruit, and so on.

✔ Create an agenda. Go over the industry, products, profits, and programs, and so on.

✔ Present testimonials. Select some members from your team to give short one- or two-minute presentations about their success with the business. Try to have three of these planned — one from every walk of the business. Someone new, a stay-at-home mom, someone who does the business as a full-time career, a working woman, and so on. Additional testimonials could be a host who had an outstanding party and wants to share how great of an experience it was.

✔ Ask each leader who is participating in the event to bring a product for the door prizes. Confirm these ahead of time.

✔ Sell raffle tickets for door prizes donated by the leaders. This will help you cover the expenses you incurred for the meeting. (Be sure to check for municipal gambling regulations. You can typically find this information online.)

✔ Assign and delegate tasks to your team such as meet and greet, registration, people to set up displays, tear down, and so on.

✔ Make a list of materials that you may need. Assign volunteers to help collect these items: name tags, pens, music, starter kit, prizes, host packets, recruiting packets, catalogs, and so on.

You're not going to use *all* these methods every time. For smaller events, you may take a different approach than your larger events. Assess the size of your venue, the size of your team, and how many guests will be attending.

When you create a venue for people to bring their guests so that they can learn more about the business opportunity, you can start signing team members for the entire organization, helping people achieve their promotions week after week.

Part V
Operating and Maintaining a Successful Business

Top Five Uses of Networking

- ✔ Grow your reach.
- ✔ Make connections.
- ✔ Get referrals.
- ✔ Seek advice.
- ✔ Boost your profile and brand.

Check out some good advice on personal development and continuous learning in an article at www.dummies.com/extras/directsales.

In this part . . .

✔ Knowing what to do with your money

✔ Holding great meetings and communicating for success

✔ Networking online and off to grow your business

Chapter 18

Managing Your Money Wisely

In This Chapter

▶ Obtaining spousal buy-in

▶ Paying yourself

▶ Avoiding some of the dangers of success

▶ Being smart about taxes

*F*our out of five representatives say they joined or are considering joining a direct sales company to make extra money. Even if you initially joined with other things in mind, like discounted or free product, a chance to earn a free trip, or the opportunity to make new friends and have some fun, every independent representative needs to learn some basics of how to handle the money. This chapter aims to convey some important money-management tips I've discovered, especially with regard to direct sales.

Whether you're wildly successful and your direct sales business is bringing in more money than you could have ever dreamed possible, or you think you're barely turning enough profit to cover filling up the gas tank, the tax benefits alone of managing and tracking your money properly make it worth learning more about tactics and facts.

Don't worry. Managing this money, whether it seems like a trickle or a tsunami, is simpler than you think. Really. I promise!

Often I find that suddenly making extra money comes as a surprise to a lot of people, even if they are part of the 80 percent who join a direct sales company *for* the money. Especially if they start making a substantial amount of money, they find themselves not knowing what to do.

Regardless of how healthy your relationship is with money, if you're like most people, managing your money, preparing for tax time, and understanding what it means to be an independent contractor can be challenging. This chapter aims to help you navigate some of these challenges so you will be better prepared.

Please note: I am not a qualified tax expert, or financial advisor, and this chapter is not meant to be a comprehensive guide to all of your money needs. In addition, I highly recommend finding a small business accountant to at least consult with when you get started, if not to handle your taxes and advise you throughout the year. Especially if you're making substantial money, seeking out qualified individuals to support you in your financial planning and your tax preparation is important. Tax laws are ever-changing, and things can get unpleasant if you proceed on your own without comprehending income tax basics. For this reason, and many others, it is imperative that you find a professional who is up-to-date on tax law and who understands direct sales and how your business works.

That said, after 35 years in direct sales and self-employment, I have a lot of experience, have made it through struggles, and have watched many other independent representatives struggle with money challenges as well.

Getting Spousal Buy-In

One of the greatest challenges with this business is getting full support or "buy-in" from your spouse, especially for women who make up the vast majority of independent representatives.

Spouses often have a natural "show-me-the-money" attitude. When you can truly show your spouse the financial details, pay for an unexpected bill, or spring for an all-expenses-paid vacation — you will typically find that your spouse is suddenly much more ready to treat your direct sales work as a business, rather than considering it just a "fun job" you have.

It can still be a "fun," extra stream of income, if that's what means the most to you. But when you can actually document the money you have made, there will actually be more support available from your spouse, whether you're a woman or a man. I interview men all the time about their wives' businesses, and their story seems to always be the same, some version of the following:

> "When she first joined, I thought she was just looking for something fun to do to get out of the house, but then I started seeing the money and I told her with a little more effort she might really be able to do something with this. Then she started making really good money and now I just try to help her wherever I can. I never had any idea it could be what it has become."

I have heard virtually that same story repeated over and over again. Once I had a team member who joined the business with a very specific goal in mind: She wanted to redo her living room. She talked about the new furniture she was going to get, the new color scheme and paint, and even the flooring. This was her burning desire as she started her business.

I urged her to open a separate checking account and a savings account and designate them for her business only. Her husband was making a significant income, so the money from her business wasn't really needed for their day-to-day living expenses. She deposited every cent she earned into her accounts, diverting 80 percent of it immediately to savings and leaving 20 percent in the checking account to cover the expenses of her business.

In less than four months, she had saved more than $3,000 and was able to order her furniture. Impressed, her husband covered the rest of the renovations, including new floors and professional painting. What was even more fun for all three of us was that he came to me soon after to learn more about what his wife could do to really ramp up her business and earn even more money! Talk about spousal buy-in!

When you diligently manage your money, you're able to shift from a "tell them" model to a "show them" model and nothing is more impactful than demonstrating success by allowing people to see the change.

Paying Yourself and Keeping Track

It is important to keep track of your commission and expenses and learn how to manage your money wisely.

To make sure you're very clear on how much you are truly earning — and to keep your records taxman-approved — you need to keep your money separate. Accountants will advise you not to "co-mingle" your funds. That means keeping completely separate accounts where all the money related to your business is kept completely separate from any of your personal income or expenses.

All the money you receive connected to your business gets put in the separate checking account you use for your business. That means *every* check and *all* the cash from your customers, as well as your commissions check from your company, is deposited into that business account. Then *all* expenses related to your business get paid out of that account, by check or with a linked debit card. If you need more money available for day-to-day expenses with your business, either open a new credit card account or designate one of your existing credit cards as your "business" credit card and use it *only* for business expenses. Pay the bill for that card using the checking account you use for your business.

Some companies issue commissions to a pre-paid debit card. Again, only use that card for business expenses. Transfer money periodically from that company-hosted debit card account to the checking account you're using for your business. It is common for people to lose track of how much they're earning when their commissions are on a debit card they're just using for expenses, especially if they're using that card for personal expenses as well. (Which, as mentioned, is a bad idea! Keep business business and personal personal.)

You may be wondering: then how do I get the money to spend for things other than my business? The easiest and most organized way is to write yourself a "paycheck" from the account you use for business. You can decide what you want your "pay" to be and write yourself a check for a set amount, such as $500 per week or $1,000 every two weeks.

Another method is to write yourself a check only when the money hits a certain threshold, for example, write yourself an $800 check (or transfer money to yourself) every time the balance reaches $1000. This way, when your business expenses are higher or your income from your business is lower, you're only taking out money that is actually available profit.

The benefit of these two methods is that you can track how much you're truly earning, after expenses, by tallying up how much you've written yourself in checks each month, each quarter, or each year.

Keep a cushion in your account for unexpected business expenses. A good rule of thumb, once you get a feel for how much you're making each month, is to keep a balance in your checking account equal to or higher than 20 percent of what you earned last month. This balance minimum is after typical ongoing expenses are paid and after you've paid yourself. This may sometimes mean paying yourself less than usual to keep a healthy balance in the checking account you use for your business.

Watch Out for Overnight Success

Another real danger I have seen over the years is that people suddenly start making a substantial income and don't know how to manage it.

If that happens, get a financial advisor, pronto!

Some people are so overcome with the results of building a large team that they don't understand that direct sales is a peaks-and-valleys business. The income they are generating today may not be the same a year or so down the road. They increase their cost of living to match their spike in income and then don't plan appropriately or save accordingly.

I married young, and we had two small children. My direct selling income was not extra — it paid our bills! If I wanted to stay home with the kids, I had to make a certain amount. We struggled month to month just to pay our bills and put some into savings. By 29, I was earning on average $10,000 a month. This was in the late 1980s, early 1990s, and was very good money for that time. It still is a substantial income for most people.

When I started making those big paychecks, it was exciting! I got a new car, and we were finally able to get a boat (we were living on a lake). Rather than asking myself whether we could afford these things, I only asked myself, "Can we afford these payments?" Of course, with that income, at that moment, the answer was, "Yes!"

My income stayed at $8,000 to $10,000 a month for quite a while, and I slipped into the mindset of believing that the money was never going to stop, that it was only going to get better. When you're working hard and maintaining best practices, this is generally true. But you're never in complete control of outside circumstances that can have an impact on the productivity of your team. I suddenly experienced a perfect storm of situations outside of my control that greatly impacted my team and created a downward spiral of income.

TIP

While my income seemed to be going away, my financial obligations didn't. I learned a difficult but vital lesson: No matter how exciting your commission income is, it's important to save, plan, and prepare for things to change; so that in the event a downturn happens, you are able to take care of your financial obligations.

One of my favorite books on this topic is *Smart Women Finish Rich* (Crown Business, 2002) by David Bach. In it, I learned some great principles for how to manage my money while times are good so that even when times aren't so good, my family and I would be fine. Because of this book, I now automatically evaluate what I'm going to do with my money. I set aside special funds for things like vacations, house projects, checking, savings, and so on.

Very often, people make more money in direct selling than they've ever earned before. And if the company is relatively new with a hot product, a rep may find herself earning $20,000 or $30,000 a month within just a couple of years. That kind of income can sneak up on people before they've begun to implement the good business practices for training and recruiting that can help sustain their business when the product is no longer a hot trend.

REMEMBER

Direct selling is like any other business; it goes through ups and downs. And while you'll be earning commission income based on the efforts of others as well as your own, you'll discover that in sales, as in life, there are no guarantees. Your company's product will not always be a hot trend. There may be a product recall, the economy may have a downturn, or you may have lower productivity when key leaders stop performing due to personal circumstances such as divorce, death in the family, critical illness, or a priority change. Any of these things can cause a significant downturn in your income.

Opening Your Eyes to Taxes

It would never fail. Every year around tax time I would lose some team members because their husbands felt their fun-time hobby was costing them more than they were making. It's often hard for people who have always traditionally worked a nine-to-five job to understand what it means to own your own business when it comes to how taxes work. This section touches on a few tax issues as they relate to direct sales. For much more on the tax implications of owning a home-based business, check out *Home-Based Business For Dummies* by Paul and Sarah Edwards (Wiley, 2010).

Withholding, refunds, and loaning the IRS money

When you have a normal job, your employer withholds your taxes — usually slightly more than you actually owe. If things go well, you get a refund check at the end of the year. If not, you end up having to write a check to pay the balance to the IRS at tax time. In direct sales, no employer is withholding your taxes.

Income tax refunds are an illusion. They just mean you overpaid your taxes during the year and gave the IRS a free loan. When the IRS refunds that money to you, it's money that you already earned and paid to them. The only difference in paying your taxes on April 15 is timing, visibility (those big checks can be alarming!), and who got to use or earn interest on that money during the year.

As an independent contractor, you are responsible for withholding a portion of your money. You can make quarterly tax payments, but until you pay the IRS, *you* can be using your income and/or earning money on it.

Tax benefits of a home-based business

The average American family, if they don't own their own business, is *overpaying* when it comes to taxes. The tax code is preferential toward business and business owners. If you currently only have W-2 income (meaning you get a paycheck from an employer that withholds taxes for you), by starting a direct sales business this year, you could save a lot on taxes — some estimate you could save $5,000 a year for an average family of four.

The direct sales business model is very tax-advantageous because so many of the expenses you already have are either fully or partially tax-deductible once you're in business for yourself. In addition, much of your daily activities can be combined with your business activities, increasing opportunities to lower your tax bill as you increase your income.

I won't go into a lot of detail on tax prep, because, again, I'm not a tax professional or financial advisor. For a lot more, I recommend checking out *Small Business Taxes For Dummies* by Eric Tyson (Wiley, 2013). And I encourage you to do more research and get in contact with a tax professional as part of building your business. That said, here are a few simple tips to get you thinking about your tax needs:

- ✔ **Set up a savings account.** In addition to having a separate checking account, it is smart to have a separate savings account that you use just for business. It's best if that account is with the same institution you use for the checking account. Each month — or better yet, each time you receive a commission check — transfer 10 to 30 percent over to the savings account immediately. Consider this your tax account. With it you're doing the tax withholding you're accustomed to with a paycheck. This is smart for a number of reasons, the most important of which is, at the end of the year, if after paying quarterly taxes you still have a balance due, you'll have it set aside and won't be stuck with a large surprise tax bill. And if you don't have taxes to pay, you'll be able to give yourself something like your own personal tax refund in the spring.

- ✔ **As your income grows, live on 80 percent or less.** This is a lifestyle tip, but all responsible lifestyle choices are ultimately tax tips when you're talking about being in business for yourself. When your profit income (what your business earns after you set aside money for taxes and pay the expenses) starts to rise over $1,000 per month, it's time to dial back how much of it you're using day to day. A smart way to do this is to gradually get to the point that you are putting half of whatever "paycheck" you're writing yourself into personal savings. This can be your emergency account, your financial cushion, or even an account you'll eventually use for investment — just don't use it for living expenses.

When you're able to eventually get to using just half of your profit day-to-day, you'll be able to prevent yourself from ramping up your lifestyle to unsustainable levels and be better protected against ups and downs. And most importantly, one year from now, two years from now, five years from now, and beyond — you will always have something to show for the work you've done now and you'll be better off, due to the effort you're putting into your business now. Let your money work for you and improve your security, rather than just relying on today's cash flow.

✔ **Keep a detailed calendar.** Much of your daily activity is related to your business when you're in direct sales. You meet a prospect for coffee. You drive two hours for a launch party. You go to the post office to mail out samples. You attend a networking lunch. Make sure you use your business account debit card or checks to pay for the coffee, the luncheon, the postage — and then also make sure these are reflected on your calendar and in your mileage log (see next bullet). Whether you have a paper calendar or a digital one, add as many details as you can, especially about who you met with and why. Later, should you need to present proof of your business deductions to the IRS, your detailed diary will be a very powerful element. Keep copies of your calendar with that year's tax paperwork.

✔ **Track your mileage in a mileage log.** When you get in your car to leave your house on your business errands, to a party, to the post office, to a networking event, or anything related to your business, write down the date, where you're going, and your starting mileage in a log. When you return home, write down the ending mileage. When you file your taxes, store each year's mileage log with that year's tax paperwork.

✔ **Pay attention to training and seek out expertise.** If there is a class or conference call on taxes for the self-employed business owner provided by your company, your team, your networking group, or by anyone else, *attend it.* If you hear of a book that people love about taxes, read it. And if there is an app or software made available to you that helps you track this information and makes you more likely to keep records, use it!

As I've urged throughout this chapter, get professional tax advice from someone who understands this business. You have a lot of tax benefits with this business; get advised well and educated so you can take full advantage of them.

Chapter 19

Meeting and Communicating

. . . .

In This Chapter

▶ Knowing the importance of monthly meetings

▶ Holding successful meetings

▶ Communicating with your leader

▶ Talking with your team

. . . .

*W*hen I was in the field, I was consistently the top seller and top booker every single month. I would go to all the monthly meetings for my team, and my leaders would always ask me to train on party/appointment bookings and sales.

After months of me consistently training at these events, I was starting to lose my enthusiasm for attending. I felt that I wasn't getting much from the meetings and I wasn't learning new things to build my own business. My leader could tell and she said something to me that I will never forget: *Don't ever question whether you should go to the meeting because either you need the meeting or the meeting needs you.*

But at one point, my bookings started falling and I hit a wall. I called some of my friends to ask what was working for them and how they were filling their calendar each month. I went to the meeting that month, and even though I was low on parties, they still asked me to train. At that meeting I shared some of the ideas my friends gave me because I didn't have any of my own success stories for that month to share.

The next meeting they didn't ask me to speak because I had zero parties and appointments booked on my calendar. I wondered who they would ask to speak and hoped that I would be able to leave with some information that could help get bookings back on my calendar.

That's when a lady on one of the other teams went up to speak on bookings. When I saw her walk to the front of the room, I remember saying to myself, "How is she going to help me? She only ever has two parties every single month!?"

Well, it turned out that she had a record-breaking month with 26 parties booked. When my leader asked her what she did to book so many parties, she said, "I really just followed what Belinda taught us at the last meeting."

That's when I realized that I wasn't doing what I was teaching. Suddenly I was in a place where *I needed the meeting*; it reenergized me and reminded me that I am in complete control of my business and that I had lost my motivation. It also taught me that if everyone would just implement one idea that they heard in a meeting, imagine what it could do to their business!

This chapter covers why meetings are important and what makes them successful. It also discusses the importance of communicating with your team and your leader.

Attending Your Company's Conference

If you're looking to take your business to the next level, then attending your company conference (or *convention, celebration, regional,* or whatever else they may call it) is a must. Not only does your company's conference give you the training you need to build your business, it will give you the big picture of the company and its mission.

There is usually a small fee to attend your company conference, but it is an investment that is well worth it.

Here are some reasons to attend your company conference

- ✔ **Sales increase:** People who attend conference typically enjoy a 35 percent increase in the fall selling season because of the motivation and training they leave with.

- ✔ **Training:** There are always multiple training sessions at conference that will help you build your sales and recruiting efforts.

- ✔ **Motivation:** Conference energizes you and gives you the motivation to create and build a successful business. Company owners and leaders in your organization often give inspiring stories that will change not only your business, but your life.

- ✔ **Friendships:** The friendships you will make with other representatives are some that will last a lifetime. You will always be able to connect with mentors and make accountability buddies.

- ✔ **New products:** Many companies use conference as a way to launch new products for the upcoming selling season. Conference attendees typically get the first look at these new products as well as the new catalog.

✔ **Speakers:** Along with the training done by corporate and field leaders, most companies hire speakers (like myself) to speak at your event. These people bring a wealth of knowledge and inspiration with them and sometimes years of success in the industry.

✔ **Trip incentives:** Many companies announce their trip incentives at conference and also offer trip points for attending.

✔ **Recognition:** Conference offers many opportunities for recognition, from top earners to promotions and earners of smaller incentives.

✔ **Gala:** *Gala night* is a very special night at conference for many people. It gives people the chance to dress their best and attend a formal event they may never otherwise have the chance to attend.

Your company's conference is an investment in yourself and can help take you and your business to the next level. Make it a yearly goal to get yourself there and budget accordingly throughout the year, setting a portion of your commission aside to help pay for the expenses. This is also something you can write off at tax time.

Planning and Attending Successful Meetings

There is a clear correlation between active healthy businesses and meeting attendance. Even though video-conference meetings are gaining in popularity, in-person meetings still garner more enthusiasm and income-producing activity than any other type of meeting. And it's easy to see why — being in a room with other enthusiastic people, sharing ideas and successes, creates motivation and momentum.

Think of a concert — you could hear the same music on your stereo, iPod or laptop, but sharing the experience with others creates an energy that simply can't be replicated in any other way.

Regardless of your previous experience with monthly meetings, you can create an energy-filled atmosphere that will generate enthusiasm and momentum in your meetings. And having value-packed meetings is important because people have many choices for what they can do with their time, and they want to feel it was time well spent.

Motivation

Motivation is *pumping people up,* and assuring them that they can reach their goals. Some people are natural encouragers, and almost everyone loves to be encouraged. The motivation segment of the meeting doesn't have to be super long, but it can include a (planned) testimony from someone who has experienced success, and what they did to achieve it. Something like this, for example:

> "I was really struggling to get appointments and parties booked, until I started doing weekly follow-up calls. Now booking is really easy for me."

Another part of motivation is encouraging people to set a goal and work toward it. If the promotion is that representatives who book and hold eight parties will earn a beautiful necklace, then encourage your team by being enthusiastic and excited:

> "Who in here is going to earn this month's gorgeous necklace? Raise your hands! Have we got at least five who are pursuing this goal? Who's with me?"

Recognition

Recognition is an important part of meetings because it creates energy and motivation for your team. People love to be recognized for their hard work and often value it even more than financial rewards.

Wondering what to recognize? Top sales and top recruiting awards are standard, but you can also recognize things like the following:

- ✔ Personal bests like Top Your Best Paycheck or Top Your Best Party Average
- ✔ Highest Party of the Month
- ✔ Highest Party Average
- ✔ Best Team Sales
- ✔ Earners of Monthly Incentive

You can also choose to recognize goal achievement awards. For example, Sarah may not have booked more parties than anyone else, but when she sets a goal for booking four shows this month and reaches the goal, it's a victory for her. At each meeting, get your team members to commit to a goal for the next month. This way you can track it to see if they have achieved it and then recognize them at the following meeting.

You can also recognize percentage increases as well as hard numbers. One thousand dollars in sales might not be a big deal to many of your teams, but when it's a 25 to 50 percent increase over her last month's sales, then it's a big deal to that representative.

Milestones are also another wonderful thing to recognize: anniversaries with the company, getting a first recruit (especially in the first 30 days), or reaching a new sales level are all recognition-worthy.

At the beginning of every meeting, I used to ask people to stand who had brought a guest. I would then get them to introduce themselves and tell the group something about their guest. This was great recognition for both parties.

Recognition can also be in the form of opening the floor for people to share something exciting about their business.

By doing coaching calls throughout the month, you will know who has exciting things happening. Call them out if they don't offer it up! Many people don't know whether or not their accomplishments are exciting enough. Recognition doesn't have to be in the form of an award. It can simply be having people stand or come to the stage.

The recognition portion of the evening will be the most memorable and exciting for many of your team members. If they're working a 9–5 job, odds are they aren't getting much recognition in their work life. And if they're stay-at-home moms, it's even less likely. So by making recognition a strong element in your meetings, you are likely to keep members coming back.

Even though this is an exciting part of the meeting, keep it moving quickly and don't devote too much time to it so that people who aren't being recognized don't lose interest.

Sharing information and important updates

At some point in the meeting, you always want to share with your team any important information or updates. These are typically the announcements from corporate and include facts on the current promotion and upcoming events.

Whatever you do, don't read this info from the company newsletter. Your team can read the newsletter anytime, anywhere. Instead, share the information in your own words and end with the announcement that is the lead-in to the evening's training. For example, if the promotion is an award for booking eight shows in a month, then the training following the information portion should be on securing parties.

Training

Linking the meeting's training to a current promotion helps train your team to tune into the meeting, because the topics build upon one another. That doesn't mean you have to be an expert on every single thing, or that all the training rests on your shoulders. The training portion of the evening is one that can be delegated to a team member or leader who does an activity particularly well.

When I sold jewelry, I held engaging and fun parties and always did well with filling my calendar and recruits. But you know what? I wasn't particularly great at accessorizing. Another team member was really great at that, and customers loved her tips. Having her present on that topic really helped the entire team. It also helped that representative feel like a valued and successful part of the team.

The training segment of the evening can also be project-based. After a short training on customer care and follow-up, you could have the attendees spend the next 15 minutes making re-order calls. Another great project is to brainstorm ideas for a recruiting flyer or opportunity event. As the team members talk about the benefits the flyer should list, those benefits will reignite their excitement as well as remind them of who they want to share the flyer with.

One thing we know about people today is that they truly like to interact. People like to share their thoughts and ideas. So, take time during this section of the meeting to get their input. One thing you can ask is, "Who has something exciting they want to share this week?"

Be creative and have fun. As long as team members learn something new or get a new perspective, the training session was a success.

Friendship

People look forward to meeting up with their friends and peers every month. Remember, even though your meetings are there to motivate and train your team, socializing is a very important aspect.

Be sure to leave time in your agenda for mingling. This is great to have at the beginning while everyone is arriving, and then again at the end. If your meeting ends at 8 p.m., don't train until 8. Train until 7:45 and allow the remaining time to be devoted to socializing.

This section of a meeting is important for new leaders as well. When people start building a team, they usually don't know how to run a successful meeting or have the resources or knowledge to hold a training session. Monthly meetings can simply be a group of people in a room to socialize and brainstorm. Many groups also choose to meet at restaurants where you can eat and meet in the same space.

A few years ago, I was asked to run monthly meetings for six months for a company in Michigan. The meeting was held across the street from a restaurant so we could walk over afterward. Once we had built leaders and they were ready to take over the meetings, I decided to do an exit survey with the group. One of the questions asked was what they liked best. I'm a good trainer, but their favorite thing was going over to the restaurant after the meeting to socialize.

The energy you create that night will leave with them and motivate them in their business. As long as you keep the meeting fun and engaging, everyone will have a good time and you will see benefits.

New products

At the beginning of a new catalog or season, your meetings should have a portion focused on product knowledge. This is where you share how to sell and demonstrate your new products. You want to give your teams tricks on how to use the product, help them with benefit selling, and brainstorm some creative ways to share the product online.

If your company offers launch kits or sends top leaders new product in advance, be sure to have this meeting before the new product launches. That gives your representatives more time to become familiar with the product as well as more time to prepare their marketing. If your company doesn't offer launch kits, then be sure to order new products as soon as they become available and have your meeting the second week after the product launches (giving you time to receive the product in the mail). That way, you're still able to showcase the product at the beginning of the month and take advantage of a larger selling period.

Culture of opportunity

At your meeting, it's a great idea to create a culture where everyone brings guests. Your monthly meeting should always be a place for team members to bring potential recruits to hear you give an effective opportunity talk and learn more about the business.

Having these potential recruits hear the other sections of the meeting, like recognition and training, shows them that this is a fun and rewarding opportunity that is open to everyone. Show potential recruits that they'd be part of a team who wants to see them succeed.

Allowing your team to bring guests really promotes group recruiting, which is a win/win. The more people added to your team each month means great success for you and for each of the members on your team who are gaining a recruit. See Chapter 17 for more on holding opportunity events.

Communicating with Your Leader and Your Team

Communication is an important part of your success. It's vital that you keep in contact with your leader as well as your team. The great thing about the direct selling industry is that you are in business *for yourself,* but never *by yourself.* Embrace the support available to you and always share your knowledge and expertise with others.

Communicating with your leader

Especially during your first few weeks, communicating with your leader or sponsor is paramount to your success. Our business is one of peaks and valleys, and your leader is there to help celebrate the peaks and help you through the valleys. Your upline has your best interests at heart and wants you to succeed, so listen to them. Profit from their advice and training. They have been down this road before, and you can avoid many pitfalls by profiting from their past experiences.

Let your leader or sponsor be your coach. They will be able to help you in a number of areas:

- ✔ **Launch party:** Your leader will help you craft the words to say to invite people to your first party, help you prepare your booking talk, and give helpful hints on how to get bookings from your first party. Your leader can also help you brainstorm and build your list of contacts for your Booking Lead Notebook (see Chapter 7 for more on this).

- ✔ **Customer feedback:** When you get a booking or positive feedback from those closest to you, call your leader or sponsor with the good news. More importantly, when someone you were certain would book or be supportive says no, call your leader and share that experience, too. They can guide you through it because chances are, it has happened to them as well. Rather than sit and worry and wonder if you're doing the right thing, tap into your leader's positivity and experience, so you can move forward and make the next call. A daily call, message, or text to your leader can be the best morale booster you have.

✔ **Parties:** After each of your first parties, call your leader to report the results: How many guests were there, who booked, who was interested in the opportunity, what were the sales like? Also share how you felt about the party: Were you comfortable with your presentation? With your booking talk? What will you change or improve for the next party? What questions do you have? What questions did your guests have that you were unable to answer?

✔ **Recruiting:** When you have a recruit lead, call your leader immediately for help with follow-up. Ask for advice — or together, place a three-way call to the lead so you can learn what to say the next time. There is no better way to learn the words to say than hearing them again and again. Soon, your leader's words will come naturally to you, too.

✔ **Goals:** Share your goals with your leader. Let your leader know what you're working for, so they can help you get there. Getting bookings from your first six parties is your very first short-term goal; but it's important that as you attain one short-term goal, you have another to replace it. Your leader can help you take the next step. If leadership is your goal, your leader will help you move quickly through the steps to achieve that goal.

✔ **Insight:** Sometimes you just need someone to listen or to share an idea or work through a plan. Your leader can lend valuable insight in these types of conversations. Other times you just need validation that you're on the right track and that you're expending your energies in the right places for your new business. Your leader is the perfect person to call for that, too.

When it comes down to it, direct sales is a simple business, consisting of a few disciplines repeated on a consistent basis. But it takes time to learn and practice. Let your leader or sponsor assist you in the process. Your leader is there to help you see beyond today's challenges, through to tomorrow's solutions. As you book more parties and add more members to your team, different situations will arise that create a unique learning and maturing environment. This means that you'll master these disciplines, too — and soon you'll be someone who can mentor others.

Communication with your team

As you bring more people into the business and grow your team, you will transition into being a leader. It's important that you establish good communication habits with your team.

You've been where they are. Share with them your success stories and how you overcame the obstacles they're currently facing.

The preceding section gives you some great ideas on what you can discuss with your team. But here are some more great ways to stay in touch:

- **Monthly meetings:** Your monthly meetings are a great way to get your team together to motivate and train. Meetings have been shown to increase your team's activity and success.

- **Facebook Groups:** You should have a Facebook Group dedicated to your team (see Chapters 11 and 16 for more on Facebook Groups). When someone is recruited, they're added to your team page, as well as any larger teams that you're also a part of. Groups are a great way to share information, training, and recognition. It's important that you add your team to your leaders' team pages as well so they can enjoy multiple training techniques and perspectives. Remember, not everyone learns the same or is fuelled by the same things. Someone on your team may connect more to another leader's training. That's not a bad thing! Remember, you're all a part of the same organization.

- **Telephone calls:** Conference calls are a great way to keep in touch with your team. You can hold them monthly for your team members who don't live in the area and can't make it to your monthly meetings. Coaching calls are a great way to check in with team members individually.

- **Email and texting:** Your communication to your team doesn't always need to be lengthy and full of training and other information. Sometimes a small text or email can go along way. Be sure to keep in contact with your team to show that you care about them and their success. There's nothing worse than only ever hearing from your leader during the last few days of the month. That's usually because they're trying to find out if you're placing an order so that they're meeting their sales quotas or if they can reach their next promotion.

People do business with people they want to be friends with. Create authentic relationships with your team members through meetings and other communication channels and you'll notice an increase in productivity and enthusiasm among your team members.

Chapter 20

Networking to Grow Your Reach

· ·

In This Chapter

▶ Seeing why networking is so important

▶ Becoming business best friends

▶ Obtaining referrals

▶ Attending networking events

▶ Assembling an advisory board

· ·

*I*n direct sales, as in any kind of business for that matter, it's important to network. Engagement and communication are how you grow a strong circle of professionals, community members, and friends. Networking is a catalyst for success.

In business, return on investment (ROI) measures the success you receive from investing in your business through actions that are monetized — advertising, for example. Return on relationships (ROR) in the business world describes the success we receive from building authentic relationships with our customers, community, and others. Establishing these relationships online, within your community, and at professional events grows your customer base and helps you reach more people every day. Always be on the lookout for community or chamber of commerce events in your area and get involved!

Networking can be scary and difficult for many people because it involves putting yourself out there and starting conversations. To help you get over your nerves at a networking event, arrive early so you can become comfortable in a small setting first. You can also bring a friend/colleague with you.

When you are in business for yourself, it's important to network for a number of reasons:

> ✔ **Grow your reach.** Networking gives you the opportunity to grow your audience and reach more people who may be interested in your service or product.

- ✔ **Make connections.** Making strong bonds is important in business for a variety of reasons. You know the saying, "It's who you know." It's so true. Knowing the right people can help you find new customers and new opportunities that will be profitable to you and your business.

- ✔ **Get referrals.** *Who do you know who . . .?* During networking events, you may not meet people who are in need of your product or service, but you may meet people who know people who would benefit from it. Networking is a great tool to gain referrals for your business that will help you increase your customers, hosts, and recruit leads.

- ✔ **Seek advice.** A networking venue like your local Chamber of Commerce is a great place to meet other successful business professionals who have already navigated some of the hurdles you may be facing. These people are great for advice and motivation.

- ✔ **Increasing profile and brand.** People want to do business with people they want to be friends with. Networking and getting yourself out there in the community will make your name known; it is a free marketing and branding technique that you should all be taking advantage of.

Introducing Yourself

At networking events, you can't sit in the corner and wait for people to come to you. Here are some easy ways to introduce yourself:

- ✔ **Stand near the bar or refreshment table.** Many people head over to the bar or refreshment table throughout the night. When you're there, it's easy to spark a conversation without having to walk up to a group of people.

- ✔ **Introduce yourself to the organizer.** Always introduce yourself to the organizers of the event and thank them for putting it together. Often, they will point you in the direction of someone they think you would benefit from speaking to or introduce you to someone else on the spot.

- ✔ **Don't be a spammer.** You don't want to "work the room" or be a business card spammer. Introduce yourself to someone and spark up a conversation — then let them introduce you to others in their circle. Having a bunch of short conversations won't help you in the long run. Instead, try to have a few, meaningful dialogues.

- ✔ **Don't be afraid to join in.** People attend networking events to meet new people and gain new connections, so don't be afraid to initiate a conversation or introduce yourself during a break in a group's conversation.

- ✔ **Find familiar faces.** If you recognize someone, re-introduce yourself and remind them how you know each other or where you saw them. You can say things like, "Hi there, my name is Belinda. I recognize you from LinkedIn and remembered that you own the restaurant Wild Orchid. I go there all the time with my family. How are you enjoying the evening?"

Business Best Friends

Business best friends is a term used to describe a relationship between two business owners — in your case, independent representatives — who share a mutually beneficial relationship.

One way to grow your reach and network with other like-minded people is by developing relationships with representatives who represent a company different than your own. You typically meet these people through social media, tradeshows, home parties (you can book a party with a consultant from a company you would be interested in working with), and other vendor events. The two of you work together to promote each other's products and services so that you can each grow your audience by tapping into each other's customer bases.

Here are some important tips to remember:

- **Same demographic:** Business best friends should always have similar demographics for their customer base. If your product line typically attracts women ages 45–55, then you should work alongside someone whose products also attract that age group. The point of a business relationship of this nature is to refer your audience to your friend when they are in need of her service or product and vice versa.

- **Different product lines:** You don't want to be in competition with your business best friends, because then you will always be taking sales away from each other. Instead, find a rep whose products complement yours. For example, a cookware company and a food company, cosmetics company and jewelry company, or decor company and cleaning company would be great matches.

- **Being authentic:** Even though I'm mentioning this last, this is probably the most important point of the three. You don't want to develop a fake relationship in order to benefit from a business best friend. Developing an authentic and trusting friendship is not only a great way to increase your reach, but to gain a friend who is like-minded and who also believes in direct sales. Friendship is one of the reasons people join companies and stay in the direct sales industry. Establishing lifelong friendships is both rewarding and fulfilling.

So, how does it actually work? Here are some ways you and your business best friend can work and benefit from each other:

- **Special giveaways on social media:** Your business should be on at least one of the following: Facebook, Instagram, Twitter, or Pinterest. Social media is a great way to reach your customers and gain new followers. Chapter 11 discusses how in the world of social media, engagement is king; engagement determines whether your content makes it into newsfeeds and ultimately who sees your posts. Engagement on Facebook for example is measured by three actions: Likes, Comments, and Shares. You should be sharing interesting content that includes calls to engagement. For example, "Like if you agree," "Comment below with your answer," and "Share this photo with your friends and family."

Contests and giveaways are great ways to increase your engagement through Likes, Comments, and Shares and get more people falling in love with your products. Most companies offer contests for people who comment on a post or submit their own content. In this case, you select a winner and send them free product. Just always be sure to check Facebook's policies on contests and giveaways. For example, Facebook permits contests focused on Comments and Likes to Comments, but not on page Likes or Shares. Contests and giveaways are especially great if you offer new products, because many of the people who already like your fan page have either tried your product or are at least familiar with it.

A great way to get your fans excited and sharing your content is to offer them something new. Work with your business best friend to offer giveaways on each other's social media. Your fans will be excited by the new product you're giving away from your friend's business, and you'll gain new, excited followers through her page.

✔ **Referral gifts:** Referrals lead to new customers, hosts, and recruit leads. Everyone at some point in their life will need your product, a fun night out with friends, or the benefits from having a home-based business. And when you meet someone at a time when they aren't interested, find out if they know someone who is.

Your business best friend can be a great tool in helping you gain referrals. The two of you can offer each other referral gifts when you refer someone (a customer, host, or recruit lead) to each other.

✔ **Open houses:** Again, the main benefit of having a business best friend is cross-promoting your products across each other's customer base and audience. Holding an open house together is a great way for you to meet new people, gain more customers and bookings, and achieve additional sales.

✔ **Advice:** Your business best friend can be an amazing resource for training, information, advice, and motivation. You can lean on each other, cheer each other on, and help each other build lasting and successful businesses. That's the amazing thing about this industry — that we all work together to help each other succeed.

Always get referrals

Networking is a great way for you to gain referrals and new business. By attending community events and other networking events you meet new people who may be interested or have a need for your product or service.

At events you must always be ready with your 30-second commercial (see Chapter 6) to share with people you meet. The idea is not just to tell them what you do, but to create an interest for your product or service.

If someone you meet at a networking event isn't interested in hosting a party or purchasing the product, it doesn't mean that they don't like you or don't believe in your business. It might just mean that the time isn't right for them right now, and that's okay. Be sure to take their business card and add them to your lead notebook. And always ask: *Who do you know who . . .?*

Who do you know who would benefit from a product like this?

Who do you know who would enjoy a fun night in with friends sampling these amazing products?

Who do you know who would enjoy additional income every month?

Finding the Right People to Network With

Not every event or situation is the right place for you or your business. It's a good idea to attend events with like-minded people or with people who are within the demographic that you are trying to sell to.

The key to networking is quality over quantity. It is far better to develop a few really close relationships and connections than a bunch of shallow ones. Say, for example, you're trying to sell a luxury car. Who would be better to network with — five financially well off adults or a hundred teenagers?

Walking around the room passing your business card out to every person you bump into usually isn't the best way to gain new business or interest. Instead, listen to what people are saying and look for cues that might suggest they would be interested in your product or business opportunity. Then approach these people, introduce yourself, and take an interest in their problem or need. You want to take the focus off of you and put it on them. It's how can you help them — not how can they help you.

Practice makes perfect. Practice your introduction at home before you venture off to a networking event. It's important to sound confident. Be clear when you speak. Don't come off like you're hand-delivering sales pitches around the room. It is 100 percent acceptable to talk business at business events, so be sure to practice ways that make your business and product sound interesting, appealing, and beneficial.

Attending community events

Attending community events shows that you care about the community and are proud of the locale you live in. Getting involved in events will also increase your business awareness. People are more likely to refer you to others if they have met you and like you. Many times after meeting you at an event, people will be quick to recommend you, your business, or your skills to other people in the community, even if they've never worked with you. They will instead refer you based on the fact that they like you and think you are someone they would like to work with. Remember, people want to do business with people they want to be friends with!

Another great reason to attend community events is to promote yourself as a local business owner. In most places, people are more inclined to help and patronize local businesses than national chains, if they can. This helps keep business in the community and helps support those who live and participate in the community.

Community events can also help you attract opportunities for fundraising. Attend community events that are charity focused and get involved. Show people you care about the community you live in and the services your community provides. Connect with the chairperson of the event and let them know that you offer an amazing fundraising opportunity that can help bring financial aid and awareness to their cause.

Using social media

With social media you can network with like-minded people and grow your fan and customer base online. Facebook, Twitter, and LinkedIn are the most effective platforms for business communication, and Instagram and Pinterest are effective for sharing photos and videos that help enhance your brand and create a desire for your product.

Most people who use Facebook, Twitter, and LinkedIn use their real names and are participating in the platform to make connections with other people. Understanding the reasoning behind why people are on these platforms and the etiquette associated with them is important to know when participating on social media.

In my *Mastering Social Media* CD I made with Karen Clark, we discuss the ways you should behave on each platform when you are trying to network and build connections. Here are some highlights:

- **Facebook:** Networking on Facebook is like attending your neighbor's backyard BBQ. You dress business-casual. You can show off bright colors and bold accessories. You also want to be friendly and start casual conversations. It is okay if the conversation leads into business, but it should never start off as business. Facebook is about creating authentic relationships with people. You should never spam people. Would you go to your neighbor's backyard BBQ with your sales pitch? Probably not. Instead, build friendships with those around you because people do business with people they want to be friends with.

- **Twitter:** Networking on Twitter is like being at a downtown metropolitan bar. There are a lot of quick conversations going on. You might run into people that you live nearby, people you work with, and even some celebrities. It's important to work the room and jump into conversations. Remember, you only have 140 characters or less, so be direct in your conversations and get to the point, as the attention span on Twitter is usually low. Remember to always use hashtags to help categorize what you're talking about. This is another great way to meet and connect with people who are interested in the same things as you.

- **LinkedIn:** LinkedIn is the most formal of the three social media platforms. LinkedIn is your resume and is similar to attending an event at your local Chamber of Commerce. The explicit intent on LinkedIn is to make business connections, so it's important that you behave in a way that draws people in. It probably isn't a good idea to have your profile picture be a photo of your dog, or of you at a party or on a beach. Your profile picture should be office-appropriate and so should your conversations. It is acceptable to reach out to people and let them know you would love to connect and discuss business together. However, you should stay away from messages that seem inauthentic and too "salesy."

Here are some general tips to remember when networking on social media:

- **Be authentic:** Be yourself! Show off who you truly are and you will attract similar people. Always be sure to be real in your conversations and develop meaningful relationships.

- **Don't spam:** Get people to care about you before they care about your business. Don't message people, especially people you don't know, with a sales pitch. People will write you and your business off if they feel they are being pressured to buy. When posting on Facebook or other social media platforms, don't post things like *Join my team! Help me earn a promotion! Only $X away from achieving my goal! Help me earn my FREE trip to Mexico!* You want people to feel like your business and your products benefit *them,* not just you. Always be personable, relatable, and positive, and people will be attracted to you.

> ✔ **Care about people:** To get people to care about you, you need to care about them. Wouldn't it be nice if your friends and customers came to you to do business instead of running away whenever you bring up the subject? Well, that's what happens when you take the time to serve instead of sell. Building relationships, offering free tips and ideas and finding out what product or service would best fill their needs are all things that will draw people to you and your business.

Want to know if you're focused on service or sales? Take a look at your posts on social media; are they focused on you or on how you can make someone else's life better?

Creating friendships

When networking, you want to create friendships with people, not just business connections. When you start with a business relationship that develops into a friendship, your bond is much stronger and will turn into a more successful business relationship in the future.

Friendship means you care about the other person. Ask questions. Ask what is happening in their life, how is business, how is their family, what are some of their favorite hobbies, and so on. Finding out these details about their life will better help you understand who they are and what their needs are.

A lot of people get nervous when it comes to networking because they think they need to be extroverts or big talkers. But the key to good networking isn't talking — it's *listening*. Listen to what people around you are saying because often times they are dropping hints that will lead you to a conversation about your business.

You may hear people say the following things:

I wish my career was more flexible.

I wish I could stay home with my daughter.

I hate missing all my son's little league games.

We need to buy a new family car.

These types of statements give you the opportunity to share what your business can offer them and the types of opportunities having a direct sales business affords.

Tips for Power Networking

When attending networking events, always be prepared and ready for business. Here are some helpful tips of things you should always be ready to do or say:

- ✔ **Always have business cards on hand.** If people are interested in your business or products, or even just staying in touch with you, they may ask for your business card. Having a business card keeps the relationship going as well as showing that you are serious about your business.

- ✔ **Always ask for business cards.** If you meet someone you would like to keep in touch with, always ask for their business card as well. And be sure to keep a pen either in your pocket or your purse. When they walk away, take a few notes on the back of their business card that you can mention when you speak to them again.

- ✔ **Be prepared with your 30-second commercial.** You want to draw people in to what you do with your 30 second commercial (see Chapter 6 for more on this). Be sure to tell people what you do, not who you are. For example, you could say, "I show homeowners how they can clean their homes using safe and environmentally friendly cleaners without harsh chemicals," instead of, "I am an Independent Group Director for [Cleaning Products Company]." The first example not only explains what you do, but shows your prospect how you might be able to help them as well.

- ✔ **Ask (and care) about what they do.** Don't make everything about you. You want to be sure to ask questions about the person you are talking to and take interest in what they are saying. You want to always be genuine and authentic in your conversations. This will help you establish a closer and more meaningful bond.

- ✔ **Find similar interests.** Finding similar interests can be a great way to keep not only the conversation going, but also the friendship. Bond over things you have in common and make plans at a later date to do them. For example, if you meet someone who loves golf, and you love golf, invite them out to play with you.

- ✔ **Ask for leads.** Just because your product or business might not be for them, it doesn't mean they don't know someone who would benefit from your opportunity. Always be sure to ask for leads, referrals, and introductions to others who may find your business interesting.

- ✔ **Probe about other events they attend.** People who attend one networking event are likely to attend others. Ask what other events they attend in the community and see if any of them sound right for you and your business.

✔ **Tweet during the event.** Twitter is great for events. Many events or networking groups usually have hashtags that they use to promote the evening. Be sure to tweet throughout the event and tag those you're meeting. If there is someone in the room you want to meet and you notice that they have tweeted, you can always respond to their tweet — which will make it easier for you to approach them at the event. Not only will tweeting help you at the event, it will show others in the community that you are involved.

Maintaining Connections After Meeting

You don't want to let your connections die or fizzle out after the event. Here are some ways you can stay connected to people you have met:

✔ **Connecting online:** Stay in touch on social media. I suggest adding your new connections to Twitter and LinkedIn only. Some people don't use Facebook for business and only for personal use, so sticking to Twitter and LinkedIn is usually best. If the event you were at was using a hashtag, be sure to tweet the people who were there using the hashtag to remind them you were there and that you look forward to connecting again.

✔ **Email and phone calls:** If you have exchanged business cards with someone, don't be afraid to email or call them to say you enjoyed meeting them and look forward to chatting more.

✔ **Setting up a meeting.** If you discussed business with someone, reach out to them to set up a meeting to discuss your business and products more. If your meeting was more casual, you can always ask them to meet for a coffee after work or for a bite to eat during a lunch break.

✔ **Staying in touch.** Continue to engage with the people you meet at events. This could involve something as small as retweeting them, commenting on a blog post they made, or endorsing them for a skill on LinkedIn. You want to make sure you always keep yourself and your business in front of them so when they are in need of your services, you will be there.

Networking is about the long game, not the short one. Developing friendships over time is rewarding.

Using the power of three

The power of three is a great way to categorize the people in your life and in your circle. You value each of these people for different reasons and have them in your life for different purposes. You should be able to realize what you need in a particular moment and who can help you achieve that.

✔ **The Hugger:** The hugger is the person who makes you feel good. They give you the confidence boost you need. You reach out to the Hugger when you need to be reassured about yourself, what you're doing, your business, and your capabilities.

✔ **The Realist:** The realist is the person who gives you the hard truth. They are not there to sugarcoat anything for you or say anything to make you feel better. They are realistic about your situation and are often unbiased and objective.

✔ **The Problem Solver:** The Problem Solver helps you answer the question *what's next?* Often times after the Hugger has helped you boost your confidence and the Realist has stated the facts of your situation, the Problem Solver helps you move forward.

Set Up an Advisory Board

You can't succeed in business alone. That's why it's important to have a group of people who essentially make up your advisory board. I divide them into three different types of people:

✔ **Mentors:** Your mentors are the people you look up to, who offer you advice and training. They are usually the people you go to when you're struggling with a certain part of your business or are looking to grow your business. These would include people like your upline leaders in your organization or successful business owners outside the direct sales industry.

✔ **Peers:** Your peers are the people you work alongside that you can brainstorm with and bounce ideas off of. These are typically people who are at the same stage as you in business. They can be within your company or outside the direct sales industry.

✔ **Connectors:** Connectors are typically outgoing and extroverted. They are great at networking and helping establish connections between others. People trust them and their recommendations. Connectors are great for you to have in your life to help refer you to people who may be interested in your business, or to people who can help you in an area you need assistance in.

You also need to be a connector for other people. For example, let's say you sell cosmetics, and you call a customer to see if she would like to re-order.

> Belinda: "Hey Karen, it's Belinda. I just wanted to touch base with you to see how you were doing with your products and if you're needing anything right now."

> Karen: "Oh, hey, Belinda, I am loving the make-up and I am almost out but I can't even begin to think about that right now. I desperately need to find someone who can repair my furnace."

> Belinda: "Karen, I actually know someone who fixed our furnace last winter and did a fantastic job. Would you like me to connect you two?"

> Karen: "Oh, my gosh! Thank you so much. Yes, please!"

The more people you know in your circle of influence, the more value you bring to your relationships. Adding value to people's lives makes people feel important and reminds them that you are important, as well.

Networking and growing your reach is important and vital to your success. If you continue to add people to your circle and nourish those relationships, you will always have an abundance of business.

Part VI

The Part of Tens

Check out a bonus Part of Tens chapter at www.dummies.com/extras/
directsales.

In this part . . .

- ✔ Avoiding common mistakes new representatives make
- ✔ Checking out some great online resources for your business
- ✔ Counting down the top benefits of direct sales

Chapter 21

Ten Mistakes to Avoid

• •

In This Chapter

▶ Understanding the most common mistakes direct sellers make

▶ Learning how to overcome common challenges

• •

This chapter covers ten key mistakes that every direct seller should avoid in their business.

Not Starting with a Strong Line-up of Events

One of the biggest mistakes when starting your business is not having enough parties, launch events, or prospecting appointments scheduled on your calendar. Most companies recommend a certain amount of activity to really get your business going. Following the recommendation creates a strong start as well as momentum for your business.

During your first 30 days, I suggest starting with four to six parties or events. People who start with only a few parties on their calendar end up with no business or slow business. Without the momentum that comes with a solid launch schedule, it is common to feel unsuccessful or lose enthusiasm for your business.

Many people settle on doing two to three parties and convince themselves that somehow they will get the parties, sales, and recruits that they need. However, they don't create the momentum they need to continue, because it is the bookings from those first six parties that will give them future business and help them create a success story for themselves.

When I first started, it was a requirement to do six parties in a two-week time frame in order to receive your starter kit. We made money very quickly, earned back our investment, grew our confidence in our business, and had a success story to share.

Another thing many representatives don't do, which is a mistake, is fail to schedule their launch party right away or never have one at all. Your launch party is the perfect way to launch your business. It is at this party that you will be able to act as both representative and host, earning commission as well as host benefits from your party sales. A launch party introduces your product to your friends and family and gives you the opportunity to book parties for them.

Start your business by making your *list of 100*. Write down people who might be interested in the product, the party, or the opportunity and make it a plan to reach out to those people. You can use my system, the Power Hour (see Chapter 5 for more), to spend 15 minutes two to three times a week just on booking calls. This will help you to continually have a full and income-producing calendar.

Being Afraid to Ask for a Party or Appointment

So many people are so afraid to hear the word no that it paralyzes them. They are unwilling to get out of their comfort zone and ask for help, the sale, or for referrals. I believe this comes from a lack of self-confidence — which is really only gained by *just doing it*.

The reality is you will get no's. It's just part of the sales process. Don't take it personally. Sometimes a no just means *not right now*.

There is also the fear of appearing to be a *salesperson*. Focusing on service instead of sales can help keep your conversations with your customers genuine and authentic.

To overcome the fear of hearing the word no, you need to consistently reaffirm your belief in your company, your product, and in yourself.

Failing to Set Goals

Setting goals is one of the key ingredients to success. When people have no idea what they want or where they want to be, it is difficult or even impossible to keep moving forward. The fear of failure or what other people think is often what holds people back from setting simple goals.

Many also feel that a goal has to be huge for them to feel validated by themselves and others. In fact, the small benchmarks are what lead us to the bigger desires we want in our lives.

Even if you don't hit your goal, you're farther ahead than where you started.

Lacking Commitment and Persistence

Not staying committed or quitting too soon is another mistake that many new direct sellers make. Representatives often feel discouraged when they miss a benchmark they set for themselves. They lose drive for their business when they realize that just like any business, a direct sales business takes time. A large percentage of people do direct sales part-time or for additional income for their family, so when they discover that it still requires work and dedication, they are more likely to quit.

Maybe the first few people they ask aren't interested in hosting a party or signing up for an auto-ship. Maybe no one shows up to their launch party. Sometimes a friend at work might say, "I tried that once, but didn't want to keep pressuring my friends." All of a sudden, that same person who was going to change her life is now justifying why she decided to quit.

It's sad that so many talk themselves out of the business before it even starts. That's why it's important to be committed. To get the results you desire from your business, you *must* be committed to giving your business the time and attitude it deserves.

Like any new job, there are going to be times when you feel uncomfortable. When that happens, some people quit because they think another product line will be easier to sell. Instead of chasing the next shiny new object, give your business time. It's not going to happen overnight. If you want results, you have to stick with it. Commitment is key.

Prejudging Customers and Prospects

In business, it's important not to prejudge anyone. Often, we decide in our minds how much someone will spend or whether someone will be a fit for the business without ever offering them the opportunity. We assume that people won't want to do business with us, buy our products, or have enough time to host a party.

You have to put your preconceived ideas about people aside and offer your products and opportunity to everyone. Let people decide for themselves what they want and don't want. You can't know what is in someone's checking account or heart simply by looking at them.

Always offer your products and services to everyone. Don't be afraid to hear no. The more no's you get means a yes is just around the corner.

Not Treating Your Business like a Business

Your direct sales business is just that — a business — and you need to treat it like one. You must set office hours, determine the days you want to work, and be consistent with that. You must always have proper business aids and supplies so that you're ready for business when it comes.

There are certain things you expect from businesses you interact with — such as your hair salon, bank, grocery store, and so on — and your customers should expect certain things from you as well.

To be successful, you must not only treat your business like a business, you must be consistent with it. Set a consistent work schedule, maintain your calendar, and consistently work on your Power Hour (see Chapter 5 for more). Use the Power Hour system two to three times a week to keep up with the important income-producing activities of your business.

Stay on top of your social media channels. When someone visits a Facebook business page only to find the business hasn't posted in days or weeks — it doesn't look great. It looks like the business or individual is lazy or inconsistent — or worse, out of business entirely.

Know your numbers. Know what your commission is, what you've sold, and what your team has sold. Be aware of whether you and your team are hitting the targets and meeting the goals you've set. And know how far away you are from your next promotion, as well as how far those on your team are from theirs.

Lacking Focus

When you're in business for yourself and work from home, getting distracted can be very easy. Being self-employed can be quite challenging for people who have only ever worked a nine-to-five job.

It's important to balance life and work and be present in whatever it is that you're doing. If you want to spend time with your family, then mark the time off and be present in that moment. If you want to work on your business, then spend time on income-producing activities, away from all distractions.

Some join multiple direct sales companies. In my training, I always stress how you can't chase two rabbits at the same time. You need to find one company you want to get serious about and build a successful business with.

Signing up with an additional company to get products at a discount is fine. But if you want to be successful in this industry, focus on building only one business.

Skipping Training and Development

Personal development and growth are essential. You must always be a student and learn as much as you can.

Too many people either think they know all the answers without having any experience — or they're too afraid to ask for help. I also see that many people don't want to invest in any kind of training.

Take advantage of training. It's usually free, or at least very affordable. Dedicate time in your week to your development. Listen to CDs, read books, watch webinars, and learn from others who have already traveled your road.

Stay in the mindset of learning because as long as you are learning, you are growing.

Neglecting Business Relationships

Building strong relationships requires time and commitment. Many representatives do not take the time to connect with their customers, hosts, and team members.

Think ROR: *return on relationships.* This business word is being used more and more by companies because they're finding that customer relationships are proving to be better at creating brand ambassadors and loyal customers than traditional advertising.

Another relationship that is important to build is the one with your upline leader. Your leaders want to see you succeed, and yet I hear from leaders all the time that they can't get their team members to answer their phones or return any messages. That they don't attend meetings and overall don't engage. Creating and maintaining a relationship with your leader is important to your overall success. Let them help you. Tap into them for their knowledge and expertise.

Depending on Friends and Family for Too Long

One mistake many representatives make is that they focus only on their friends and family and eventually exhaust their customer base. In the beginning, family and friends either purchase products at your launch party or agree to host a party for you. And at your parties, instead of going in trying to book *their* friends and expand your circle, you may forget your booking talk and focus only on sales.

A successful party or event is not based on just what you achieve in sales. A successful event is one that has average to above average sales, recruit leads, *and* new bookings or appointments for your calendar.

As I've said a few times in this book, think about *who do you know who . . .?* A friend or family member may know someone who would love your products or services. *Always* ask for referrals from people and focus on booking new parties to expand your circle.

Filling your calendar with events, appointments, and parties is vital to your success. A full calendar is a healthy calendar.

A leader I know at one company ran into this problem at the very beginning of her cosmetics business. The first thing she did was write down 100 names of people that she knew who might be interested in the product. This is something I suggest everyone do — create a lead notebook. But she only focused on sales, not bookings. Within a few days, she had sold $1,500 worth of products to her family and friends by showcasing the company's most popular product. When she realized she had exhausted her family and friends, she realized she didn't have anywhere to move forward. Instead of contacting 100 people to purchase one item, she would have been better off contacting 20 people to book a party. That would have resulted in higher sales for her and a large booking chain in the long run.

Your family and friends are usually the first people who will help you with your business, but they're not the ones who will take your business to the next level. Always be on the lookout for your next recruit, host, and customer.

Chapter 22

Top Ten Resources for Direct Sellers

In This Chapter

▶ Top resources you can utilize for your business

▶ Marketing, getting educated, and communicating more easily with apps and websites

T his chapter covers ten key resources you can use for your business.

Step Into Success

After having been in this industry for 35 years, worked with hundreds of companies and literally thousands of independent representatives, I am confident that my company, Step Into Success, offers some of the best resources for training and consulting in the industry.

In this book, we are covering so many of the basics for the direct sellers, but I also offer an array of programs that focus on follow-up, host coaching, my proven system the Power Hour, how to build a million-dollar organization, how to plan and execute interviews and opportunity events — and so much more. Whether you're new to direct sales, looking to revive your business, or want to take your successful business to the next level, I have a collection of training programs that will help you succeed.

If you're a leader looking for training to help motivate your downline or a corporate representative looking to add valuable industry training at your next event or convention, live-event training is for you!

I also offer a digital academy where you can sign up for classes to learn the latest in digital marketing and applications. Experts in social media and digital marketing teach you the ins and outs of social media, how to keep your business organized online, and how to successfully achieve sales and recruits through social media. Step Into Success is truly a one-stop shop for all your direct sales needs.

I also provide consulting for direct sales companies to assist them with training programs and guides, compensation plans, incentives, weekly conference calls, and webinars. I also provide personal coaching for the executive team.

Visit stepintosuccess.com for more information.

Time Management

Time-management tools are a great way to keep on top of your to-do lists. With these apps and resources, you can set up tasks and reminders from your computer, tablet, or phone. You can create multiple lists, set priorities, get push notifications, and even share task lists with others.

Tasks are important to set for yourself daily, weekly, and monthly. Schedule your Power Hour times using these apps as well as your personal priorities and responsibilities. Time-management tools are also great when planning events with other leaders in your team because many apps give you the ability to share task lists with others.

Here are three I suggest you try:

- Any.Do (www.any.do)
- EasilyDo (www.easilydo.com)
- Wunderlist (www.wunderlist.com)

Another great time-management resource is marGo (www.margo.me). marGo is the first invitation service designed specifically for direct sellers. marGo offers mail, email, text, Facebook posting, voice broadcasting, and invitation images. marGo provides three touches before a party to help ensure your in-home or virtual party is well attended, and two touches after the party to capitalize on post-party orders, bookings, and recruiting.

Organization and File Sharing

Organization and file-sharing tools help you keep your business documents in one place and easy for you and your team to access. With these tools, you have the ability to take notes, track tasks, and save anything you find online. The app syncs everything together between your phone and your computer automatically, meaning you can access your information from anywhere.

You can also invite others to view your work. That's great for sharing your training documents with new recruits and people on your team. You can also store images that you use for marketing and online parties.

Some great resources worth trying include the following:

- Dropbox (www.dropbox.com)
- Evernote (www.evernote.com)
- Google Drive (www.google.com/drive)
- Trello (www.trello.com)

Team Communication and Online Meetings

Keeping in contact with your team is important to your success. There are many resources available out there for you to hold conference calls as well as online webinars. Online meetings work as additions to your monthly meeting, especially if your team isn't local to you.

You can also use these resources to hold opportunity calls where you can invite prospects to join to learn more about the opportunity from a top leader in the organization. Here are some I suggest:

- Free Conference Call (www.freeconferencecall.com)
- Fuze (www.fuze.com)
- Google Hangouts (http://plus.google.com/hangouts)
- GoToMeeting (www.gotomeeting.com)
- Meet.fm (www.meet.fm)
- Skype (www.skype.com)
- Zoom (www.zoom.us)

Social Media Communication and Management

Social media management applications help you view, schedule, and post to all of your social media sites. Applications like Hootsuite and Buffer allow you to plan posts in advance with their scheduling options so you can spend less time on your social media accounts.

They also give you the opportunity to stay consistent with your social media and share content across a variety of platforms in a few simple clicks. You can also measure your return on investment (ROI) using their analytics and reporting. These tools are for anyone who wants to take their social media and engagement to the next level.

- Buffer (www.buffer.com)
- Hootsuite (www.hootsuite.com)
- Meet.fm (www.meet.fm — for virtual parties and communication with online party guests)

Video Creation

Video is an amazing tool for your business. Video creation apps give you the ability to share videos or post your own videos from your phone to your YouTube channel and social media platforms.

Share video testimonials, product demonstrations, and training using videos. The following resources allow you to record, edit, and share your videos while on the go:

- iMovie (www.apple.com/ios/imovie)
- Screen-Cast-O-Matic (www.screencast-o-matic.com)
- Skype Qik (www.skype.com/en/qik)

Images and graphics

There are many excellent resources for creating free or very affordable graphics. With these apps and websites, you can create many types of images, especially for sharing on social media. You can choose from pre-set images such as Facebook post, Twitter heading, and so on. You can also create custom images of any size.

And you can create things like postcards, thank-you cards, and posters. Check out some of my favorites:

- ✔ Canva (www.canva.com)
- ✔ Pic Collage (www.pic-collage.com)
- ✔ PicMonkey (www.picmonkey.com)
- ✔ Red Stamp Cards (www.redstamp.com)
- ✔ WordSwag (www.wordswag.com)

Newsletters and Email

Not all direct sales companies offer customer newsletters on your behalf, so it's important to send out monthly reminders to your customers. These newsletters and emails can cover things like the opportunity, monthly specials, product highlights, tips, host benefits, and so on. You can also use these newsletter and email applications to stay in contact with your team and downline.

Another great idea is to have a newsletter specifically for your loyal customers and VIP hosts. Give them the first sneak peak at new products and specials.

Here are some resources to try:

- ✔ AWeber (www.aweber.com)
- ✔ Constant Contact (www.constantcontact.com)
- ✔ iContact (www.icontact.com)
- ✔ MailChimp (www.mailchimp.com)

Business Expenses and Money Management

Track your mileage, store your receipts, and keep more of your money!

These resources and tools will keep your expenses organized and help you keep more of your money when it comes to tax time:

- ✔ Accountable Solutions (www.costamesataxreturn.com)
- ✔ Deductr (www.deductr.com)

- Expensify (www.expensify.com)
- J.F. DePetris, CPA (http://www.jfdcpa.com)
- Mint (www.mint.com)
- QuickBooks Online (www.quickbooks.intuit.com)
- TaxBot (www.taxbot.com)

Website and Blog Creation

Most direct sales companies will offer you a website (for free or for a small fee) where you can set up online parties as well as sell products online through an e-commerce system. But many representatives opt to set up an additional website or blog to share content and interesting information with their customers and fans.

Blog posts work great for sharing on social media and encouraging engagement. You can share video tutorials, interesting facts, and product information through your blogs. Check out three of my favorite (and free) platforms:

- Blogger (www.blogger.com)
- Wix (www.wix.com)
- Wordpress (www.wordpress.com)

Chapter 23

Ten Benefits of Direct Sales

In This Chapter

▶ Finding out the benefits of owning and operating a direct sales business

▶ Discovering how you can create an income, develop personal growth, and work when you want

This chapter covers what I consider to be the top ten benefits of owning and operating a direct sales business.

Increase in Income

Whether your business is a way to supplement your income, replace a full-time salary, or enjoy financial freedom, your direct sales business can help you achieve your goals depending on the time and effort you put into your new business. You can choose to give yourself a pay raise at any time simply by increasing your efforts. Many people enjoy above-average earnings in this industry compared to many others.

It is also a business where your previous experience or education does not play a significant part in what you are able to earn or achieve.

People use their direct sales business to pay for things like the following:

- ✔ Children's sports teams and classes
- ✔ Household expenses
- ✔ Car or home insurance
- ✔ Mortgage or rent
- ✔ Debt and credit card payments
- ✔ Vacations and other luxury items
- ✔ Retirement

Your direct sales business gives you the opportunity to write your own paycheck.

Flexible Schedule

Direct sales works for you whether or not

- ✔ You work a full-time job.
- ✔ You're trying to make a little money in a short amount of time.
- ✔ You're a stay-at-home parent who wants to work around the family's schedule and not give away 75 percent of income to daycare.
- ✔ You're a college student who wants to work around a class schedule.
- ✔ You're a retiree who wants to start something new and/or supplement a pension.

Direct sales meets the needs of lots of different individuals and circumstances. Your direct sales business gives you the opportunity to create your own business hours and work your schedule around your existing priorities and responsibilities.

Be Your Own Boss and Work from Home

In direct sales, you work for yourself and don't have to answer to anyone. You have the support and encouragement of many others, including your company, but you have the ability to choose when you want to work.

You also have the opportunity to schedule vacations, take off special holidays, attend special events with your family, and participate in community events. Ultimately, you can spend your time in the areas that matter most to you.

Working from home has many benefits, including saving on expenses related to working outside the home. You can wear whatever you want to "work" — though I do find that people who get dressed and ready for their day are more productive. You can work wherever you want, whenever you want. Working from home allows you to stay on top of household chores, responsibilities, and run errands at times that suit you.

And lastly, because you're in charge of your success and of how much you want to work, you can give yourself a pay raise whenever you choose.

Friendships and Relationships

When you join direct sales, you suddenly have a whole new group of like-minded friends who share some of the same interests as you. For people moving to a new area, it is a great way to meet a new group of friends.

In addition to the friendship, you get support from your team and from your company. In direct sales, your colleagues want to see you succeed and encourage you to do so. Your promotion within your company is not at the expense of someone else, because there is enough room for everyone to achieve success. Representatives have the ability to grow at their own pace and create their own definition of success. All this adds up to a friendly and supportive community not only within your company, but within the industry as a whole.

Incentives and Recognition

Everyone loves recognition. In fact, many surveys show that the number one thing people value in a job — above income — is being recognized and appreciated for a job well done.

In direct sales, you are continually being recognized for your achievements, from the smallest shout-outs on your Facebook page to the product rewards in your Fast Start program — plus the many ongoing programs throughout the year. There really is nothing better than being recognized by your company and your peers.

Incentives can be an incredible way for you to receive and experience things you would not otherwise have had the chance to. Special electronic devices, jewelry, accessories, and all-expenses-paid vacations to very desirable locations all over the world are all things you can achieve with your company, just for working your business.

Business Skills

Your direct sales business will help you learn many different business skills that will help you in all areas of your life. This is especially true for the college student as well as those dreaming of owning their own business. There really is no better training for someone looking to develop multiple skill sets, such as the following:

- ✔ Time management
- ✔ Organization
- ✔ Presentation skills
- ✔ Speaking skills
- ✔ Money management
- ✔ Party planning
- ✔ Effective coaching
- ✔ Sales techniques
- ✔ Customer service

Personal Growth

Many people experience a surge of self-confidence through their business. You can see them transform before your eyes.

People who could not talk in front of others are now comfortable with public speaking. People who were afraid to venture from home can now travel anywhere. And people who often shied away from team situations are now moving into leadership roles. Many reps have told me they've even been promoted in their day jobs because their manager or employer saw such a positive change in them.

Increased self-esteem, believing in yourself, patience, empathy, and being an encourager of others are all positive changes people see through direct sales. Your direct sales business can help you become more well read and well traveled through the many incentive trips you can earn. All this allows you to connect, engage, and increase your circle of influence.

Mentorship

Being a mentor and having a mentor are two of the greatest benefits you can enjoy in life. Sometimes knowing where to find a mentor or how to be a mentor to someone else can be difficult, but it is a natural fit in direct sales.

Your upline leader or sponsor many times will become a great mentor to you, and you will learn things not only about your business but about yourself. As you build relationships, you'll find that you'll have many different mentors. And because of the friendships you build, you will receive mentoring on a variety of topics other than just business.

Many people have been where you are and have gone where you want to go. As you build a team, you will become a mentor to others. Becoming a mentor is very rewarding and can in fact mean as much to your life as the income you generate. Knowing you made a difference and had an impact on another person's life is priceless.

Discount on Products

For many people, being able to purchase product at a discounted price is a big benefit — especially if it is a consumable product that you use on a regular basis. For others, direct sales is a way to get all the things they want over a period of time at a discounted price. If you really love a product, it only seems natural that you will share it with others. This gives you the opportunity to earn some income at the same time.

You will also be privy to all the newest products on the market before other customers are. This is a huge plus for people who like to stay ahead of trends and be the first to get their hands on the hottest new product.

Tax Benefits

Having a home-based business or being in business for yourself comes with some tax benefits. It is also a great way to keep more of your money throughout the year. Of course it's important to seek out a professional in your area who can assist you with this. You can enjoy deductions on things like the following:

- ✔ Automobile
- ✔ Business supplies
- ✔ Percentage of mortgage or rent
- ✔ Personal development
- ✔ Trips related to your business
- ✔ Utilities

Index

• *Numerics* •

2+2+2 method, 83, 231–235
3 Ps, 35–38, 294–296
30-second commercial, 58, 99–101,
    212, 323, 327
80% rule, 307

• *A* •

A or B questions, posting on Facebook, 186
accountability buddy, 87
Accountable Solutions (website), 343
advertising, 185
advice
  from business best friends, 322
  seeking through networking, 320
advisory boards, setting up, 329–330
agenda, for events, 297
albums, creating in Facebook Groups, 283
announcing your business, 284
Any.Do (website), 340
appearance, 58
appointments
  about, 44
  asking for, 334
  getting one-on-one, 211–212
  scheduling, 113–118
  securing, 118–123
  selling with one-on-one, 210–211
apps, 205–207
asking
  for appointments, 334
  for bookings, 124, 129
  for interviews, 262–264
  for leads, 327
  for parties, 334
attending
  community events, 324
  company conference, 310–311

host coaching on, 167–168
  meetings, 311–316
attitude
  about, 55
  importance of, 55–63
  overcoming self-doubt, 63–66
  roadblocks, 66–70
attracting new team members, 239–260
attributes, needed for direct selling,
    19–22
audience
  building on Twitter, 197–198
  finding your, 183
  knowing your, 182
authenticity
  importance of, 321, 325
  as strength of Facebook, 182
automatic income, 14, 42
auto-ship, 11
avoiding
  blame, 68–69
  denial, 68–69
  mistakes, 333–338
  resignation, 67
AWeber (website), 343

• *B* •

Bach, David (author)
  Smart Women Finish Rich, 305
back-up launch party/show, 145
being your own boss, as benefit of direct
    selling, 346
belief, cornerstones of, 64
benefit selling, 162
benefits
  of direct selling, 345–349
  of recruiting, 240–243
  for recruits, 247–252
  tax, 306–308

"Best Buy Syndrome," 98
blame, avoiding, 68–69
Blogger (website), 202, 344
blogs
  about, 201–205
  content through, 181
  resources for, 344
bonus booking dates, 129
booking games, 129–130
Booking Lead Notebook, 116–118, 267
booking leads
  following up with, 224–226
  notebook for, 116–118, 267
booking seeds
  about, 126–127, 155
  discussing on Facebook party, 193
booking talk
  about, 127–128, 129
  giving your, 158–160
booking tree, 129
bookings
  about, 109–110
  asking for, 124, 129
  booking seeds, 126–127, 155, 193
  booking talk, 127–128, 129, 158–160
  controlling calendar, 111–113
  15 minutes on, 81–82
  importance of, 110–111
  overcoming common objections, 130–132
  power questions, 125–126
  reasons for, 123–125
  scheduling, 113–118
  securing, 118–123, 128–130
  tips on, 132–137, 157
booster call, 173–174
boss, being your own, as benefit of direct
    selling, 346
brand
  awareness on Twitter, 196
  building on Pinterest and Instagram, 195
  increasing through networking, 320
Briggs Meyers, 279
Buffer (website), 342
building
  albums in Facebook Groups, 283
  audience on Twitter, 197–198

Booking Lead Notebook, 116–118
brand on Pinterest and Instagram, 195
confidence, 65–66
content, 183
a culture of opportunity at
    meetings, 315–316
customer relationships, 203
desire, 152–153, 160
excitement, 169–170
fan base, 183
friendships, 326
graphics, 286
interest, 261–262
momentum for future business, 115–116
more desire for products, 157–158
self-esteem, 65–66
vision in others, 274–275
business
  announcing your, 284
  sharing, 213
  treating like a, 336
business best friends, 321–322
business cards, 92–93, 327
business expenses, resources for, 343–344
business hours, 268
business model, explaining the, 292–293
business opportunity, 141
business relationships, importance
    of, 337–338
business services, incorporating, 207
business skills, as benefit of direct
    selling, 347–348
business starter kit
  about, 8–9
  available at events, 297
buying cues, ability to recognize, 21

• C •

calendar
  controlling, 111–113, 308
  setting goals for, 112–113
call to engagement, 187
Canva, 206, 343
capturing social sales, 200–201
caring about people, 326

casual approach, to bookings, 118–119
catalogs
  about, 94
  for launch party, 143–144
challenging new recruits, 283–288
check-in table, at events, 297
checklist, for Facebook party host, 191–192
checkout, 161–163
choices, implications of your, 87
choosing
  direct sales companies, 31–40
  social media, 179
  what to say, 158–160
church, as a customer resource, 135
classes. *See* home parties
cleaning products, sharing, 217
closing
  about, 161–163
  discussing on Facebook party, 193
  parties, 174–175
closing talk, 272
clothing, finding services to introduce, 220
clubs, as a customer resource, 134
coach, knowing when to, 276–278
cold markets
  about, 222
  customer service, 223–224
  getting referrals, 223
  likeability, 222–223
  trustworthiness, 222–223
cold recruit leads, 228–231
college students, as recruits, 250
commenting on posts, 192
commissions, 303–304
commitment
  lack of, 335
  as a strength, 86
communication
  about, 309–310
  digital, 280
  electronic, 280
  on Facebook, 180–182
  resources for, 341, 342
  skills in, 19–20
  with your leader, 316–317
  with your team, 318

community building, on Twitter, 181
community events, attending, 324
companies
  about, 31–33
  belief in, 64
  considerations for, 33–35
  saturation, 40
  start-up, 38–39
  "three P's," 35–38
company conference, attending, 310–311
company programs, 268
company training, reviewing, 144
comparing yourself to others, 70
competition, watching your, 184
conducting interviews, 261–268
confidence, building, 65–66
connections
  maintaining after meetings, 328–329
  making with networking, 320
  online, 328
  on Twitter, 196
connectors, on advisory board, 329–330
consistency
  for blogs, 204
  power of, 86–88
Constant Contact (website), 343
consumer sales, on Pinterest, 180–182
contact information, on catalogs, 94
contacts, life cycle of, 221
content
  creating, 183
  posting on Facebook, 186
contests
  on social media, 321–322
  on Twitter, 196
controlling
  calendar, 111–113, 308
  money, 301–308
  perfectionism, 67–68
  procrastination, 67–68
conversations
  engaging in, 58–59
  on Facebook, 180–182
  starting, 215–216
cosmetics, finding services to
    introduce, 219

cover photo, in Facebook Groups, 283
creating
  albums in Facebook Groups, 283
  audience on Twitter, 197–198
  Booking Lead Notebook, 116–118
  brand on Pinterest and Instagram, 195
  confidence, 65–66
  content, 183
  a culture of opportunity at
      meetings, 315–316
  customer relationships, 203
  desire, 152–153, 160
  excitement, 169–170
  fan base, 183
  friendships, 326
  graphics, 286
  interest, 261–262
  momentum for future business, 115–116
  more desire for products, 157–158
  self-esteem, 65–66
  vision in others, 274–275
culture of opportunity, creating at
    meetings, 315–316
custom content
  creating, 194
  posting on Facebook, 186
customer care
  about, 21–22
  providing, 137
  recruiting and, 259
customer feedback, communicating with
    your leader about, 316–317
customer information slip, at events, 297
customer relationships, creating, 203
customer re-orders, 49
customer service
  being systematic about, 223–224
  enhancing, 184
  15 minutes on, 83
  on Twitter, 196
customers
  following up with, 227–228
  going where they are, 134–136
  pre-judging, 335–336

• D •

dates
  booking for Facebook parties, 191
  choosing for launch party/show, 143
  knowing your, 130
dealing with 'no,' 59–60
debut. *See* launch party/show
decision, as one of Five D's of Setting
    Intentional Goals, 77
decor products, sharing, 217
Deductr (website), 343
demographics, 321
demonstrations, 195. *See also* parties
denial, avoiding, 68–69
DePetris, J.F. (CPA) (website), 344
descriptive selling, 162
designing graphics and invitations, 205–206
desire
  building for launch party, 143
  creating, 152–153, 180–182
  as one of Five D's of Setting
      Intentional Goals, 77
destination, as one of Five D's of Setting
    Intentional Goals, 78
details, as one of Five D's of Setting
    Intentional Goals, 77–78
determination, as one of Five D's of Setting
    Intentional Goals, 78
developing skills, 83–88
development, importance of, 337
digital communication, 280
direct sales. *See* direct selling
direct selling. *See also specific topics*
  about, 7–8
  benefits of, 345–349
  first steps in, 14–17
  flexibility with, 23–26
  how it works, 8–10
  model history, 27–29
  models for, 10–14
  personal attributes and skills needed
      for, 19–22
  resources for, 339–344

on social media. *See* social selling
success of, 17–18
Direct Selling Association (website), 33
#directsales hashtag, 199
Direst Selling Association, 43
discounted products
as benefit of direct selling, 349
as a reason for bookings, 123
as reason for hosting parties, 151
distributing promo cards, 216
door prizes, at events, 297
downline, 39
dressing for success, 102–103
Dropbox (website), 341

• *E* •

EasilyDo, 206, 340
eCheat Sheet (website), 3
80% rule, 307
electronic communication, 280
elevator pitches, 99–101
Ellsworth, Belinda (author), 73
email
about, 280
maintaining connections through, 328
resources for, 343
team communication via, 318
encouraging decisions during group
recruiting, 296
engaged
in conversations, 58–59
keeping hosts, 168–176
enhancing personal shopping
experience, 218–220
enthusiasm, sharing, 56–58, 191
event parties, 24–25
events
planning, 296–298
promoting in Facebook Groups, 283
recruiting at, 291–296
staging, 296–298
strength of, 333–334
tweeting during, 328
using, 185
Evernote (website), 116, 206, 341

excitement
building, 169–170
maintaining in hosts, 168–176
showing, 58–59
executing show-on-the go, 215
Expensify, 207, 344
"extras" (website), 3

• *F* •

Facebook
about, 182
Business Page setup, 185–187
communication on, 180–182
conversation on, 180–182
hosting parties, 189–193
for networking, 325
recruiting on, 260
strengths of, 182–185
using personal account for personal
branding, 187–189
website, 182, 260
Facebook Groups
about, 280
team communication via, 318
using for teams, 282–283
Facebook jail, 194
Facebook time-out, 194
face-to-face meetings, 281–282
facts, posting on Facebook, 186
family, depending on, 337
fan base, building, 183
Fast Start
about, 78
incorporating programs, 273
Fast Track, 78
file sharing, resources for, 341
Files tab, in Facebook Groups, 283
financial freedom, as a benefit for recruits,
248, 293–294
finding
business after relocating, 136–137
people for networking, 323–326
silver lining, 60–61
your audience, 183
"Five Cs of Social Media," 180–182

flexibility, with direct selling, 23–26
flexibility of time, as a benefit for recruits, 248–251, 294
flexible schedule, as benefit of direct selling, 346
Flight Plan (Tracy), 72
Flint, 207
focus
    lack of, 336–337
    power of, 84–85
    as a strength, 85
follow-up
    about, 221–222
    with booking leads, 224–226
    cold markets, 222–224
    with customers, 227–228
    for Facebook party, 193
    with hosts, 226–227
    importance of, 288
    with recruit leads, 228–231
    recruiting and, 259
    re-servicing, 235–236
    2+2+2 method, 231–235
    warm markets, 222–224
food and beverage products
    finding services to introduce, 220
    sharing, 217
free auto-ship, 13
Free Conference Call (website), 341
free products
    as a reason for bookings, 123
    as reason for hosting parties, 151
friend requests, sending to hosts, 191
friendliness, on blogs, 205
friends/friendships
    as a benefit for recruits, 251, 294
    as benefit of direct selling, 347
    bringing, 268
    creating, 326
    depending on, 337
    enlisting for bookings, 121–122
    inviting, 287
    from networking, 326
    as reason for attending company conference, 310
    as reason for attending meetings, 314–315

as a reason for bookings, 124
    as reason for hosting parties, 151
front-end loading, 43
full-time workers, as recruits, 249
fun
    as a reason for bookings, 123
    as reason for hosting parties, 151
fundraising, 25, 197
Fuze (website), 341

• **G** •

gala night, as reason for attending company conference, 311
getting
    referrals, 223
    spousal buy-in, 302–303
giveaways
    discussing on Facebook party, 193
    on social media, 321–322
giving presentations, 156–158
global nature, of direct selling, 32
goal achievement awards, recognizing, 312
goals
    about, 19, 71, 75
    communicating with your leader about, 317
    intentional, 76–78
    scariness of, 75–76
    setting, 334–335
    setting for calendar, 112–113
    setting for others, 274–275
Google Drive (website), 341
Google Hangouts (website), 341
GoToMeeting (website), 341
grand opening. *See* launch party/show
graphics
    creating, 286
    designing, 205–206
    resources for, 342–343
"ground floor opportunity," 38
group message, 176
group recruiting
    about, 289–290
    encouraging decisions during, 296
    planning events, 296–298

recruiting at events, 291–296
staging events, 296–298
types of opportunity events, 290–291
groupings, showing in, 163
Groups (Facebook). *See* Facebook Groups
groups, using, 185
growing your reach, 319
growth, sustaining, 221–236
guests
   about, 48
   as best customers, 49
   as new recruit leads, 49
   recognizing, 313
   scheduling bookings from, 110
gyms, as a customer resource, 134

• H •

habits, 86
hashtags, 198–200
herbal hours. *See* home parties
home, working from, as benefit of direct
   selling, 346
home parties. *See also* launch party/show
   about, 11, 23, 140
   appeal of, 150–152
   asking for, 334
   booking talk, 158–160
   checkout, 161–163
   closing, 161–163, 174–175
   communicating with your leader
      about, 317
   creating desire, 152–153
   giving presentations, 156–158
   history of, 149–150
   hosting, 122–123, 149–163
   opening talks, 153–156
   recruiting talk, 161
   upselling, 161–163
home-based business, tax benefits
   of, 306–308
Hootsuite (website), 342
host coaching
   about, 165–166
   on attendance, 167–168

excited, engaged, and informed
   hosts, 168–176
   15 minutes on, 81
   motivation for, 166–167
   online, 176
   on outside orders, 167–168
host packets, 95–96
host-appreciation events, 291
host-coaching package, 192
hosting
   about, 149
   building desire for, 160
   Facebook parties, 189–193
   parties, 122–123, 149–163
hosts
   about, 11, 48
   following up with, 226–227
   as most likely next recruit, 49
   sending friend requests to, 191
   thanking, 155
hot recruit leads, 228–230
'The Hugger,' 329
Hybrid model, 12–13, 51–52

• I •

"I don't have any time - I'm too busy"
   objection, 131
"I think I just want to do a catalog party"
   objection, 131–132
icons, explained, 2
iContact (website), 343
identifying target audience, 219
images, resources for, 342–343
iMovie (website), 342
incentive programs, 71, 78–79
incentive trips, 79
incentives, as benefit of direct selling, 347
income
   as a benefit for recruits, 248, 293–294
   as benefit of direct selling, 345–346
increasing
   search engine visibility, 202
   visitors to your website, 202
independent contractor, 306
independent representatives, 8

industry, belief in, 64

industry expert, positioning yourself as an, 202–203

industry trends, discussing on Facebook party, 193

information, sharing at meetings, 313

informed, keeping hosts, 168–176

insightful
  being, 184
  communicating with your leader about, 317

Instagram
  about, 194–195
  creating desire on, 180–182

intentional goals, setting, 76–78

interest, creating, 143, 261–262

Internet age, 27–28

Internet resources
  Accountable Solutions, 343
  Any.Do, 340
  AWeber, 343
  Blogger, 202, 344
  Buffer, 342
  Canva, 206, 343
  Constant Contact, 343
  Deductr, 343
  DePetris, J.F. (CPA), 344
  Direct Selling Association, 33
  Dropbox, 341
  EasilyDo, 206, 340
  eCheat Sheet, 3
  Evernote, 116, 206, 341
  Expensify, 207, 344
  "extras," 3
  Facebook, 182, 260
  Flint, 207
  Free Conference Call, 341
  Fuze, 341
  Google Drive, 341
  Google Hangouts, 341
  GoToMeeting, 341
  Hootsuite, 342
  iContact, 343
  iMovie, 342
  increasing visitors to your, 202
  Instagram, 194
  LinkedIn, 260

MailChimp, 343
marGo, 340
Meet.fm, 341, 342
MileIQ, 207
Mint, 344
Pic Collage, 205, 343
PicMonkey, 206, 343
Pinterest, 194
QuickBooks Online, 207, 344
Red Stamp Cards, 205, 343
resources for, 344
Screen-Cast-O-Matic, 342
Skype, 341
Skype Qik, 342
Step Into Success, 340
TaxBot, 344
Trello, 341
Twitter, 195
Wix, 344
Word Swag, 206
Wordpress, 344
WordStream, 185
WordSwag, 343
Wunderlist, 206, 340
YouTube, 260
Zoom, 341

interpersonal skills, 20

interviews
  about, 261
  asking for, 262–264
  beginning of training, 267–268
  conducting, 261–268
  creating interest, 261–262
  hearing 'no,' 265
  indecision in, 265
  what to say, 264, 266–267

introducing yourself, 320

introductory party. *See* launch party/show

inventory loading, 43

invitations
  designing, 205–206
  to events, 296

inviting
  compared with recruiting, 243–244
  friends, 287
  people to launch party/show, 144–145

IRS loans, 306
#itworks hashtag, 199

• J •

#jamberry hashtag, 199
jewelry, finding services to introduce, 220
jump-starting your business, 114

• K •

kick-off. *See* launch party/show
kitchenware, finding services to
    introduce, 220

• L •

launch party/show
  about, 11, 23, 140
  appeal of, 150–152
  asking for, 334
  assisting recruits with, 272–273
  back-up, 145
  booking talk, 158–160
  checkout, 161–163
  closing, 161–163, 174–175
  communicating with your leader
      about, 316, 317
  creating desire, 152–153
  giving presentations, 156–158
  history of, 149–150
  hosting, 122–123, 149–163
  importance of, 141–142
  inviting people to, 144–145
  opening talks, 153–156
  planning, 139–148
  preparing for, 142–144
  recruiting talk, 161
  of recruits, 268
  scheduling, 267
  two-booking method, 145–148
  upselling, 161–163
launching new team members, 271–273
leaders
  attending launch parties with, 144
  being a, 74

communicating with your, 316–317
  learning from, 144
leading teams, 269–288
leads
  asking for, 327
  booking, 116–118, 224–226, 267
  compared with recruits, 246–247
  getting leads from, 133
  losing, 256–259
less, settling for, 66–67
"Let me check with my friends first"
    objection, 130
likeability, 222–223
LinkedIn
  for networking, 325
  recruiting on, 260
  website, 260
links, posting on Facebook, 187
live presentations, 23
loans, IRS, 306
local events, on Twitter, 197
locating
  business after relocating, 136–137
  people for networking, 323–326
  silver lining, 60–61
  your audience, 183
locations, for events, 296

• M •

MailChimp (website), 343
maintaining
  calendar, 308
  connections after meetings, 328–329
making connections with networking, 320
malls, as a customer resource, 135
managing
  calendar, 111–113, 308
  money, 301–308
  perfectionism, 67–68
  procrastination, 67–68
marGo (website), 340
material, organizing, 206
Meet.fm (website), 341, 342
meetings
  about, 309–310
  attending, 311–316

meetings *(continued)*
attending company conference, 310–311
face-to-face, 281–282
maintaining connections after, 328–329
monthly, 318
planning successful, 311–316
setting up, 328
mentoring
as benefit of direct selling, 348–349
defined, 276
team members, 278–279
mentors, on advisory board, 329
mileage, tracking, 308
MileIQ, 207
milestones, recognizing, 313
Mint (website), 344
mistakes, to avoid, 333–338
mixers. *See* parties
MLM (multi-level marketing). *See* network marketing
#MLM hashtag, 199
models, for direct selling, 10–14
mom groups, as a customer resource, 134
momentum, building for future business, 115–116
money management
about, 301–302
getting spousal buy-in, 302–303
overnight success, 304–306
paying yourself, 303–304
resources for, 343–344
saving, 185
taxes, 306–308
tracking your pay, 303–304
monthly meetings, 318
motivation
as reason for attending company conference, 310
as reason for attending meetings, 312
multi-level marketing (MLM). *See* network marketing
multitasking, as a strength, 85
"My friends are partied out" objection, 130–131
"My house isn't big enough" objection, 131

• N •

nail art, 216
name, practicing your, 155
needs and desires, fulfilled by direct selling, 293–294
neighbors, as a customer resource, 135
Network Marketing model
about, 10–11, 41–42
one-on-one appointments in, 211
people best suited for, 45–46
recruiting in, 42–44
sharing products and opportunities, 44–45
success tips for, 46–47
networking
about, 214–215, 319–320
business best friends, 321–322
distributing promo cards, 216
finding people for, 323–326
introducing yourself, 320
maintaining connections after meetings, 328–329
power, 327–328
product on hand, 217–218
promotables, 216–217
setting up advisory boards, 329–330
show-on-the go, 215
social media for, 324–326
starting conversations, 215–216
wear-to-share, 216–217
networking groups, as a customer resource, 134
#networkmarketing hashtag, 199
newsletters, resources for, 343
next available dates, knowing your, 103–105, 113
'no,' dealing with, 59–60

• O •

objections, overcoming, 130–132
office space, 89
one-on-one selling
about, 148, 209–210
with appointments, 210–211

enhancing personal shopping experience, 218–220

getting appointments, 211–212

networking, 214–218

what to do and say, 213–214

online connections, 328

online host coaching, 176

online marketing, 25

online meetings, resources for, 341

online parties, 25, 140–141

open houses, 140, 322

opening talks, 153–156, 272

opportunities, sharing, 44–45, 49

opportunity events

holding, 289–298

promoting, 297

types of, 290–291

opportunity packets, 95–96

opportunity seeds, 261

order checkout, tips on, 272

organization, power of, 88–89

organizational products, finding services to introduce, 220

organizing

about, 285

material, 206

resources for, 341

outside orders, host coaching on, 167–168

overcoming self-doubt, 63–66

over-invite, for launch party/show, 143

overnight success, managing an, 304–306

overpaying, 306–307

● *p* ●

parties. *See also* launch party/show

about, 11, 23, 140

appeal of, 150–152

asking for, 334

booking talk, 158–160

checkout, 161–163

closing, 161–163, 174–175

communicating with your leader about, 317

creating desire, 152–153

giving presentations, 156–158

history of, 149–150

hosting, 122–123, 149–163

opening talks, 153–156

recruiting talk, 161

upselling, 161–163

Party Plan model

about, 11–12, 29, 47–48

one-on-one appointments in, 213

people best suited for, 50

recruiting in, 48–49

sharing products and opportunities, 49

party presentation, 49

patience, 20

paying yourself, 303–304

Pearson, Pat (author)

Stop Self Sabotage, 65–66

peers, on advisory board, 329

people, finding for networking, 323–326

percentage increases, recognizing, 313

perfectionism, managing, 67–68

persistence, lack of, 335

personal attributes, needed for direct selling, 19–22

personal branding, 187–189

personal growth

as a benefit for recruits, 252, 294

as benefit of direct selling, 348

commitment to, 22

personal shopping experience, 26, 218–220

personalities, working with different, 279–282

phone calls, 280–281, 328

photos, for blogs, 204

Pic Collage, 205, 343

PicMonkey, 206, 343

pinning posts in Facebook Groups, 283

Pinterest

about, 194–195

consumer sales on, 180–182

planning

events, 296–298

launch party/show, 139–148

show-on-the-go, 96–99

successful meetings, 311–316

planting seeds, for recruiting, 253–256

play groups, as a customer resource, 134

point system, 191

points game, 192

policies and procedures, knowing your company, 181

positioning yourself as an industry expert, 202–203

positive, on social media, staying, 62

positive affirmation, 155

posts
  commenting on, 192
  on day of Facebook party, 192–193
  pinning in Facebook Groups, 283

potential recruits, interviewing, 264–268

power
  of consistency, 86–88
  of organization, 88–89

Power Hour, productivity and, 79–83

power networking, 327–328

power questions, 125–126

practical skill sets, 71

practice
  about, 114–115
  for launch party, 144

preferred customer rate, 13

pre-judging, 244–245, 335–336

pre-party orders, 192

pre-party posts and invitations, 190–191

presentation skills, 20–21

presentations
  about, 44
  giving, 156–158
  live, 23
  tips on, 272

private messages, to hosts, 192

'The Problem Solver,' 329

procrastination, managing, 67–68

product launches, 291

product lines, 321

product on hand, 217–218

productivity
  about, 71
  Power Hour and, 79–83

products
  belief in, 19, 64
  building more desire for, 157–158
  discounted, 123, 151, 349

discussing during group recruiting, 294–295

discussing on Facebook party, 193

as door prizes at events, 297

finding services to introduce, 219–220

free, 123, 151

as one of "three P's," 35–36

selling, 110

sharing, 44–45, 49, 213

products, new
  as reason for attending company conference, 310
  as reason for attending meetings, 315

profile, increasing through networking, 320

profitability, as one of "three P's," 36–37

profits, discussing during group recruiting, 295–296

programs
  discussing during group recruiting, 295
  as one of "three P's," 37–38

promo cards, distributing, 216

promotables, 216–217

promoting
  events in Facebook Groups, 283
  opportunity events, 297

prospects, pre-judging, 335–336

purposeful conversation, 50

pyramid scheme, 43

• *Q* •

Quick Start, 78

QuickBooks Online, 207, 344

• *R* •

raffle tickets, at events, 297

reach, growing your, 319

readiness
  about, 91–92
  business cards, 92–93
  catalogs, 94
  dressing for success, 102–103
  host packets, 95–96
  knowing next available dates, 103–105

opportunity packets, 95–96
show-on-the-go, 96–99
30-second commercial, 99–101
'The Realist,' 329
realtors, as a customer resource, 135
recognition
  as a benefit for recruits, 251, 294
  as benefit of direct selling, 347
  milestones, 313
  as reason for attending company
    conference, 311
  as reason for attending meetings,
    312–313
recruit leads, following up with,
  228–231
recruiting. *See also* group recruiting
  about, 239–240
  benefits for recruits, 247–252
  benefits of, 240–243
  communicating with your leader
    about, 317
  compared with inviting, 243–244
  customer care, 259
  discussing on Facebook party, 193
  at events, 291–296
  15 minutes on, 82
  follow-up, 259
  losing leads, 256–259
  in Network Marketing model, 42–44
  parts of, 240
  in Party Plan model, 48–49
  planting seeds for, 253–256
  rules of, 243–247
  on social media, 259–260
recruiting packets, at events, 297
recruiting seeds, 155, 157
recruiting talk, 161, 245–246, 262
recruits
  assisting with launch parties, 272–273
  benefits for, 247–252
  challenging new, 283–288
  compared with leads, 246–247
  launch parties of, 268
  sponsoring, 269–288
Red Stamp Cards, 205, 343

referral gifts, 322
referrals
  from business best friends, 323
  getting, 220, 223
  from networking, 320
  using social networks for, 133
refreshments, at events, 297
refunds, tax, 306
relationships, as benefit of direct
    selling, 347
relevance, in hashtags, 199
relocating, finding business after,
    136–137
Remember icon, 2
research, on Twitter, 196
re-servicing, 26, 110, 235–236
residual income, 14, 42
resignation, avoiding, 67
resources
  for blogs, 344
  for business expenses, 343–344
  for communication, 341, 342
  for direct selling, 339–344
  for email, 343
  for file sharing, 341
  for graphics, 342–343
  for images, 342–343
  for management of social media, 342
  for money management, 343–344
  for newsletters, 343
  for online meetings, 341
  for organizing, 341
  for social media, 342
  for team communication, 341
  for video creation, 342
  for websites, 344
restaurants, as a customer resource, 134
retirees, as recruits, 250–251
return on relationships (ROR), 337
reviewing company training, 144
risks, taking, 69
roadblocks, 66–70
role model, being a strong, 62–63
ROR (return on relationships), 337
RSVP, for events, 297

• S •

sales increase, as reason for attending company conference, 310
salons, as a customer resource, 134
sampling, 45
saturation, myths about, 40
saving money, 185
savings account, setting up, 307
schedules
    flexibility of, as benefit of direct selling, 346
    setting, 111–112
    tips on, 273
scheduling
    appointments, 113–118
    bookings, 113–118
    launch parties, 267
    posts on Facebook, 187
school, as a customer resource, 135
Screen-Cast-O-Matic (website), 342
search engine optimization (SEO)
    for blogs, 204
    increasing, 185
search engine visibility, increasing, 202
securing
    appointments, 118–123
    bookings, 118–123
'see the people,' 119–121
selecting
    direct sales companies, 31–40
    social media, 179
    what to say, 158–160
self-doubt, overcoming, 63–66
self-esteem
    as a benefit for recruits, 252, 294
    building, 65–66
self-talk, 65
selling
    with one-on-one appointments, 210–211
    products, 110
    through your blog, 203–204
SEO (search engine optimization)
    for blogs, 204
    increasing, 185
service recovery paradox, 63, 184

service seminars, 291
services, finding to introduce products, 219–220
setting
    goals, 334–335
    goals for calendar, 112–113
    goals for others, 274–275
    intentional goals, 76–78
    schedules, 111–112
settling for less, 66–67
setup
    advisory boards, 329–330
    Facebook Business Page, 185–187
    Facebook Events, 190
    meetings, 328
    savings account, 307
sharing
    business, 213
    enthusiasm, 56–58, 191
    information at meetings, 313
    opportunities, 44–45, 49
    products, 44–45, 49, 213
    3 Ps, 294–296
    updates at meetings, 313
shop from home, 28
showcases. See parties
showing excitement, 58–59
show-on-the-go
    executing, 215
    planning, 96–99
shows. See home parties
sign-in sheet, at events, 297
silver lining, finding, 60–61
skills
    developing, 83–88
    needed for direct selling, 19–22
Skype (website), 341
Skype Qik (website), 342
Small Business Taxes For Dummies (Tyson), 307
Smart Women Finish Rich (Bach), 305
snail mail, 281
social media
    contests on, 321–322
    creating interest on, 262
    direct selling on. See social selling
    giveaways on, 321–322

for networking, 324–326
recruiting on, 259–260
resources for, 342
staying positive on, 62
using in blogs, 204
social networks, using for referrals, 133
social proof, 28–29
social selling
about, 28–29, 177–178
apps, 205–207
blogging, 201–205
capturing social sales, 200–201
choosing social media, 179
Facebook, 182–194
"Five Cs of Social Media," 180–182
Instagram, 194–195
Pinterest, 194–195
Twitter, 195–200
solution oriented, being, 61
spa products, sharing, 217
spammer, 320, 325
speakers, as reason for attending company
conference, 311
specificity, in hashtags, 199
sponsor, 9, 127
sponsoring. *See also* recruiting
about, 239–240, 269–271
launching new team members, 271–273
recruits, 269–288
spousal buy-in, getting, 302–303
staging events, 296–298
starter kit
available at events, 297
for launch party, 143
tips on, 272
starting conversations, 215–216
start-up companies, considerations
for, 38–39
stay-at-home moms, as recruits, 249
staying in touch with connections, 328
Step Into Success, 339–340
Stop Self Sabotage (Pearson), 65–66
strengths
of events, 333–334
of Facebook, 182–185
StrengthsFinder, 279
success, dressing for, 102–103

success stories, 212
sustaining growth, 221–236
systems, 45

• T •

take-a-looks, 290–291
taking risks, 69
target audience, identifying, 219
tastings. *See* parties
tax benefits, of direct selling, 349
TaxBot (website), 344
taxes
about, 306
benefits of home-based business,
306–308
IRS loans, 306
refunds, 306
withholding, 306
team leaders
about, 269–271, 274
becoming a trainer, 275–276
building vision in others, 274–275
challenging new recruits, 283–288
communicating with your, 318
Facebook Groups, 282–283
knowing when to coach, 276–278
mentoring team members, 278–279
setting goals for others, 274–275
working with different
personalities, 279–282
team meetings, 291
team members
attracting new, 239–260
finding potential, 111
launching new, 271–273
mentoring, 278–279
reassuring your, 136
teams
leading, 269–288
resources for communication with, 341
technological aptitude, 22
telephone calls, 280–281, 318
testimonials
about, 44, 212
for events, 297
posting on Facebook, 187

texting, 280, 318
thank-you notes, 175
30-second commercial, 58, 99–101, 212, 323, 327
3 Ps, 35–38, 294–296
time
  choosing for launch party/show, 143
  flexibility of, as a benefit for recruits, 248–251, 294
time management, 206, 340
Tip icon, 2
tools, 45
topicality, in hashtags, 200
tracking
  mileage, 308
  your pay, 303–304
Tracy, Brian (author)
  Flight Plan, 72
trade shows, 23–24
trainer, becoming a, 275–276
training
  attending, 308
  beginning of, 267–268
  importance of, 337
  as reason for attending company conference, 310
  as reason for attending meetings, 314
traveling salesmen, 27
Trello (website), 341
trip incentives, as reason for attending company conference, 311
True Colors Personality Test, 279
trunk shows. *See* home parties; parties
trustworthiness, 222–223
tweeting, during events, 328
Twitter
  about, 195
  building audience on, 197–198
  community building on, 181
  hashtags, 198–200
  for networking, 325
  reasons for using, 196–197
  website, 195
2+2+2 method, 83, 231–235
two-booking method, 145–148
Tyson, Eric (author)
  Small Business Taxes For Dummies, 307

• U •

updates
  sharing at meetings, 313
  on Twitter, 196
upline mentors, 9
upselling, 161–163

• V •

vanishing auto-ship, 13
vendor events, 23–24
video-conference calls, 280–281
videos
  posting on Facebook, 186–187
  resources for, 342
viral, going, 183–184
virtual office, 11, 284–285
vision
  about, 19, 71, 72
  building in others, 274–275
  changes in your, 73–74
  of Ellsworth, 73
  helping others with their, 74
visitors, increasing to your website, 202
volunteers, at events, 297

• W •

warm markets
  about, 222
  customer service, 223–224
  getting referrals, 223
  likeability, 222–223
  trustworthiness, 222–223
Warning! icon, 2
weak-tie relationships, 183
wear-to-share, 216–217
weave dating, 113
website links, posting on Facebook, 187
websites
  Accountable Solutions, 343
  Any.Do, 340
  AWeber, 343
  Blogger, 202, 344
  Buffer, 342

Canva, 206, 343
Constant Contact, 343
Deductr, 343
DePetris, J.F. (CPA), 344
Direct Selling Association, 33
Dropbox, 341
EasilyDo, 206, 340
eCheat Sheet, 3
Evernote, 116, 206, 341
Expensify, 207, 344
"extras," 3
Facebook, 182, 260
Flint, 207
Free Conference Call, 341
Fuze, 341
Google Drive, 341
Google Hangouts, 341
GoToMeeting, 341
Hootsuite, 342
iContact, 343
iMovie, 342
increasing visitors to your, 202
Instagram, 194
LinkedIn, 260
MailChimp, 343
marGo, 340
Meet.fm, 341, 342
MileIQ, 207
Mint, 344
Pic Collage, 205, 343
PicMonkey, 206, 343
Pinterest, 194
QuickBooks Online, 207, 344
Red Stamp Cards, 205, 343
resources for, 344
Screen-Cast-O-Matic, 342
Skype, 341
Skype Qik, 342
Step Into Success, 340
TaxBot, 344

Trello, 341
Twitter, 195
Wix, 344
Word Swag, 206
Wordpress, 344
WordStream, 185
WordSwag, 343
Wunderlist, 206, 340
YouTube, 260
Zoom, 341
"why" story, 286–287
withholding, tax, 306
Wix (website), 344
Word Swag, 206
Wordpress (website), 344
WordStream (website), 185
WordSwag (website), 343
working from home, as benefit of direct
    selling, 346
workshops. *See* home parties
Wunderlist, 206, 340

• *Y* •

yourself
  belief in, 64
  comparing to others, 70
  introducing, 320
  paying, 303–304
  positioning as an industry
      expert, 202–203
  reassuring your, 136–137
YouTube
  recruiting on, 260
  website, 260

• *Z* •

Zoom (website), 341

Dedication

To those who have mentored me throughout the years, and to the thousands I have had the privilege of mentoring, thank you for sharing all of your success stories. To each and every person who has a dream of making their life better through this amazing industry, it has always been and remains my goal to bring you the best tools to make that dream a reality.

About the Author

Belinda Ellsworth is the premier motivational speaker, sales trainer, and expert for the direct sales industry. She has trained thousands of independent sales representatives, managers, and executives and has worked with more than 100 different direct sales companies. With more than 30 years of experience in the industry, Belinda is the corporate consultant, motivational speaker, and trainer companies and top field leaders turn to again and again. Belinda is also recognized among her peers throughout the direct sales industry as the recipient of the 2015 DSA Ethos Partnership Award, given by the Direct Selling Association, for her contribution and expertise within the industry.

Author's Acknowledgments

I want to thank my family for their love and encouragement in all that I do and for their patience while I was completing this book. Thanks to my husband Chris and my daughter Tiffany for their help with the editing and writing.

Thanks to my team at Step Into Success: Donna, Lydia, Karen, and Tiffany. Your hard work and dedication allow me to do what I love best — teach others to succeed.

A very special thanks to the team of writers I've worked with through the years who all came together to make this project its absolute best: Lindsay Tompkins, Jenna Lang, and Martha McBride. It has been an absolute pleasure working with you. Lindsay, I will forever be grateful for your hard work and dedication.

I especially want to thank the team at Wiley for giving me this amazing opportunity and for their dedication in bringing quality work to readers. Special thanks to Stacy Kennedy, acquisitions editor, and Corbin Collins, my amazing editor. Thank you for making this an incredible learning experience.

Thanks to Martha McBride of Words Are My Life, our technical editor, for the time, effort, and authenticity she brought to this book.

Finally, thank you to my other direct sales friends who offered an ear and advice when needed.

Publisher's Acknowledgments

Acquisitions Editor: Stacy Kennedy

Editor: Corbin Collins

Technical Editor: Martha McBride

Production Editor: Kinson Raja

Cover Image: © Andrew Parfenov/ iStockphoto